Political Theory

To
Raphs and Issy

Political Theory

A Beginner's Guide

Pete Woodcock

polity

First published in 2020 by Polity Press

Polity Press
65 Bridge Street
Cambridge CB2 1UR, UK

Polity Press
101 Station Landing
Suite 300
Medford, MA 02155, USA

ISBN-13: 978-1-5095-3133-2
ISBN-13: 978-1-5095-3134-9 (pb)

A catalogue record for this book is available from the British Library.

Library of Congress Cataloging-in-Publication Data
Names: Woodcock, Pete (Peter Stewart), author.
Title: Political theory : a beginner's guide / Pete Woodcock.
Description: Cambridge, UK ; Medford, MA : Polity, [2020] | Includes
  bibliographical references and index. | Summary: "In this highly
  accessible new introductory textbook, Pete Woodcock examines the
  fundamental questions of political theory. He takes students
  step-by-step through the most important answers given by history's most
  famous thinkers to the most essential questions in politics, on topics
  ranging from liberty and justice to gender and revolution"-- Provided by
  publisher.
Identifiers: LCCN 2019024002 (print) | LCCN 2019024003 (ebook) | ISBN
  9781509531332 (hardback) | ISBN 9781509531349 (paperback) | ISBN
  9781509531363 (epub)
Subjects: LCSH: Political science--Philosophy.
Classification: LCC JA71 .W68 2020 (print) | LCC JA71 (ebook) | DDC
  320.01--dc23
LC record available at https://lccn.loc.gov/2019024002
LC ebook record available at https://lccn.loc.gov/2019024003

Typeset in 9.5 on 12pt Utopia Std by
Servis Filmsetting Ltd, Stockport, Cheshire
Printed and bound in Great Britain by CPI Group (UK) Ltd, Croydon

The publisher has used its best endeavours to ensure that the URLs for external websites referred to in this book are correct and active at the time of going to press. However, the publisher has no responsibility for the websites and can make no guarantee that a site will remain live or that the content is or will remain appropriate.

Every effort has been made to trace all copyright holders, but if any have been overlooked the publisher will be pleased to include any necessary credits in any subsequent reprint or edition.

For further information on Polity, visit our website:
politybooks.com

Contents

Acknowledgements   vi

Chapter 1: Introduction   1

Chapter 2: What is the nature of politics?   10

Chapter 3: Is humanity nasty or nice?   31

Chapter 4: Why should I obey the state?   51

Chapter 5: Is democracy the best form of government?   70

Chapter 6: When can my freedom be restricted?   90

Chapter 7: What would a just society look like?   104

Chapter 8: Why have women been ignored in the history of political
                thought?   129

Chapter 9: When is revolution against government justified?   145

Chapter 10: Conclusion: Ideologies   160

Index   176

Acknowledgements

This book is the result of teaching I have delivered at the University of Huddersfield, and prior to that at the University of Southampton; I am in the debt of colleagues and students at both institutions that have endured my endless wittering on the subjects contained within these pages. I appreciate how lucky I am to spend my working life discussing these things with you all.

Whilst writing this book I have sought refuge in the University of Huddersfield's library, the Leeds Library, and Lindley Library (Kirklees), and have benefitted greatly from the expertise of the staff of those institutions, and the tranquillity of the surroundings.

Numerous colleagues have provided me with a sounding board for ideas throughout the years whilst working on this project, but in particular Catherine McGlynn, Shaun McDaid, Leonie Jackson, Russell Bentley, David Owen, and Michael Bacon deserve special mention. George Owers and Ian Tuttle from Polity have worked beyond the call of duty in making the final product vaguely coherent. Needless to say, despite all this assistance, any errors contained herein are entirely mine.

Most of all I would like to thank my mother, Viv Woodcock, and my much missed father, Lloyd Woodcock for the help and support they have provided me throughout my learning journey; I hope that creating a book to pass on knowledge is some small recompense for all that I have taken from others. And much love to my kids Raphs and Issy for keeping me smiling when the writing got tough; they might be impressed if this book results in my YouTube channel getting more views.

Please follow me on Twitter for supporting activities and media: @petewoodcock

1
Introduction

KEY QUESTIONS

(1) Why should we study the history of political thought?

(2) What are the contents of this book?

Purpose of this book

On a hot summer's day in 1749 the polymath Jean-Jacques Rousseau decided to walk the six miles from Paris to Vincennes to visit his friend Denis Diderot who was imprisoned there for his persistent criticism of the government. Taking a break, he opened his newspaper and glanced upon an advert for the Academy of Dijon's essay writing competition; entries were invited to the question 'has the progress of the sciences and arts done more to corrupt morals or improve them?' (Rousseau, 1953: 327). Rousseau outlines the effect that seeing this question had on him in his letter to the statesman/philosopher Lamoignon-Malesherbes. His head began spinning as thousands of ideas flooded into his mind of how he could answer this question, he burst into tears, and then collapsed under a tree where he remained for an hour and a half contemplating the philosophical issues that arose from the question. He was thereafter unable to do anything other than work on his essay. He could not sleep, so spent the night-times meditating on the essay, writing sentences in his head which he would dictate to his secretary in the morning. Perhaps this reminds you of yourself when writing an essay (other than the bit about the secretary).

When he had finished his essay, he sent it to the Academy of Dijon thinking it 'the most feebly argued, the most deficient in proportion and harmony' of anything that has 'proceeded from my pen' (Rousseau, 1953: 329). It won first prize and is a classic in the history of political thought, known thereafter as *Discourse on the Arts and Sciences*. Its central theme, that far from improving morals, the arts and sciences have corrupted man's[1] natural goodness, would be one that Rousseau returned to many times, and one we will discuss below.

Such is the impact of political theory. The artistic epiphany and breakdown that Rousseau suffered is probably not the reaction that you or I have when coming across an interesting theoretical political question; if you are reading this as part of your studies, it is unlikely that an essay question has had this effect on you, nor is it likely that an advert in a paper would produce this reaction. Nor is Rousseau's method of writing, even if one has a secretary, necessarily a way in which many of us can work productively. It is not necessary to have this reaction to regard political theory as being interesting, or even useful.

I was a very boring child. I became interested in politics at a very early age, spent my pocket money on political manifestos, and watched the news diligently every evening over dinner, and discussed the key issues raised with my family. The politics that I was interested in then, however, was the political reporting you see on the news, that is to say basic British politics. It wasn't until I became an under-graduate student at the London School of Economics that I was introduced to the history of political thought, and it immediately became my passion. Learning about political theory opened my eyes to a new way of discussing politics. No longer do I see it as being about individual politicians, about parties and pieces of legislation; instead, I now like to think of it as about **ideas, arguments, and justifications**. Understanding the history of the ideas that we cherish so dearly today and how they developed, whilst also noting how relatively recently those ideas have occurred, fascinates me. Likewise, noting how political theory greats such as Plato, Jean-Jacques Rousseau, Thomas Hobbes and Karl Marx would criticize the political ideas by which we live today, albeit from entirely different angles and viewpoints, fascinates me. We should all of us examine the basic philosophical underpinnings of the way in which we live our political lives today.

I am an extremely lucky man in that I am able to make a living teaching the subject about which I am passionate to students at the University of Huddersfield in Yorkshire, England. I no longer wish to simply learn about the history of ideas; I want to teach and enthuse others about the subject. I have been able to discuss all of the ideas contained within this book with many cohorts of students at the Universities of Southampton and Huddersfield, and I've arranged this text in the hope that you might become as fascinated by the topic as I am. Like so many other activities in life, one learns more about the subject the more one teaches it. Students ask different questions, apply them to different life experiences, and interpret the ideas in different ways. I have learnt far more about political theory from my students than they have ever learnt from me, and as a consequence this little book is a modest attempt to give something back to the discipline, in the

---

1 I use man here as it is the word that Rousseau uses – we can be pretty sure that he does mean man, rather than as a misguided shorthand for people. This is normal in the history of political thought until relatively recently. I can understand how you might find this irritating, but there is no sense in dressing up the sexism of the time as anything else.

hope that others may find it a useful guide to access the life-changing knowledge that is contained within the history of political thought.

As a lecturer in political theory, I also think that there is something useful about the discipline for us in the contemporary world. We have become more ideologically polarized over the past few decades, and political discourse has become harsher, and more personal in its vitriol. Disagreement is inevitable in pluralist democratic societies, and this disagreement is nothing to be scared of in and of itself. I hope, however, that discussions around central theoretical political issues might go some way towards making political discussions more genteel and civilized.

So the overall purpose of this book is to provide an introductory guide to some of the key questions in the history of political thought, and to provide a good sound knowledge of the ideas held by the key thinkers in political theory. I have written it in a particular way to attempt to make it accessible to anyone embarking on a journey of knowledge in political theory.

Why should we bother with the history of political thought?

Virtually everyone discussed in this book is dead; many long since so. So why should we find their discussions of politics useful in our modern world? Obviously, seeing as how I have written 80,000 words on the topic, I think they are **interesting**, and I strongly suspect that they are **useful**, but it is worth reflecting on precisely why this might be the case before we go any further.

To some of you, the question of interest and usefulness might be separate. We do not necessarily think watching *Downton Abbey* is useful, nor do we necessarily think this of a Shakespearean play or a novel by Goethe. We might engage with these things for the interest in and of themselves rather than helping us understand the present; we might enjoy it for the historical information it provides or the entertainment it brings. Likewise, one might be interested in the political ideas of historical figures and that that interest is sufficient reason to study them. This seems fine to me up to a point. Some of you might be interested in history, so to understand that John Locke's outline of contractual government whose powers are limited by the pre-political powers of the individual was a contribution to debates on the Glorious Revolution in England would be of some interest. Here historical insight might be enough.

Others might be looking at these thinkers and debates in an attempt to understand why, say, Republicans in the United States view the political world differently to Democrats, or why the Labour Party is distinct from the Conservative Party in the UK. So here, studying political theory might have a contemporary use as opposed to only historical interest. A key use for the history of political philosophy is to show the genesis of the ideas that we hold today, and illustrate the changes and variations that they have gone through over the years. Take democracy for example; it is perhaps useful to know that the system of liberal representative democracy with universal suffrage that is dominant in the contemporary world is distinct from the direct democracy with limited citizenship that was practised in its first incarnation in ancient Athens. Also thinkers such as Rousseau provide us with a vocabulary to critique contemporary democracy if we do not think it extends sufficiently far. When using this justification for studying the history of political thought, we should be wary of presentism, the notion that all history is leading up to us, and avoid viewing the past through our concepts and concerns.

Another way to study the history of political thought is to focus not on how our ideas have been shaped over time, but instead recognize just how different political concepts were in the past, and to use this as a critical activity. When women were completely ignored in politics, when, without irony, slave owners could write that all men were created equal, when others suggested that the monarch was put there by God and was the only person with any legitimate power, it is too easy to just say 'how could they believe that' and move on. The thing is that people did believe in these things; and they believed in them just as much as you or I believe in those political things that we believe in. The critical activity therefore rests in this; just as we are viewing ideas from the past with some incredulity, so too will people reading textbooks like this is a few hundred years look on us with amazement that we could think or act politically in a certain way. We should reflect on our beliefs and wonder what future generations will judge us harshly on. The history of political thought here is not history for its own sake, nor a history to show us how we became who we are, but rather a thought experiment urging us to be critical of the ideas commonly held today.

Activity 1. Outline three commonly held beliefs in society today that you feel a student of political theory in 500 years will find problematic.

(1)

(2)

(3)

Reasons to study the history of political thought

1) For simple historical interest
2) To see how the ideas we have today have developed
3) To acquire critical skills to assess our society

How to use this book

This book has been organized to be a useful study guide for anyone interested in learning about political theory, be they a school or college student, or an autodidact who wishes to learn the basics on their own. No prior knowledge is assumed on the part of the reader, so the hope is that if the subject interests you, you can just jump straight in. It is a book for everyone, not only for people with substantial existing knowledge on this subject, or for that matter, any other. Perhaps you are studying political theory as part of a course at college or university. Perhaps you have become interested in politics recently, and wish to learn about how some of the central figures of political theory have addressed the issues that you are now grappling with. Or perhaps you simply wish to learn about something new. Whatever your personal learning goal is, my aim in this book is to give you a good solid understanding of the basics of political theory, which you can then build upon perhaps by picking up the primary works of the thinkers discussed within these pages.

Attempts have been made throughout the book to give real-life examples of some of the dilemmas that we address in these pages, and these examples have been chosen with the aim of helping you understand a topic better, and show how the debate contained herein, is applicable to everyday life. Whereas political theory is quite an intellectual pursuit, we should never lose sight of the fact that it should be about real, everyday life; political theory should help us in everyday moral or ethical dilemmas, it should allow us to talk and think politically, and it should aid us in the ability to be good citizens and question political power wherever it may exist. We are not talking about abstract notions here; we are discussing things that happen around us every day.

The book has been organized around key political questions, questions such as 'what is the nature of the just state?', and 'why should I obey the state?' It is organized in this manner, rather than a thinker-by-thinker structure (i.e. a chapter on Plato, a chapter on Hobbes and so on) to allow you to see the contributions made by various philosophers to similar topics. This structure should better allow you to compare and contrast the thinkers, examine their views on similar topics, and therefore to adopt a critical attitude to their ideas, by showing how they would critique one another.

This book might look slightly different from similar textbooks on the history of political thought. You will not be faced with a wall of text, but rather you might notice some features which are unique to this book. Firstly, each chapter commences with some key questions which you might want to consider before starting the chapter proper. Then within each chapter, you will notice at various points certain keywords or phrases will be emboldened; this is because I feel that these points are crucially important to the discussion in hand. You will also notice small text boxes which give brief summaries of discussions scattered throughout each chapter, and larger text boxes which give you more information on an individual thinker that we are discussing, giving you brief biographical details and the like. You can dip in and out of these sections as best fits your method of learning.

Crucially there are also activities after every section within the book. These activities are designed to solidify your reading, and encourage you to reflect on what you have read. You may choose to do these activities as you read through each chapter, or you may like to do them when you have completed the chapter; it is up to you – do what you feel is best. At the end of each chapter are some text-based questions; these are, perhaps, slightly trickier than the activities contained within each chapter. The text-based activities contain some short excerpts from key texts discussed in the book, with some questions attached. I ask that you read the text, then attempt the questions.

Contents of this book

Each chapter in this book, as mentioned above, is organized around a central question in the history of political thought. They are as follows.

What is the nature of politics?

We begin by examining what acting politically entails, or what should people engaged in politics do? We will find a large variety of responses across the history of political thought. This chapter will commence with a discussion of the Greek philosopher **Socrates** and his life and thought. He argued that the individual should always strive for knowledge of the virtues, and that the unexamined life is not worth living. There is something inherently human and vital to discussing the very type of questions that we will be tackling in this book together. We will then go on to examine the work of the Florentine writer **Machiavelli**, who will argue that the chief goal of any politician should be glory, both for themselves and for the state. If one achieves glory, you can be forgiven immoral acts you have committed along the way. The **utilitarian** school of moral thinking will then be introduced, which posits that happiness, rather than glory, should be the driving feature of all government policy and political action. **Immanuel Kant** will then be introduced as a counterbalance to both Machiavelli and the utilitarians. Politics must always bend the knee to morality for Kant, that is to say that acting morally is always more important that achieving glory and/or happiness. The chapter will conclude with a discussion of **Max Weber** and his guidance that passion is an insufficient quality to succeed in politics.

Is humanity nasty or nice?

This chapter will compare and contrast the works of English philosopher **Thomas Hobbes** and the Genevan **Jean-Jacques Rousseau**. Hobbes will illustrate that in their natural condition man is violent and nasty, and left to their own devices, that is to say without a state, they will end up killing one another. **Rousseau** will counter that man's anti-sociability is not a product of nature; indeed, he claims that in his natural state man is good if not moral, but rather a product of civilized man. Civilization has corrupted our innate goodness. We will also briefly examine here the thoughts on the nature of good and evil by German philosopher **Nietzsche**, who argues that these concepts are not unchangeable over time, and that which we call good these days is often life destroying.

Why should I obey the state?

This chapter begins by examining the **social contract theory** of **Thomas Hobbes** and his near contemporary **John Locke**. Although they both ultimately say that all obligation to obey the state rests upon consent, the type of consent and the powers of the sovereign differ greatly between them. It will then examine some critiques of liberal social contract theory, namely those of **Rousseau**, **Hume** and **Pateman**.

Is democracy the best form of government?

This chapter will examine some of the challenges that exist around discussions of democratic thought. It will firstly compare and contrast **Athenian direct democracy** to our contemporary understanding of politics, noting the central differences between the two being a limited citizenry as well as the lack of representatives. It will then outline **Edmund Burke's** arguments in favour of representative democracy, and in particular non-delegated representatives who are not obliged to pay too much attention to their electors in between elections. We will then go on to examine some of the challenges to democracy, namely **James Madison's** federalist paper number 10, which argues that the size of the proposed US republic would prevent faction, before overviewing **de Tocqueville's** and **Mill's** concerns about the tyranny of the majority. We will see that Mill suggests that whereas everyone should get one vote, some people should get more than that.

When can my freedom be restricted?

This chapter will discuss a number of debates around the nature of freedom in society. It will commence with **Isaiah Berlin's** distinction between positive and negative liberty; that there have been two different ways in the history of political thought that freedom has been conceptualized. This will be challenged by **Gerald MacCallum** who will argue that there is only one concept of freedom, and **Quentin Skinner's** assertion that there are three. The chapter will end with a discussion of **John Stuart Mill's** Harm Principle, the notion that the just state should only ever stop someone from doing things that directly and physically harm someone else. The state, nor anyone else for that matter, has no right to ban someone from doing that which only harms themselves, or that which offends other people.

What would a just society look like?

In this chapter, we will examine different notions of justice in society. We will commence with **Plato's** assertion that justice involves a harmonious state when each does that which best suits them; everyone in society has a role, but these roles are not equal. This will be contrasted to **Aristotle's** notion of justice as balance. We will then examine justice more in terms of the distribution of goods, and outline **John Locke's** famous defence of a natural right to private property, and show how this was critiqued by **David Hume** and **Thomas Paine**. Next, we will move on to the debate between **John Rawls** and **Robert Nozick**, two Harvard colleagues, about the nature of justice. We will see that Rawls argues that justice is arrived at via a mind game in which the participants do not know how they will be affected as individuals, which ends up as a defence of the social democratic state. Nozick, on the other hand, will argue that justice means that the only permissible state is that which defends individual property rights.

Why have women been ignored in the history of political thought?

This chapter will attempt to show why so many of the thinkers mentioned above are men. It will begin with **Rousseau's** argument about the natural inequalities between men and women, before critiquing this with the ideas of **Mary Wollstonecraft** and **John Stuart Mill**. Wollstonecraft and Mill will argue that there are no natural differences between men and women, and, where differences exist, it is due to women's inability to access social goods such as education and improving work, as well as their lack of rights. The chapter will conclude with **I.M. Young's** contention that there are differences between men and women when it comes to ethical and political reasoning, but the male forms of reasoning are universalized. So liberal democratic culture is inherently biased towards men.

When is revolution against government justified?

Here we will overview a number of responses to when it is acceptable to overthrow the government. It will begin with the debate between **Edmund Burke**, who argues that revolution is only justified if one is restoring a set of rights and privileges that have been denied you, and **Thomas Paine**, who argued that only political institutions based upon reason are permissible. The chapter will end with a long overdue examination of **Karl Marx**, who will show that revolution is the natural driving force of societies, and overthrowing the capitalist regime is not only justifiable, but the only way one will achieve a communist society.

Conclusion: Ideologies

The book will conclude by highlighting the links between thinkers outlined in the discussions above, and the main world ideologies, namely **liberalism**, **conservatism** and **socialism**.

Methodology

Some methodological liberties have been taken with the contents of this book in an attempt to make it accessible and user friendly. One criticism that can easily be levelled at the chapter structure above is that I am taking thinkers from different societies, in different ages, responding to different political events, and moulding them together as if they were discussing the same political issues when they clearly were not. The history of political thought then becomes a dinner party with the various thinkers talking to one another, which is, of course, highly anachronistic. The only marginal defence I can make of my position here is that, in a number of the debates, people were responding to near contemporaries. John Locke was responding to Hobbes, Aristotle to Plato, Paine to Burke, Wollstonecraft to Rousseau and Nozick to Rawls. Rousseau was addressing Hobbes, although there was a century between them, and Nietzsche was addressing Socrates from the distance of well over a millennium. The convenience of structuring the book in this manner to use as an introductory text does, I hope, partially absolve any methodological qualms the reader may have.

Also, the book does focus on what might be referred to as the received canon of texts. Of course, these canonical texts are only elevated amongst others as we continually address them as such; we teach those texts that we have been taught ourselves and so the canon is perpetuated. Again, my only defence against this charge is that as this book is intended to provide an introduction to beginners to political theory it is best to focus our attention on those texts considered central to understanding the discipline. Readers might do well to reflect upon why dead, white, European males dominate this canon and challenge this.

Works cited

Rousseau, J.J. (1953) *The Confessions*. London: Penguin.

2

What is the nature of politics?

KEY QUESTIONS

(1) Does living a political life involve constant reflection on the nature of justice?

(2) Does glory act as a constraint to what a prince may do in Machiavelli's writings?

(3) Is morality derived from the motivations behind an act, or the consequences of them? How might this apply to politics?

(4) Can one become a politician and remain morally innocent, or must one get one's hands dirty?

(5) Is passion a good thing in politics?

We all think we know what politics is; but what is the purpose of it? Why do we, as a species, do it, and what is its end? If you went up to the first person you met on the street and asked them what politics is, the likelihood is that they would give the response that it is the stuff that goes on in Washington, DC/Westminster/Canberra/Brussels or similar; and that is a perfectly plausible account of what politics is in the contemporary world, but it doesn't really help us with what it is for.

In 2012, the city of New York proposed a change to its health codes prohibiting sales of sugary drinks in sizes of more than 16 ounces (around 0.5 of a litre) in the city upon health grounds. One would be able to buy/sell diet or milk-based drinks in any size you liked, but sugary drinks would be limited to 16 ounces due to the calories contained therein, in an attempt to limit citizens' sugar intake and promote healthy living. There is an inbuilt assumption here that one of the purposes of politics and government is to protect the health of the citizens of a country, and the attempt by the City of New York to limit the sales of large sugary beverages is hardly new in this regard. Around the world cigarettes are taxed (often heavily) to discourage smoking, alcohol is restricted and taxed, many drugs are flat out banned, whilst subsidies might be given to organizations that put on physical activities. One can prohibit certain things that may lead to poor health to actively stop someone gaining access to them, one can tax them to discourage people from buying them, or, in New York's case, one can restrict the size of sale; of course, one could always buy two or three drinks, but perhaps this is unlikely. Poor diet and lack of exercise lead to poor health in the population, increased strain on medical budgets, and many/most governments see it as their business to combat this. To put it another way, many/most governments see the overall health of the population to be one of the things that politics is for; it is one of the tests of a successful administration that health statistics are on the rise.

Others might argue that this is none of the state's business, and that policies such as this are instances of the nanny state. This account would argue, perhaps, that politics is for defending rights, protecting property and liberty, and administering the state; what people want to drink, smoke or do in their own time is none of government's business.

The City of New York's proposal failed to be implemented, not because it was determined that it was an overreach of the City's powers, but rather because it would only affect businesses licensed by the City, and many locations inside the city were licensed by the state and were not subject to City regulations on this issue. Equity was at stake here; certain businesses would have been free to sell sugary drinks by the bucket load, whilst others would have restrictions placed upon them, and this would have led to an unequal marketplace. Fairness in the application of principles was deemed a more important goal of politics than health.

Chapter overview

This chapter aims to begin our reflections on politics by examining what politics is about? What type of aims should we have from politics? How has politics been conceptualized? This chapter will commence in ancient Athens, then move from Renaissance Florence to nineteenth-century England, then hop over to Germany, before travelling across the Atlantic to the United States in the 1970s, before returning to Germany. As you might expect from such a journey, the ranges of responses to the question 'what is politics about?' are varied.

Our first discussion will be a brief examination of the life of Socrates and to see how he placed a search for justice at the heart of politics, and thought that we should all regard this quest as being central to our lives. Indeed, he became a martyr for this quest. We will then examine Machiavelli's advice to politicians outlined in his work *The Prince*. We will see here that it is not morality that should be at the heart of politics, as it is pointless always being moral as a prince because if you do you will lose your position to someone who is not as good as you. This does not mean to say that the prince can do anything to keep his power though, as, for Machiavelli, glory is the purpose in politics, and glory places restraints on what a ruler can do.

We will then begin a comparison among utilitarian philosophers such as Bentham and Mill, who will argue that politics should be about bringing the greatest amount of happiness possible in politics. This will be contrasted with Kant, who argues that morality is the most important thing in politics. We will see that there exists between Kant and the utilitarian theorists a significant difference in how we formulate the nature of a moral act, with Kant focusing purely on the motivations behind an act, and the utilitarians examining the consequences of an act. Walzer will provide us with a potential halfway house between these competing perspectives on morality with his notion of dirty hands.

The chapter will conclude with an overview of Max Weber's cautionary note against pure passion in politics, noting as he does that, with a centralized state with a monopoly of the use of legitimate force, this should be balanced with responsibility and a sense of purpose.

Socrates and the examined life

Socrates wrote nothing down, and the accounts we have on him are spartan, so it might seem strange to start a chapter on the nature of politics in a book on political theory with someone who leaves us with nothing to examine. It is rather his life that gives us a lesson in the nature of politics; he was a badass. He questioned whatever beliefs he wanted, cared not one iota for money or possessions, actively opposed the form of government in Athens at the time, and did not care who he upset in the process. The only Greek who comes close to beating him in the rock and roll stakes is Diogenes, who lived in a barrel and would walk around the marketplace in daylight with a lamp in the search for an honest man. Philosophy was not a subject to be abstractly studied in the classroom or the library for Socrates; it was to be lived. If one discovered a virtue, the notion that you should act differently to that virtue would have baffled him.

In *The Apology*, an account of the trial of Socrates, where he was being prosecuted on the charge of corrupting the youth of Athens, written by his devoted student Plato, Socrates outlines why it would be no good for them to exile him from Athens. Socrates was a controversial figure who questioned many of the religious and political beliefs that were dominant in the ancient Greek democracy. He philosophized on the street, gained adherents and enemies alike, and asked searching questions about the nature of virtue. He argued that if exiled he would just continue doing precisely that which he had done hitherto in another place:

> Perhaps someone may say, 'But surely, Socrates, after you have left us you can spend the rest of your life in quietly minding your own business.' This is the

hardest thing of all to make some of you understand. If I say that this would be disobedience to God, and that is why I cannot 'mind my own business', you will not believe me – you'll think I'm pulling your leg. If on the other hand I tell you **that to let no day pass without discussing goodness and all the other subjects about which you hear me talking and examining both myself and others is the very best thing that a man can do, and that life without this sort of examination is not worth living**, you will be even less inclined to believe me. (Plato, 1993: 63, my emphasis)

Socrates is saying here that 'discussing goodness' is what we should all be doing every day, and, if we do not do this, we are wasting our lives. Those of us who get up, go to work, go home, watch TV, go to the pub, then go to sleep without thinking about, or better yet discussing with our peers, the nature of justice and politics, are not really living lives that are meaningful in any way. Discussing the kind of issues that are in this book is what makes life worth living. Consider this, when you attempt the activities throughout this book (especially if you do them with friends), you are not just testing your knowledge, or providing yourself with an *aide-mémoire*, you are living a meaningful life for Socrates.

> The unexamined life is not worth living for Socrates. We should, on a daily basis, question the nature of justice and morality, and we should live our lives according to our conclusions.

Socrates developed what has become known as the Socratic method as a way to examine concepts and beliefs; you can see this method at work in any of the Socratic dialogues written by Plato, and his use of him in *The Republic*. The Socratic method involved Socrates cross-examining his interlocutor, generally asking for a definition, then perhaps another example. If you are studying at college at the moment, you may have witnessed the Socratic method from your tutor without knowing it. Its purpose was to bring clarity of definitions and concepts in a search for truth, but often Socrates would try to show how the definitions and additional examples his colleague raised showed how their original assertion was false. As well as illuminating, they could sometimes destroy.

Socrates often tried to show how beliefs and contentions held by those he was talking to were in fact false. Nothing was worse for Socrates than claiming to know something which you did not know, or thinking you knew a lot when you did not. This is known as the Socratic irony, that the wisest people realize that they know nothing. Acceptance of the world of things which one does not know is a virtue for Socrates. He is not, however, defending ignorance here; far from it. What he is attacking is the pomposity and sophistry of those who claim to know more than they do. This is a political point, as he thought that in Athenian democracy, too much power was given to those who either knew nothing, or knew less than they claimed to know.

In response to this, Socrates developed the Craft Analogy. Politics should be seen as analogous to crafts. If your car broke down this morning, you would not take a vote amongst your friends about how to fix it; you would take it to a mechanic who is an expert in fixing cars. Likewise, if your mobile phone died, you would not necessarily canvass opinion from all and sundry as to how to fix it; you would take it to a specialist. So it is with the leadership of the state; it should be left to those with the most skill in that particular craft, people like Socrates, rather than being in the hands of everyone in a democracy. Plato would develop this point further in *The Republic*, but it is obviously undemocratic; not everyone has the skill to lead for Socrates, not everyone questions the nature of justice and leads an examined life, qualities needed as a minimum for leadership.

Activity 1. Please attempt the tasks below:

(1) When was the last time you had a philosophical or political discussion with your friends or family?

(2) What would Socrates think of your response to task (1)?

(3) What did Socrates mean by the Craft Analogy? What do you think of it?

Machiavelli and glory

Niccolò Machiavelli was, prior to his writing career, a practising politician. In 1498 he was appointed Second Chancellor to the Florentine republic; roughly equivalent to posts such as Secretary of State in the United States or the Foreign Secretary in the UK, as it dealt with foreign policy. As a result, Machiavelli travelled Europe and met many of the leading politicians of his day and age. When the Medici returned to Florence and disbanded the republic, Machiavelli was accused of plotting to kill one of the Medici, imprisoned, tortured, and eventually exiled from Florence. It was when living on a farm that he took up writing, and completed *The Prince* and *The Discourses on Livy* amongst other things.

Machiavelli was, Oppenheimer notes, 'the first philosopher to define politics as treachery' (2011, xiii).

> If the prince was to follow the Christian virtues all the time, he would become predictable – and end up losing his position, probably to someone less good than him. So it is vital that the prince learns how not to be good sometimes.

The Prince takes the popular Renaissance literary form of an advice-book for princes, a scholar providing advice to a prince on how they should govern, a manual, or idiots' guide if you will, on what a prince should do when in power. Other instances of this type of work are Castiglione's *The Courtier*, for example. In some ways *The Prince* takes the typical form of an advice-book for princes, but in one crucial way it 'revolutionised the *genre*' (Skinner, 1978: 118). Most of his fellow authors argued that a prince should be virtuous, and by this they mean that they should always follow the Christian virtues. Machiavelli also thought a prince should be virtuous, but he meant it in an entirely different way. He meant it to mean virtuoso, or, to put it another way, skilled. If one refers to a virtuoso pianist, we mean that they are skilful at playing the piano, not that they are a moral pianist (even if perhaps they are). Likewise, the prince should be skilful as opposed to always moral.

Following the Christian morals was not necessarily bad in and of itself for Machiavelli; indeed, perhaps the prince should generally follow them. The problem arose for Machiavelli if the prince *always* followed them, he always kept his word, he always paid his debts, and so on. This would be because the prince would then become predictable, and his political opponents would always know what he was going to do, and he would be deposed. So if the prince wanted to keep hold of his position, he must learn how to sometimes do the opposite of the Christian morals; this was the skill that he must learn. It might be fine to always be moral if we always know that our opponents would be likewise; but they won't and therefore we shouldn't.

> [T]he gulf between how one should live and how one does live is so wide that a man who neglects what is actually done for what should be done learns the way to self-destruction rather than self-preservation. The fact is that a man who wants to act virtuously in every way necessarily comes to grief among so many who are not virtuous. (Machiavelli, 1961: 91)

When Michelle Obama responded to criticisms of her and her husband, she famously urged her supporters not to resort to cheap shots by saying 'when they go low, we go high'. Machiavelli would have had no problem with a politician generally staying high, but if one always stays high, one becomes predictable. It is always necessary for the politician to learn how to sometimes go low. Imagine for a moment that you, literally you, with your fair mindedness and a programme for social justice, wanted to become a political leader. All your friends, family and political supporters want it likewise; but everyone knows that you will face stiff competition from people wanting to put their schemes into place. Indeed, perhaps those schemes are the exact opposite of yours and will leave people

Machiavelli

Machiavelli was born in 1469 in Florence, modern-day Italy but then a city state, to a prominent, but not very wealthy, family. During Machiavelli's lifetime, Florence oscillated between being a republic and being ruled by the Medici family, a dynasty of bankers and art patrons. As part of his duties in the Florentine republic, he met leading political figures of the day such as Cesare Borgia, Louis XII and Pope Alexander VI. It was here he became interested in the manner in which political rulers acquired and ruled their territories.

After the return of the Medici he was imprisoned and tortured for his alleged involvement in an assassination attempt. He then went to live on his farm outside of the city of Florence, where he started writing.

Machiavelli is best known for his work *The Prince*, which shows how princes should govern, and the *Discourses*, where he shows how republics should govern. It is in dispute as to which he favoured.

worse off than your proposals. In this scenario, what is better? For you to not play the game of politics, remain virtuous and pure, but the people who would have benefitted from your proposals to be worse off. Or for you to play the game of politics, do a questionable act every now and again, and for your proposals to be put into action and for people to be better off? This is the dilemma that Machiavelli suggests is the real stuff of politics. One must, as a politician, learn not to always be like a fox (crafty, wily, cunning), nor always like a lion (scary, dominant), but instead learn the skill to judge when to act like a lion and when to act like a fox. You certainly cannot be successful in politics by being good all the time. 'You can make this generalization about men', Machiavelli states, 'they are ungrateful, fickle, liars, and deceivers', you cannot trust them, so governing by being good all the time will never work (Machiavelli, 1961: 96).

The enemy of the skilful prince is fortune; and many thought that any prince could be thrown off course by bad luck. Indeed, Stoic thought was popular when Machiavelli was writing; and Stoicism placed a lot of emphasis on luck. After you had prepared yourself for a certain activity, if luck prevented you from suc- ceeding, Stoic philosophy invited you to shrug your shoulders and accept that so much of the world is out of your control. Machiavelli completely rejects this. Whereas fortune does indeed control a lot of one's life (half of it, he suggests), it will control far more of the life of a weak unskilled prince than a skilled manly man. Fortune favours the brave, for Machiavelli. So he suggests:

> She shows her potency where there is no well regulated power to resist her, and her impetus is felt where she knows there are no embankments and dykes built to resist her. (Machiavelli, 1961: 130–1)

So far from our discussion, we might be tempted to conclude that the purpose of politics for Machiavelli is for the prince to keep power, and that the prince is entitled to do anything to do this. This is not the case, even though his reputation often makes people think this is so. The purpose of politics for Machiavelli is glory; to be a glorious leader and to lead a glorious state. *The Prince* is full of examples of leaders from Machiavelli's time and from antiquity that he thinks we can learn from. What politicians should do is learn from these leaders about the nature of glorious leadership in the hope that future generations might look to your example to learn about politics. Like an art student who copies an old master to learn the excellence of painting, Machiavelli invites the reader to attempt to provide future generations with an example of glory to follow.

Take his description of Agathocles, the man who showed 'much audacity and physical courage' to rise from an obscure position to become King of Syracuse, for example (Machiavelli, 1961: 62). To take power, he rounded up the politicians and wealthy citizens and had them summarily executed, and faced no internal opposition thereafter. He held on to power for some time, and won many magnificent military victories, so in some ways might be seen as the archetypal Machiavellian ruler, showing as he did ingenuity to tame fortune. This is not, however, Machiavelli's conclusion on his reign. Machiavelli states that it 'cannot be called prowess to kill fellow citizens, to betray friends, to be treacherous, pitiless, irreligious. These ways can win a prince **power but not glory**' (Machiavelli, 1961: 63, my emphasis).

The fifteenth-century Italian politician Cesare Borgia, on the other hand, receives high praise from Machiavelli. In particular, he singles out one episode in his career that was worthy of special mention of praise, indeed singling it out as worthy of 'close study and imitation by others' (Machiavelli, 1961: 57). Borgia captured Romagna (an area in the north of modern-day Italy) and appointed his trusted servant Remirro de Orco to govern the area. Romagna had a history of anarchy in the past, so Borgia instructed de Orco to govern sternly and assert the authority of the state. Borgia's instructions were carried out well and de Orco 'pacified and unified' the area 'winning great credit for himself' in the process (Machiavelli, 1961: 57). Borgia sensed a problem. The objective of restoring law and order had been achieved, but due to the severe methods de Orco had used, methods that were at Borgia's insistence, there was a growing sense of hatred towards Borgia in the area. Borgia's methods here deserve to be quoted in full:

Agathocles vs Borgia

Agathocles was cruel and merciless – and although he held onto his power, he was not glorious as he is remembered as a tyrant. Borgia on the other hand committed a savage act, but is remembered as a glorious ruler. Glory places a limit on what the prince can do for Machiavelli.

> Knowing … that the severities of the past had earned him a certain amount of hatred, to purge the minds of the people and to win them over completely he determined to show that if cruelties had been inflicted they were not his doing but prompted by the harsh nature of his minister. This gave Cesare a pretext; then, one morning, Remirro's body was cut in two pieces on the piazza at Cesna, with a block of wood and a bloody knife beside it. **The brutality of this spectacle kept the people of the Romagna for a time appeased and stupefied.** (Machiavelli, 1961: 57–8, my emphasis)

So Borgia managed to restore order to an area he had conquered by installing a minister to do just this, and when the criticism of these methods started to be aimed at him, he had the minister killed and his body displayed in the town square so that his subjects would think that he had listened to them. Machiavelli thinks that this is marvellous. But precisely how is this different from the criticisms that he levels at Agathocles? The answer lays in glory. Agathocles was remembered as a tyrant who murdered many of his citizens and largely destroyed the areas under his control. He is not the type of ruler that future students of power and politics would wish to emulate. Borgia is remembered as 'severe yet loved, magnanimous and generous' and the leader of a glorious state, and precisely the type of leader who we should copy and learn the virtues of politics from (Machiavelli, 1961: 61).

Far, then, from Machiavelli thinking that the prince can do anything he wants in order to protect his position, Machiavelli thinks that glory rather than the Christian virtues places restrictions on the actions of a prince. Brutal, faithless acts are permitted as a means to an end to a glorious state. As he discusses in his *Discourses on Livy* when discussing Romulus' murder of his brother Remus, 'when the act accuses him, the result should excuse him; and when the result is good, as in the case of Romulus, it will always absolve him from blame' (Machiavelli, 1950: 139). Whereas it might not be morally right to murder one's brother, the resulting founding of Rome, the eternal city, means we can forget this transgression. **The end does not always justify the means, but if the ends are glorious the means can be justified.** Glory is the purpose of politics for Machiavelli, and the nature of man and politics is such that, in order to bring about a glorious state, it is necessary to do some things which are not quite so good.

So Machiavelli presents us with a **consequentialist** account of politics and morality. We cannot determine from his works a right or wrong set of political actions, and the virtue of a prince is to be able to do the right thing at the right time; to have the skill to be able to make political judgements based upon necessity. Therefore, the rightness or wrongness of an act cannot be determined by its intentions, motivations or adherence to a moral code, but rather from what occurs as a result of them. If a prince's achievements lead to a strong state with artistic and financial achievements, and that prince is then remembered as one to study and attempt to emulate for future generations, then he can be forgiven the occasional act that might otherwise be considered contrary to morality. If you are remembered solely for your breaches of morality and you achieve little else than power, then you will not be regarded as glorious.

Activity 2. Please attempt the activities below:

(1) Why did Machiavelli think Agathocles was a tyrant and Borgia was glorious? Is there a contradiction here?

(2) Why does Machiavelli think that a prince should not always follow the Christian virtues?

Utilitarianism and happiness

Whereas Machiavelli is a consequentialist, not all consequentialists are similar to Machiavelli. Perhaps the dominant body of thought in the history of political thought that judges the morality of an action by its consequences is utilitarianism, a body of thought which has a lot to say about the nature of politics as well. It is a complex body of thought that spans many thinkers and contains many variations of thought. At its core, however, utilitarianism argues that **the morality (or lack thereof) of an act should be judged based upon the amount of happiness that the act produces.** Utilitarians were often political reformers who proposed policy revisions in everything from punishing criminals to more recently giving all one's disposable income to charity.

In perhaps the founding text of utilitarian moral thinking, *An Introduction to the Principles of Morals and Legislation*, Jeremy Bentham outlines his 'principle of utility'.

> Nature has placed mankind under the governance of two sovereign masters, *pain* and *pleasure*. It is for them alone to point out what we ought to do ... By the principle of utility is meant that principle which approves or disapproves of every action whatsoever according to the tendency it appears to have to augment or diminish the happiness of the party whose interest is in question: or, what is the same thing in other words to promote or to oppose that happiness. I say of every action whatsoever, and therefore not only of every action of a private individual, but of every measure of government. (Bentham, 2012: 1–2)

In some ways this should not appear too controversial – no one is opposed to pleasure and in favour of pain as a general rule; but what Bentham is saying here

Utilitarians question the helpfulness of rights in discourses around politics. For them it is better to talk of people's happiness, or their interests. It is not so much that they would support active breaking of rights, but more that they feel discussion of other issues would lead to better results.

is that this should be the grounding principle as to what politics should be about. Above, we have seen how Machiavelli thinks that politics is about glory; later on in this book we will see how Hobbes thinks politics is about stability, and how Paine suggests that the protection of rights is the proper aim of politics. For Bentham, it is about promoting pleasure and avoiding pain. An action is therefore good if it brings happiness, and bad if it results in pain; therefore, the rightness or wrongness of an act is determined by its consequences as opposed to its motivations.

Let us take the following thought experiment. Suppose you are taking an afternoon stroll past a duck pond in your local park on a sunny summer's afternoon. You hear a commotion and look up and notice that a child has fallen into the pond and is in trouble; you immediately think that it is a moral law beyond question that you should assist children in peril, remove your jacket, dive into the pond, and rescue the child. Is this a moral act? Very few would doubt that it is. If you are a Kantian (precisely what this means will be discussed below, but for our purposes it means someone for whom universal morality consists of universal laws based upon motivations), the fact that your intentions were pure and universal make this moral. If you are a rule-based utilitarian like J.S. Mill (again more on this later, but broadly it means that utility is best brought about by enforcing certain laws as opposed to making lots of individual calculations), again it appears moral as the rule that we should assist children in peril seems to be one that would increase overall happiness. And Bentham would certainly regard it as moral, although he would probably think the motivations and rule are largely irrelevant, and the crucial issue was the pleasure of the child at being rescued and the avoidance of pain.

But let us twist the example a little bit. Suppose you were taking the same stroll on the same sunny summer's day, and you heard the same commotion, and noticed the same child in peril in the pond. But this time you did not immediately remove your jacket and dive into the pond to rescue the child because you thought there was an irrefutable moral law commanding you to do so. Instead, you glanced up and noted that nearby the child in need was Justin Bieber, or Cardi B, or George Clooney, or Christina Hendricks, or whatever celebrity you think is attractive. You think to yourself, 'if I jumped into this pond and rescued the child, then Justin/Cardi/George/Christina or whoever would notice me, think I was brave, and maybe take me out to dinner as a reward'. So you remove your jacket, jump into the duck pond, and rescue the child. Is this still a moral act? Kant would almost certainly say not, as your actions were based upon potential consequences rather than motivations, and based on laws that cannot be universalized. You would have used that child as a means to an end rather than them being an end in and of themselves. Likewise, Mill, although a utilitarian, might have a problem with attempting

Utilitarianism

Jeremy Bentham is generally regarded as the founding father of utilitarianism. Bentham was born in 1748 in London, and educated at Oxford. In addition to his writing on utilitarianism, he was a leading social reformer of his day. Whereas he was an opponent of natural rights arguments, he nevertheless supported the notion of legal rights when they could be said to increase the overall happiness of the people.

You can still visit Bentham to this day. Bentham played a role in founding University College London, and left his body to the college. His mummified remains are displayed in the main reception area.

Other utilitarians include father and son team James and John Stuart Mill and Henry Sidgwick. It still has proponents in the contemporary world, with the works of Australian philosopher Peter Singer, who uses the idea to support vegetarianism and giving all of our disposable income to charity.

to apply the rule that we should 'rescue all children who are in the vicinity of attractive celebrities' as one to promote general utility. Bentham would probably think that this was still a moral act, and despite the quibbles over motivations and rules, the end consequence is that the child was rescued so the happiness is equal to the scenario when the child was rescued for purer motives. For Bentham, those things that promote happiness are good, and those that lead to pain are bad; this applies just as much to politics and government legislation as it does to ethics.

Utilitarian philosophers critiqued a large array of social and political policies when they were writing. For example, they championed reforms of the punishments that prisoners received; not upon the grounds of morality or rights, *per se*, but more on the overall manner in which they worked and the results that they brought about. One such reform was that of lowering the punishments associated with crimes such as theft. Utilitarians in Britain in the late eighteenth and early nineteenth century noticed a problem with sentencing. Offences that we would regard as minor today such as theft might still be punishable by death. So the problem was that if you are caught stealing a pig, you have absolutely no incentive to go quietly and accept your punishment; if the punishment for stealing a pig is the same as killing the person who caught you stealing the pig, then you might as well fight your way out of the situation. You would have little to lose at this point, and the overall happiness would be improved by more lenient penal laws. Again, these proposals were put forward not because of human rights concerns, but to produce more happiness.

And this is the key contribution of utilitarianism to debates surrounding the nature of politics: contrary to many liberal thinkers such as Paine and Rawls (who we will address later in this book) who argue that the purpose of government is to protect rights, utilitarians do not really think we have rights. Bentham regarded the notion of rights as rhetorical nonsense on stilts. As a consequence of this, the purpose of politics is to promote happiness not rights. There are a number of ways in which protecting rights might lead to less happiness overall. Take the famous Trolley Problem. You are by a railway track and you notice that a train is out of control and is hurtling towards, and if unhindered will surely kill, a group of five people on the track ahead of it. Now suppose you could not stop the train, but you could pull a lever that would move the train onto another track, but that this act would certainly kill one person who was on that track. So you could do nothing, and five people would die, or you could take an action, and that action would result in one person dying. The overall happiness would probably be greater if you took an action that killed one person (or saved four lives to put it in a more positive way), but does not the one person have a right to life?

Governments take actions that lead to some people suffering all the time. Winston Churchill left Coventry undefended from Luftwaffe raids in the Second World War despite knowing that it was going to be attacked. He got the information from the captured Enigma machines, whose code had been deciphered by Alan Turing and his team at Bletchley Park, and feared that if he defended Coventry too rigorously, the Germans would suspect that their code had been broken, change it, and all strategic advantage would be lost. This would prolong the war, and possibly result in greater loss of life. Likewise, Truman had to consider this when the option of using the atomic bomb was available to him. American troops were in the process of island hopping on the Japanese archipelago at the time, and the hope was the dreadful firepower of atomic bombs would bring the war to a swifter conclusion and consequently save lives despite the terrible casualties. The residents of Coventry and Hiroshima at the time may dispute this philosophical sleight of hand.

These are extreme examples. When a government decides to give a shipbuilding contract to a port here, rather than there, its actions will negatively affect some citizens for the greater good. Similarly, if a person's family home is demolished to make way for a motorway, wind turbines spoil the view from your study library, roadworks cause your commute to be extended by 20 minutes every day for the summer, and so on. Sometimes politics involves trade-offs between people's interests. Whereas utilitarians don't think people have rights, they do think they have interests, and these interests need to be borne in mind when discussing politics and ethics.

Whereas Bentham's notion of rights being 'nonsense on stilts' leads to the possibility of me being horsewhipped in front of all of the readers of this book if they find it dull and it brings them happiness, most utilitarians would look to protect liberties even though they would conceptualize them differently from rights-based liberal thinkers. J.S. Mill was a rule utilitarian, meaning that he thought that overall we would be happier as a society if we applied certain types of rules. The 'Harm Principle', which we will discuss later in this book, is an example of such a rule; we will be happier as a society if we are allowed to do as we please even if certain aspects of that liberty causes us to be unhappy. So the ability to speak our mind freely trumps the hurt we might get if we are offended by something someone says whilst exercising their free speech. Mill also thinks that happiness is more complicated than it might seem, and thinks there are different levels of happiness. You might be happy after spending two hours watching *Storage Wars* on TV, but the quality of happiness is better if you spend that two hours reading the classics of the history of political thought. He justifies this with the highly questionable proposition that anyone who has known the more cerebral pleasures in life would not go back to the more basic pleasures. But do not college professors like football, or medical doctors basketball?

Activity 3. Please attempt the following tasks:

(1) Why does Bentham think that rights are nonsense on stilts?

(2) What is meant by rule utilitarianism?

(3) Do you think that the person rescuing the child in the pond due to the attractive celebrity close by was committing a moral act?

Kant, Walzer, morality and dirty hands

Immanuel Kant has no time for utilitarianism, or consequentialism of any flavour for that matter. For him, politics must always 'bend the knee' to morality, that is to say that morality is more important than politics and we should do what is right even if this makes us less happy than if we did not.

For Kant, for something to be ethical it has to be able to be universalized, to be made a universal law of nature that we would ourselves accept if it happened to us. So, whereas I may not want to pay my friend back the $10 they lent me last week, if I universalize this, and suggest that my other friend to whom I lent $20 last week need not pay it back to me, I may like this less. Let us take this back to the

Kant

Immanuel Kant was born in Königsberg in Prussia (now called Kaliningrad in modern-day Russia). He was educated at the University of Königsberg, and it has been claimed that he never left the city during his entire life. His daily routines were so regular that he was often referred to as 'the Königsberg clock' as you could tell precisely what time it was by his daily routines. Also he became used to the fact that one of the students attending his lectures had a button missing on his jacket. One day he attended with a new button sewn on; Kant allegedly asked him to remove it.

Kant's impact on the history of philosophy, morality and, perhaps to a lesser extent, politics has been massive. The political theorist John Rawls who we will meet later in this book, for example, is a Kantian. Leading contemporary theorist Will Kymlicka is a Rawlsian, so also indebted to Kant. So Kant's influence has lasted throughout the centuries.

discussion of the child in trouble in the duck pond that I mention above. In the first scenario, where you rescue the child because it is right to help children in need, this is clearly a law that can be universalized; we should all help children in need of assistance. So this is a moral act. The second scenario, where you rescue the child in the hope of gaining the attention of your attractive celebrity, cannot be universalized. We should all rescue children who get into distress in close proximity to a celebrity that you find attractive does not have quite the same ring to it as the previous example. As you are basing your actions on their consequences rather than their motivations, it cannot be a moral act.

Kant calls this process of universalizing laws 'The Categorical Imperative': for Kant, it is necessitous to be moral if we are to be autonomous; that is to say to make laws for ourselves. If we allow consequences of acts to influence our actions rather than if that act is good in and of itself, we start to allow those consequences to control us and do not act freely. We must always, therefore, not do unto others what we would not have them do unto us.

Kant's contemporary Benjamin Constant raised a problem with this categorical imperative around lying. We should all be truthful and not tell lies according to Kant as, if we tell lies, we are accepting that others can tell us lies, and we would not want this. Constant asks us to imagine what we would do if a friend was visiting us at our house, and there is a knock on the door, and we answer to find a murderer there asking about our friend's whereabouts. Are we not entitled to lie to the murderer? Is a murderer really entitled to the truth? Could we not universalize the notion that we should not tell murderers our friend's whereabouts? Kant thinks not, defending the duty to tell the truth at all times. He states that suppose you did lie to the murderer about where your friend was, and the murderer turns around and leaves your porch, only to meet your friend who has made his escape; would you not be endangering him? Being truthful is always the best policy.

But does politics really operate like this? Let us go back to the dilemma that Winston Churchill faced in the Second World War that we discussed above. Churchill knew that the Luftwaffe were planning a bombing raid on Coventry, and had to decide whether to defend Coventry and run the risk of the Germans changing their codes, or allow it to be bombed in the hope of using the code to defeat the Germans by winning the war more quickly. Lives were at risk either way; civilians in Coventry and soldiers (many conscripted) in the war in general. Now we could debate what the best course of action here might be, but is it obvious that either (a) one is morally right, and/or (b) one would have clearly better consequences than the other? It seems to me that this is a judgement call that neither deontology not consequentialism can help us with.

Michael Walzer acknowledges this political problem of ethics in his 1973 essay 'Political action: the problem of dirty hands'. Politicians, he outlines, exist in a different moral environment to the rest of society. This isn't because they are more or less moral than the rest of us or those in other professions, but rather because the nature of their role requires them to make certain types of decisions. Politicians are different from other people. Firstly, unlike other professions such as business people, politicians do not 'merely cater to our interests; he acts on our behalf'; secondly, through tax, laws, etc. the 'successful politician becomes the visible architect of our restraint'; and thirdly, via the police and the army, politicians can use 'violence and the threat of violence' (Walzer, 1973: 162, 163). Other people or professions might do one or two of these things, but not all three. As a consequence of this, politicians find themselves in moral and ethical situations that are unlike those that other people face. It is impossible to remain morally innocent in such a position.

Walzer introduces the notion of dirty hands to the debate around morality in politics; that a good person needs to necessarily get their hands dirty if they are to be a politician, they will, by virtue of their position, need to do things which others will not. But this idea is neither consequentialist nor Kantian. If you as a politician do something, like, say, sacrifice the people of Coventry to protect the Enigma codes, something that you would not do if you were an accountant or a dentist and would clearly be wrong if you did, you are getting your hands dirty in recognition of the fact that it would otherwise be wrong. Your position meant that you had to make a decision that might in other situations have been wrong, but that is the stuff of politics. This is not a consequentialist theory though, as if an act leads to a good outcome, then the acts that lead up to it were good, meaning that you do not have anything to get your hands dirty with. You acted morally.

Dirty hands

The normal rules of morality that apply in our everyday lives do not apply to politicians due to the nature of the decisions they have to take. For Walzer, it is impossible to keep your hands clean and be a politician.

Activity 4. Please attempt the questions below:

(1) Do you think that you should be able to lie to the murderer asking for your friend? What conclusions do you draw from this about Kant's theory?

(2) Can you become a politician and remain morally pure?

Weber

Max Weber's account of the nature of politics in his 1919 essay *Politics as a Vocation* focuses less on the morality of politics than the attributes that a politician needs in order to be a successful leader. Max Weber, widely considered to be one of the founding fathers of modern sociology, was a leading figure in the antipositivism school of thought, meaning that he did not think that the social sciences could be studied in the same way as the natural sciences. Social things did not necessarily have simple causes, and elements such as culture and religion have a large impact on social phenomena. Indeed, his most famous work, *The Protestant Ethic and the Spirit of Capitalism*, was based on these themes. He was involved in politics in his later years, around the time that he wrote *Politics as a Vocation*, and as such these works can be seen as a commentary on politics at that time.

The state, according to Weber, 'is a human community that (successfully) claims the monopoly of the legitimate use of physical force within a given territory' (Weber, 1946: 4, italics supressed). Weber begins his discussion with this definition, illustrating that the business of politics is always about force, therefore there is considerable responsibility attached to it and it should thus be treated seriously. The modern state has centralized, and bureaucratized, the process of governance. Rather than the personal rule of the time of Machiavelli, with lower-level administrators like de Orco having a certain amount of ownership of their actions, in the modern state power is shifted upwards and bureaucrats, often professional civil servants simply enforcing the decisions made above them, are shifted lower down the system.

For Weber, **being a politician involves balancing the three essential qualities, (1) passion, (2) a sense of responsibility and (3) a sense of proportion**. One needs passion in what you are doing in order to drive through change, and to prevent politics from becoming merely an academic discussion as opposed to actually doing something. Passion is also useful to gain adherents to your cause, and to motivate people when change is necessary. But passion in and of itself is problematic, as you cannot (nor perhaps should you) achieve things by will alone. Here, the senses of responsibility and proportion will help the politician deliver on the issues that they care so much about, whilst also remembering how close they are to the form of legitimate violence.

> For Weber the business of being a politician involves balancing three qualities: (1) passion, (2) a sense of responsibility and (3) a sense of proportion. Conviction on its own was insufficient.

In the age of ideological polarization and populism that we live in today, Weber's argument needs some consideration. Across the world we are increasingly being attracted to charismatic politicians, often from outside of the traditional political class, that adherents see as being able to shake up the political system for the better. Weber would not necessarily have regarded this as being a good thing. Whereas passion and the ability to persuade people of the need for change is not a bad thing in and of itself, it always needs to be measured with a sense of responsibility and proportion for government to be successful and balanced.

Activity 5. Please attempt the tasks below:

(1) Why does Weber think that passion alone is insufficient to be a successful politician?

(2) Make a list of some politicians you think are conviction politicians. Have they achieved what they set out to?

Conclusion

So we have seen in this chapter a variety of responses to the question 'what is the nature of politics?'

For Socrates, it was the perusal of justice and living an examined life. Likewise, Kant placed morality at the centre of politics, arguing that politics should always bend the knee to morality. For Kant, we should always live as if our actions should become a universal law. So for both Socrates and Kant, politics, morality and the way we live our life are intrinsically linked. Passion for causes is a necessary but insufficient quality in a politician for Weber; passion must always be measured with responsibility and sense of purpose. If it isn't (if, say, a sense of justice is all a politician has), then little might actually get done.

For Machiavelli, politics is about glory – concentrating too much on morality would cause you to lose your position if you were a prince; concentrating on it too little would make you remembered as a tyrant. For Machiavelli, the real skill of politics was judging when to act, and in what manner. For Bentham (and to a certain extent Mill), politics was about bringing happiness to as many as possible, meaning the rightness or wrongness of an act was not determined by its moral justifications, but rather its consequences. Walzer notes that a politician cannot remain morally innocent; there is something about the position that means one has to get one's hands dirty, but this is not to deny that there is a moral dilemma involved.

Throughout this book there will be more discussions that pertain to the nature of politics. For Hobbes it is security, for Burke preserving the best of the past for the future, for Paine the protection of rights, for Rawls the ability to make impartial laws about justice, and so on. So whereas this chapter concludes here, this does not mean to say that these are the last words on the nature of politics in this book.

Works cited

Bentham, J. (2012) *An Introduction to the Principles of Morals and Legislation*. New York: Cosimo Classics.

Machiavelli, N. (1950) *The Prince and the Discourses*. New York: The Modern Library.

Machiavelli, N. (1961) *The Prince*. London: Penguin.

Oppenheimer, P. (2011) *Machiavelli: A Life Beyond Ideology*. London: Continuum.

Plato (1993) *The Last Days of Socrates*. London: Penguin.

Skinner, Q. (1978) *The Foundations of Modern Political Thought: Vol. 1, The Renaissance*. Cambridge: Cambridge University Press.

Walzer, M. (1973) 'Political action: the problem of dirty hands', *Philosophy & Public Affairs*, 2(2), 160–80.

Weber, M. (1946) *Politics as a Vocation*. New York: Oxford University Press. Available at https://archive.org/details/webermax18641920politicsasavocation/page/n3

Text reading activities

Aristotle on citizenship, *The Politics*, Book III, part IV, available at https://classicalwisdom.com/greekbooks/politics-by-aristotle-book-iii/2/

There is a point nearly allied to the preceding: Whether the virtue of a good man and a good citizen is the same or not. But, before entering on this discussion, we must certainly first obtain some general notion of the virtue of the citizen. Like the sailor, the citizen is a member of a community. Now, sailors have different functions, for one of them is a rower, another a pilot, and a third a look-out man, a fourth is described by some similar term; and while the precise definition of each individual's virtue applies exclusively to him, there is, at the same time, a common definition applicable to them all. For they have all of them a common object, which is safety in navigation. Similarly, one citizen differs from another, but the salvation of the community is the common business of them all. This community is the constitution; the virtue of the citizen must therefore be relative to the constitution of which he is a member. If, then, there are many forms of government, it is evident that there is not one single virtue of the good citizen which is perfect virtue. But we say that the good man is he who has one single virtue which is perfect virtue. Hence it is evident that the good citizen need not of necessity possess the virtue which makes a good man.

The same question may also be approached by another road, from a consideration of the best constitution. If the state cannot be entirely composed of good men, and yet each citizen is expected to do his own business well, and must therefore have virtue, still inasmuch as all the citizens cannot be alike, the virtue of the citizen and of the good man cannot coincide. All must have the virtue of the good citizen – thus, and thus only, can the state be perfect; but they will not have the virtue of a good man, unless we assume that in the good state all the citizens must be good.

Again, the state, as composed of unlikes, may be compared to the living being: as the first elements into which a living being is resolved are soul and body, as soul is made up of rational principle and appetite, the family of husband and wife, property of master and slave, so of all these, as well as other dissimilar elements, the state is composed; and, therefore, the virtue of all the citizens cannot possibly be the same, any more than the excellence of the leader of a chorus is the same as that of the performer who stands by his side. I have said enough to show why the two kinds of virtue cannot be absolutely and always the same.

But will there then be no case in which the virtue of the good citizen and the virtue of the good man coincide? To this we answer that the good ruler is a good and wise man, and that he who would be a statesman must be a wise man. And some persons say that even the education of the ruler should be of a special kind; for are not the children of kings instructed in riding and military exercises? As Euripides says:

No subtle arts for me, but what the state requires.

Kant on politics and morality, 'On the Opposition Between Morality and Politics with Respect to Perpetual Peace', available at https://www.constitution.org/kant/append1.htm

To such dubious consequences we are inevitably driven if we do not assume that pure principles of right have objective reality, i.e., that they may be applied, and that the people in a state and, further, states themselves in their mutual relations should act according to them, whatever objections empirical politics may raise. Thus true politics can never take a step without rendering homage to morality. Though politics by itself is a difficult art, its union with morality is no art at all, for this union cuts the knot which politics could not untie when they were in conflict. The rights of men must be held sacred, however much sacrifice it may cost the ruling power. One cannot compromise here and seek the middle course of a pragmatic conditional law between the morally right and the expedient. All politics must bend its knee before the right. But by this it can hope slowly to reach the stage where it will shine with an immortal glory.

Bentham on the happiness principle, From Bentham, J. (2012) *An Introduction to the Principles of Morals and Legislation.* New York: Cosimo Classics, p. 1

To this denomination has of late been added, or substituted, the greatest happiness or greatest felicity principle: this for shortness, instead of saying at length that principle which states the greatest happiness of all those whose interest is in question, as being the right and proper, and only right and proper and universally desirable, end of human action: of human action in every situation, and in particular in that of a functionary or set of functionaries exercising the powers of Government. The word utility does not so clearly point to the ideas of pleasure and pain as the words happiness and felicity do: nor does it lead us to the consideration of the number, of the interests affected; to the number, as being the circumstance, which contributes, in the largest proportion, to the formation of the standard here in question; the standard of right and wrong, by which alone the propriety of human conduct, in every situation, can with propriety be tried. This want of a sufficiently manifest connexion between the ideas of happiness and pleasure on the one hand, and the idea of utility on the other, I have every now and then found operating, and with but too much efficiency, as a bar to the acceptance, that might otherwise have been given, to this principle.

Question 1: Do you agree with Aristotle when he says that a 'good citizen need not of necessity possess the virtue which makes a good man'? Why/why not?

Question 2: Can you think of any instances whereby your duty as a citizen overrides your duty as a good man/woman?

Question 3: Where would utilitarianism leave human rights?

3

Is humanity nasty or nice?

KEY QUESTIONS

(1) How would humanity act if there was no state power acting over them?

(2) Is there a natural law that would guide our actions in the absence of state-made law?

(3) Is humanity's competitiveness natural, or is it society that makes us competitive?

A popular genre of videos to watch on YouTube when life is getting you down are those around the theme of 'faith in humanity restored' which tell of times when people have done something over and above that which is expected of them. If one ever becomes jaded about the nature of humanity, they are worth viewing. They show motorists stopping their cars and helping senior citizens cross the road, police officers buying shoes for homeless people, restaurant patrons giving generous tips to their servers, people paying for needy people's shopping, and athletes in the heat of competition helping out their opponents. They give us hope, despite the evidence that is all around us, that inherently humanity is good and that we will help one another out.

That said, nearly every post-apocalyptic film or TV show tells us that after the government collapses due to nuclear war, natural disaster, zombie attack or the like, society will become chaotic, with each individual looking after themselves alone, and cooperation and kindness will go out of the window. The acts of kindness and humanity noted above, these post-apocalyptic stories might suggest, are dependent upon the maintenance of a state, and humanity without this state will descend into an everybody-for-themselves free for all.

We have probably all been in a conversation about political or social issues when someone has justified their point by shrugging, and then just saying 'well that's just human nature isn't it'. It is probably the oldest political argument in the book. The nature of humanity, and the type of government that we should have based upon this, is the subject of much debate. Conservative politicians, for example, might well favour tough law-and-order policies, giving additional powers to the police and enacting more laws to keep the peace. They often do this as they feel humanity is naturally imperfect and self-interested, and the best way to keep the peace is to ensure offenders are caught and put in jail, and that potential law breakers are scared stiff by the powers of the state.

Left-wing thinkers, on the other hand, might think that humanity is naturally good, and if we are competitive, greedy and selfish these days, it is because society has made us this way. It is not necessary to extend the powers of the state to keep people in order, these people might think; far better to spend money on education, on social mobility, on helping people to get jobs. Removing the harsher edges of competition and uncertainty would allow people to cooperate and live together peacefully.

Our judgement about what the natural state of humanity is, therefore, is a crucial area of ethical reasoning that impacts upon our broader understanding of policy and politics.

Chapter overview

This chapter will examine some responses by key thinkers in the history of political thought about what the nature of humanity is, and in particular how they will act in the state of nature. We will discover, however, that even what constitutes the state of nature is up for much debate. We will begin with an overview of the reflections of the seventeenth-century English philosopher **Thomas Hobbes** on the matter. He will argue that in their original state men are equal and free, but that the lack of a state over us will inevitably lead to a state of war between all men. This isn't because they are inherently evil, but rather because this is an entirely rational response in a time when there are limited resources and no law to protect oneself from attack. Also Hobbes will argue that the state of nature is simply humanity without a sovereign power over them; so logically we could go into the state of nature in the future should the state collapse.

Hobbes will then be contrasted to his near contemporary and countryman **John Locke**, who will argue that, although there are inconveniences to the state of nature, humanity would not be lawless in that condition; but rather it would be guided by the laws of nature that ensure we would not harm another person in their life, liberty or property.

We will then examine the response to this by the eighteenth-century Genevan polymath **Jean-Jacques Rousseau**, who will argue that Hobbes, far from discussing natural man, is rather describing social man, or perhaps more accurately men who have been formed by society rather than natural man. To discuss natural man, one needs to cast one's mind back in time to when man was a hunter and gatherer, leading a solitary existence. Rousseau will suggest that natural man was naturally free and happy, and neither desiring the company of other men, nor wishing to harm them. It is society that has corrupted them and made them vain, selfish and desiring domination over one another.

We will then examine an entirely different argument put forward by the nineteenth-century German philosopher **Friedrich Nietzsche**, who will suggest that concepts such as good and evil are bound up in a struggle between the powerful and the powerless, and that much of what Western philosophy describes as being good or evil comes from a position of weakness and is life destroying. So the concepts of good and evil are constructs based upon power rather than having any real basis in nature.

Thomas Hobbes

Thomas Hobbes witnessed (albeit from the relative safety of Paris) the effects of the English Civil War when the Parliamentarian forces led by Thomas Fairfax and Oliver Cromwell challenged and defeated Charles I's army, leading to the overthrow of the state and the eventual trial and execution of the King in 1649. Monarchs being deposed in a dynastic dispute was moderately common. For one to be removed, put on trial, and executed by their own subjects was unheard of in seventeenth-century Europe. Charles I's father, James I of England, when discussing kings, stated that 'even by God himself they are called gods' (James VI and I, 1986: 107). It was not the business of subjects to second guess the manner

Thomas Hobbes

Thomas Hobbes was born in April 1588 in Gloucestershire, England, his mother allegedly frightened into childbirth on hearing the news of the sighting of the Spanish Armada off the English coastline. Fear, it is said, became a constant in his life and philosophy.

He was educated at Oxford, and joined the household of the Earl of Devonshire as a tutor. During his time with the Devonshires, he spent a lot of time in Paris immersing himself in the intellectual culture of the time, becoming especially interested in geometry and the sciences.

Hobbes lived most of his life in England with the Devonshires at Harwick Hall in Derbyshire. He was an early proponent of running as a form of exercise, and thought it healthy to binge drink until he vomited; he lived until he was 91.

Hobbes's most famous work *Leviathan*, published in 1651, is perhaps the most complete overview of his political theory.

in which they govern. The war split the country, pitting brother against brother and father against son, and destroying political order across the country.

Thomas Hobbes was a royalist in the build up to the Civil War, as were his employers the Wentworth family, with whom he lived at Hardwick Hall in Derbyshire and acted as a tutor to the family. When war broke out, the Wentworths, with Hobbes in tow, travelled to France to avoid the conflict. Hobbes was appalled that a stable government had been overthrown and that law and order had been subverted. As we shall see over the next couple of chapters, above all Hobbes favoured stable order, or rather he argues that the rational individual should consent to a strong and stable state to avoid the problems associated with a collapse in order. He was, however, an atypical royalist. He will argue that political power originates in individuals who are by nature free and equal, that the state is an artificial creation of these individuals, and that the political power of this state rests in the consent of the governed. These are not propositions that Charles I or the majority of his supporters could have supported.

The reason Hobbes so favoured a strong and stable political order, as we shall now go on to examine, is because he thought that humanity in its natural state would be unable to live sociably together and would compete to such an extent **that life without a state would be a state of war 'and such a warre, as is of every man against every men'** (Hobbes, 1985: 13). It is in our rational self-interest, he thought, to seek a way out of human's natural state.

The state of nature

The state of nature, for Hobbes, is not a historical place that we have developed out of (as Rousseau would later argue). When we think of humanity's origins we may conjure up in our mind images of cavemen hunting and gathering and painting on cave walls. This was not what Hobbes meant. Hobbes conceived of our natural state as simply society without a sovereign power over it. This may have occurred in the past, but for Hobbes we could easily return to the state of nature in the future should the state and political order collapse. So the state of nature is not something we have emerged from for Hobbes, but rather a place that the threat always exists that we could return: it is a constant threat.

Hobbes was fascinated by science and the scientific method. Science often involves reducing things to their smallest component parts and building upwards: looking at the nature of atoms in substances, or DNA in organic material. In using the state of nature, Hobbes was attempting to reduce politics to its smallest component parts, namely men and their nature. It is hard to stress enough how radical this was in the seventeenth century when political discussions were often seen as a subset of religious thinking, as God's place in the constitution of politics was generally taken for granted. So aside from what Hobbes actually says about politics, his method is ground breaking for its time.

And what he says, as we shall see throughout this book, is pretty radical as well. Hobbes was not a liberal (the term liberal did not emerge until the nineteenth century) and his political doctrine is not one that many liberals could adhere to, but many of the methodological assumptions made by Hobbes would be used by many thinkers whom we would regard as liberal. Hobbes will outline that in their natural state, humans are equal and free and capable of reason, and using that reason they will contract with one another to form a political power that will then use the powers transferred to them. This structure will be repeated by many thinkers in the history of political thought, albeit in a different manner.

> It is due to this assertion that humanity in the state of nature is free and equal that Hobbes is regarded as an early liberal despite his illiberal political conclusions.

The nature of humanity

Humans in their state of nature are:

- **Free:** with no state, and therefore no government, no laws to obey and no police officers to enforce them, men are fully entitled to do as they please as nothing can really be said to be wrong until 'they know a law forbids them', and in the state of nature there can be no law (Hobbes, 1985: 187). As a consequence, every man has a right to everything in the state of nature.
- **Equal:** when one builds an argument around equality in the contemporary world, one might argue that everyone has equal moral worth, or to use the words of the Declaration of Independence that 'all men are created equal'. This is not Hobbes's argument, which is far more pessimistic. **He argues that all men are equal as each could kill one another.** Certainly, some people would be stronger or quicker and therefore harder to kill, but Hobbes suggests that this is not that much of an advantage if someone plotted against someone (say by hiding and jumping out from behind a bush with a weapon, therefore taking the stronger person by surprise) or by ganging up on someone.

> For as to the strength of the body, the weakest has strength enough to kill the strongest, either by secret machination, or by confederacy with others, that are in the same danger with himself. (Hobbes, 1985: 183)

As we might infer from Hobbes's discussion of the nature of equality, he does not think this condition of freedom and equality is a positive thing. Anarchist thinkers such as William Godwin might argue that humanity is perfectly capable of living together peacefully without a state to keep the order, but Hobbes does not concur with this. He says that the nature of humanity means that violence will inevitably occur for three reasons. Firstly, competition: there would be scarce resources in the state of nature and, as there are no laws or police officers to protect one's property, violence will pretty much be the only way to get one's hands on the things one wants (or perhaps even for basic necessities like food and shelter). Secondly, men are diffident in the state of nature; as there are no police to protect us, we would constantly be on edge to protect ourselves, our families and our possessions. This might lead to violence, as we might conclude (rightly or wrongly) that someone presents a threat to us and attack them pre-emptively. Finally, the desire for glory, to look good to other people, might lead a cause for glory. We cannot in the state of nature issue a libel writ aimed at someone we feel has defamed us, and violence might be the only way to save face. Likewise, a criticism or insult is more likely to lead to violence in the state of nature as we will not face any legal consequences for any action we might take.

Consequently, in what is certainly the most famous passage in *Leviathan*, Hobbes describes the full horror of the state of nature:

> In such condition, there is no place for Industry; because the fruit thereof is uncertain: and consequently no Culture of the Earth; no Navigation, nor use of the commodities that may be imported by Sea; no commodious Building; no Instruments of moving, and removing such things as require much force; no Knowledge of the face of the Earth; no account of Time; no Arts; no Letters; no Society; and which is worst of all, continuall feare, and danger of violent death; And the life of man, solitary, poore, nasty, brutish, and short. (Hobbes, 1985: 186)

It is worth spending some time reflecting on the full ramifications of the passage above. Hobbes is effectively saying that **everything we hold dear depends upon a state to enforce law and order** and that therefore life in the state of nature would not just be violent and brief, but also that the things that make our lives interesting and meaningful would be unachievable. Why would you design and build a nice house if it could be taken from you by force the minute it is finished, with no potential chance for remedy? Why would you grow crops if, likewise, they could be taken from you? Why would you bother setting up a business when it and any money you had made from it could be taken from you? Why would you bother to engage in any endeavour in this climate?

Activity 1. Reread the quote above from Hobbes. Outline why he argues that the state is so important to us.

Some of you might regard Hobbes as being overly pessimistic about the nature of humanity here. You might think, for example, that whereas some people would take the opportunity of no social order to steal other people's property or attack them violently, others wouldn't. More importantly perhaps, you think that **you** would not do this. So perhaps one might argue that it is not humanity that would act in this way, but just that simply a few people would act like this; so human nature isn't systematically bad. Hobbes would no doubt admire your positivity on the nature of humanity, but point out that in the state of nature you would have no way of knowing who would attack you and who wouldn't. And it would be impossible to simply sit out the war of all men against all other men as eventually you would get challenged and have to fight back. It isn't that one is being particularly evil in participating in the war in our natural state; it is entirely rational to do so. To those who have a rosier view of human nature, Hobbes responds:

> Let him therefore consider with himselfe, when taking a journey, he armes him-selfe, and seeks to go well accompanied; when going to sleep, he locks his dores; when even in his house he locks his chests; and this when he knows there bee Lawes, and publike Officers, armed, to revenge all injuries shall be done him; what opinion he has of his fellow subjects ... *Does he not there as much accuse mankind by his actions, as I do by my words*? (Hobbes, 1985: 186–7, my italics)

So Hobbes here suggests that if you locked your door of your house before leaving for lectures this morning, if you put a lock on your bike when you arrived on campus, if you keep your especially valuable items in a locked briefcase hidden under your bed in your dorm room, you are implicitly agreeing with his view on human nature.

Activity 2. What does Hobbes mean when he says 'does he not there as much accuse mankind by his actions, as I do by my words' in the quote above? Are there times when you accuse humanity by your actions?

The state of nature, however, is not the end of the story for humanity (just as well you may think), as despite his pessimism about the state of nature, Hobbes thinks we are capable of reason; and it is this rationality that will save us. Enlightenment thinkers such as Voltaire and Diderot would, some 100 years later, start placing reason at the centre of their political philosophy, arguing that political institutions that did not pass the test of reason (i.e. arguments based on tradition or religion) were baseless. In some senses Hobbes was an Enlightenment thinker before his time as he shows how by using reason we can remove ourselves from the state of nature.

Reason would allow mankind to deduce the first law of nature, which is that 'every man, ought to endeavour Peace, as farre as he has hope of obtaining it; and when he cannot obtain it, that he may seek, and use, all helps, and advantages of Warre' (Hobbes, 1985: 190). To paraphrase Hobbes here, he is saying that we can deduce using our reason that the main law of nature is that we should protect ourselves. The best way to do this, given what we know so far about the state of nature, is to seek peace with our fellow men to get out of this condition. Where this is not possible, we can do whatever (and he means whatever) is necessary.

This is interesting for three main reasons. Firstly, this law of nature is not God's law as many authors prior to and after Hobbes would invoke in their uses of the concept; rather, it is what we, using our reason, can deduce from society around

> Hobbes isn't claiming that mankind has an 'evil gene' or is corrupted by original sin. He is saying that without a state it would be entirely rational to act in a selfish manner as we would have no idea how others would act and there would be no recourse to law.

us. Once again, we see Hobbes the political scientist – he is talking about working out political principles from what we can observe from society around us rather than discussing what God intended for us or what natural law dictates that we do. Secondly, this reinforces our view of Hobbes as not making the point that we are nasty in the sense of being inherently evil or selfish, but rather that the use of violence in the state of nature, when one cannot seek peace, is an entirely rational and understandable thing to do given the lack of sovereign power over us. Thirdly, it shows that we are capable of realizing that we should avoid this state of nature at all costs; and the rational person can realize it is in his (and others') self-interest to avoid it.

Men can deduce the second law of nature from the first; it shows us how to get out of the state of nature, and it is the first step towards the social contract that will create the sovereign power. The second law of nature is:

> That a man be willing, when others are so too, as farre-forth, as for Peace, and defence of himselfe he shall think it necessary, to lay down this right to all things; and be contented with so much liberty against other men, as he would allow other men against himselfe. (Hobbes, 1985: 190)

If everyone continues to have a right to everything, given the likely causes of quarrels Hobbes has outlined already, the state of war will continue. If everyone gives up their right to everything, there is a chance for peace. Hobbes says people can either simply renounce their right to something, or they could transfer their right to someone else. We will see in the next chapter that Hobbes suggests that the rational person will transfer their right to everything to the sovereign power, and this is the only way to keep the peace.

So we have seen from Hobbes a pretty pessimistic view of how humanity would behave in the state of nature. In the state of nature, human progress will stall and life will be horrible and brief. However, it is worth stressing that Hobbes's claim is not that humanity is biologically programmed to act in a barbaric way; there is no evil gene argument here, or notion of original sin. Indeed, Hobbes points out that men are capable of reason in the state of nature, and it is this reason that causes there to be a war of all men against all other men. With no sovereign power to keep people in order and to right wrongs, with everyone having a right to everything and a broadly equal hope of achieving it, violence becomes a rational and perfectly legitimate form of action. But the very reason that causes us to be violent also shows us that the best way out of the state of nature is to lay down our right to everything.

The structure of Hobbes's argument – free and equal men in the state of nature, the discovery of natural laws, ending with a contract that transfers powers to a civil authority – is followed by many contractarian thinkers who followed him;

none more so than John Locke. Whereas in many ways Locke's arguments look similar to Hobbes's, it is in the nuance that they differ, and crucially he will begin the link between social contract and human rights that put him firmly in the liberal tradition (although, to be historically accurate, we must stress that Locke neither described himself as a liberal, nor did he talk of human rights). We will see here, and when we discuss him later on to examine the right to revolution, that Locke asserts that, due to the nature of humanity, there are things that no government can do.

John Locke

Much like Hobbes, John Locke argued that humanity in the state of nature was equal and free. There was certainly less enmity in Locke's account than in Hobbes, but men were certainly rivals in the state of nature. The crucial difference between the two thinkers was the origin and content of the state of nature. You may remember that the content of Hobbes's laws of nature was quite thin; it told us that we should protect ourselves and would nudge us to seek peace. Also Hobbes says we discover this law of nature using our reason; just as by using reason properly we can discover scientific laws like gravity or the speed of light, we can also find social laws. We are not dependent upon divine revelation for this.

For Locke, the **laws of nature** were commandments from God, **that we should never harm another person in their life, liberty or property**. So life in the state of nature is not the lawless moral void that Hobbes describes, but rather that even without a government there were laws to which we should all adhere. There was, for Locke, a pretty obvious problem to this state of nature, however; although most people would adhere to the laws of nature, some would break them, and without a government there would be no one to enforce them and punish transgressors.

John Locke

John Locke was born in 1632 in Somerset, England, to Puritan parents; his father would fight for the Parliamentarians in the English Civil War. He graduated from Oxford having studied medicine, and took a job in the household of Anthony Ashley Cooper, 1st Earl of Shaftesbury as his personal physician. As Anthony Ashley Cooper was a prominent politician at the time, this meant that Locke became involved in the Whig politics of the day and age.

Locke had always been interested in philosophy, and as well as his political works, most noticeably his Second Treatise of Government, he wrote works on the nature of the self and of understanding. As a philosopher, he was a leading exponent of empiricism. Until the latter part of the nineteenth century, his political works were generally ignored and he was known as a philosopher rather than as a political theorist.

Locke's natural law

For Locke there were rules that would govern us in the state of nature, that we should not harm another's life, liberty or property. The problem was that it was left to us to enforce it – and we would probably punish those who had harmed us too greatly, plus we don't want to spend time enforcing laws – it would bore us.

Consequently, Locke argued that **without a government, we all had the right to enforce the laws of nature**, and to punish offenders to the extent of deterring them from breaking the laws in future. This also has two chief problems for Locke. Firstly, we do not want to spend our time enforcing the laws of nature; we want to spend our time working, or seeing friends, or listening to music, or whatever it is we enjoy; enforcing the laws of nature is a burden on our time. If you doubt this, look at the lengths that people will go to to avoid doing jury service. Secondly, Locke thinks we are not very good judges in our own cases, meaning that we are likely to see attacks on our person or property as being more serious than attacks on other people. This will mean that if someone steals something from us, we are likely to punish that person more harshly than a more neutral authority might think that they should be. These two inconveniences of the state of nature are the things that will push us to contract to form a civil authority to interpret and enforce the state of nature. We will see more of this later in the book. However, crucial to this civil organization is that as no one within the state of nature has any rightful power over another person's life, liberty or property, it would follow that neither should the civil authority.

So Locke's state of nature is not as bad as Hobbes's state of war, as natural law would guide our actions for the most part. It is inconvenient, however, and something we should seek to avoid so we can progress politically and economically.

We must now turn our eye to perhaps the sternest critic of Hobbes's view of the natural condition of humanity, to Jean-Jacques Rousseau who in his work *A Discourse on the Origin of Inequality* will argue that man is naturally good, and that if mankind seems different from that today, it is because society has corrupted him. In our discussion of him we will see that although Rousseau takes a different view on most things from Hobbes and Locke, the structure of his argument is actually very similar; the philosophical devices he uses – state of nature, laws of nature, the push towards a contract – are all still there.

Activity 3. Outline the differences and similarities between Locke and Hobbes on the state of nature below:

Similarities	Differences

Jean-Jacques Rousseau

Rousseau's discussion of natural man continues themes that he had already discussed in his first work of political theory, *Discourse on the Arts and Sciences*. There, he argues that the supposed goods of society, such as the arts and the sciences, have corrupted our natures, and have reduced our freedom, as they make us 'build our happiness on the opinion of others' rather than leaving us to find it 'in our own hearts' (Rousseau, 1993: 29). Likewise, he will argue in the *Discourse on the Origin of Inequality* that society has robbed us of our natural innocence and goodness and increased our psychological dependence on one another, which has in turn made us vain and selfish. As such, Rousseau, often described as a central Enlightenment thinker, cuts a strange figure amongst his contemporaries, as he thinks our reason is so impaired; it is not just monarchs, priests and bosses that enslave us, but also society itself.

Natural goodness

Rousseau declares in his oft-quoted passage in chapter 1 of *The Social Contract* that man 'is born free; and everywhere he is in chains. One thinks himself the master of others, and still remains a greater slave than they' (Rousseau, 1993: 181). Man is naturally free but contemporary society has enslaved him.

Rousseau begins the *Discourse on the Origin of Inequality* with a none too subtle dig at Hobbes, stating that the 'philosophers, who have inquired into the foundations of society, have all felt the necessity of going back to the state of nature; but not one of them has got there' (Rousseau, 1993: 50). This is Rousseau's

---

Jean-Jacques Rousseau

Jean-Jacques Rousseau was born in Geneva (then a city state) in June 1712; his mother died shortly after giving birth due to complications from the delivery. He had little formal education, and after his father fled Geneva when he was 13, he took a variety of jobs including that of a watchmaker before entering the household of Louise-Eléanore, Baronne de Warens. It was here he learnt about philosophy, the arts and music, and he became a tutor within the household.

He became friends with the French philosopher Diderot, for whom he wrote entries for his *Encyclopédie* on music.

In addition to works on political theory, Rousseau wrote novels. *La Nouvelle Héloïse* was a best seller, and *Émile* is arguably the basis of much modern pedagogy, as it argued that we should not teach children things, we should teach them how to learn.

Rousseau's ideas have been widely cited as one of the causes of the French Revolution.

first critique of Hobbes, that the attributes he describes to natural man (or rather man in the state of nature) are actually those of man in society. Rousseau certainly thought that people were greedy and selfish, but he thinks Hobbes is wrong to ascribe this to their natural state. Indeed, Hobbes would have little concern with this criticism as we could re-enter the state of nature tomorrow if sovereignty collapsed; it is a logical rather than historical argument. Rousseau, however, argues that natural man was **different to contemporary man and would have lived differently to social man, and as a consequence we should take a more historical view of the natural condition of mankind.**

Natural man was solitary – not needing other people to go about their hunter-gatherer-style existence. Rousseau suggests man would be 'dispersed in the woods among other animals' with 'no fixed habitation' with 'the same persons hardly [having] met in their lives' (Rousseau, 1993: 64). Indeed, man would not have even been able to speak to one another when they did meet, as man in this condition would have had no need of language. Natural man was free as he depended upon no one, and also, Rousseau asserts, he was happy. He was happy as everything he wanted was provided for by nature. He was not unhappy that he didn't have fancy clothes, smartphones, cars and the like because he had no knowledge of these things. Rousseau points out that whereas we might think a solitary hunter and gatherer must not be as happy as modern man, he points out that 'we cannot desire or fear anything, except from the idea we have of it' (Rousseau, 1993: 50). Rather, Rousseau suggests man in his natural condition has few wants, and those wants are readily provided for by nature; the things he fears are rudimentary dangers:

> The only goods he recognizes in the universe are food, a female, and sleep: the only evils he fears are pain and hunger. (Rousseau, 1993: 61)

So in this condition we do not want the same things modern man wants, and we do not fear many of the things (status anxiety, stress over essays, etc.) that modern man fears. So we are happy and free, wanting for little and desiring less.

There are no laws in the state of nature, nor are there any morals; for morals can only exist in society, for Rousseau. If one suggests the moral law 'you shall not covet your neighbour's house, wife or property', this implies that you have a neighbour, that private property exists, and that the institution of marriage exists, none of which would be the case in the state of nature. This does not imply that men are immoral in the natural condition, as immorality requires a moral code to break, but men are without morals, they are amoral. Rousseau, a committed Catholic who would later argue that atheists should be prohibited citizenship on the grounds of being anti-social, thinks that the development of morals is one of the good things that comes out of society; but this does not mean that the state of nature would become like the all-out war of Hobbes's natural condition. This is because although man may not be moral, he lives by the maxim of natural goodness.

We are self-interested certainly, in that we have a desire to avoid hunger and pain, but this does not lead us to fight one another; quite the opposite in fact.

> ### Rousseau and morals
>
> Morals develop in civilized society for Rousseau. This means that in man's natural state he is amoral (without morals). Whereas Rousseau thinks civilization is generally corrupting, the adoption of morals is one good facet of it. Indeed, Rousseau was a Catholic who would later argue that atheists could not be citizens as they could not believe in anything bigger than themselves, and as a result would be anti-social.

Nature has given mankind 'a sense of compassion' which gives us 'an innate repugnance at seeing a fellow-creature suffer' (Rousseau, 1993: 75, 73). This does not hamper our self-interest, but rather it is our self-interest that makes us pity the animal as we imagine how we would not like being in pain. So our self-interest boosts our natural compassion. As Rousseau puts it, compassion is 'stronger, the more the animal beholding any kind of distress identifies himself with the animal that suffers' (Rousseau, 1993: 75). It is this link that ensures that the natural condition of mankind is a peaceful place:

> It is then certain that compassion is a natural feeling, which, by moderating the activity of love of self in each individual, contributes to the preservation of the whole species. It is this compassion that hurries us without reflection to the relief of those who are in distress: it is this which in the state of nature supplies the place of laws, morals, and virtues, with the advantage that none are tempted to disobey its gentle voice. (Rousseau, 1993: 76)

There will almost certainly be disputes in the state of nature. These disputes will be small, centred on an object that someone desires, and easily resolvable. Crucially for Rousseau, these disputes would not be about dominance and power as the stakes would be so small. Suppose in the state of nature, Rousseau asks us to imagine, someone came and stole the fruit and game that you had hunted and gathered for your dinner, or came to forcibly remove you from the cave you used for shelter. How would this person be 'able to exact obedience' in a world without property (Rousseau, 1993: 81)? Rather if you are driven from one cave you can go and find another; one's wants in the state of nature are so small and one's freedom so great that the loss of something will not set up an enmity between people, but an inconvenience to overcome. The simplicity of the state of nature makes it virtually impossible for the strong to gain dominance over the weak.

> Working together with others increases our psychological dependence upon one another, and in so doing makes us want to look good to others. This turns our self-love from simply wanting to protect ourselves to vanity. This is the first step to making us greedy and competitive.

> Again, should I happen to meet a man so much stronger than myself, and at the same time so depraved, so indolent, and so barbarous, as to compel me to provide for his sustenance while he himself remains idle; he must take care not to have his eyes off me for a single moment; he must bind me fast before he goes to sleep, or I shall certainly either knock him on the head or make my escape. (Rousseau, 1993: 81)

So man in his natural condition, for Rousseau, is free and happy, as he relies on no one else, and his few wants are readily supplied by nature. He is without morals, but is naturally good. He wishes to preserve himself and avoid pain and hunger, but this self-love is tempered by natural compassion which does not want to see other creatures suffer. Whereas disputes may occur, the possibility for domination and servitude is slight, meaning that the state of nature is a peaceful place. Unfortunately, Rousseau does not think that this condition has endured, or to put it another way, although man may be naturally free and good, this does not mean to say that they are now. Man is naturally good but corrupted by society, and we need to now go on to examine how this corruption occurs.

Activity 4. Outline below the reasons why humanity would be happy, content, and peaceful in the state of nature despite the lack of possessions and society.

Corruption by society

Over time, men ceased to live solitary lives in the woods and came together in societies. People began to realize that there were tasks, such as felling a tree to turn it into a bridge, that they could achieve better together than they could apart. From doing this, men start to live in communities, languages are formed to communicate, they start monogamous relationships with women and take a role in raising their children, and they start living social lives. Consequently, they start becoming dependent upon one another, not just in the literal sense of requiring one another to do other tasks, but also in a psychological sense of wishing others to have a good opinion of them. We start to live our lives through the eyes of others. This, Rousseau asserts, 'was the first step towards inequality, and at the same time towards vice' (Rousseau, 1993: 90).

It is at this time that we start to become vain, obsessed with our standing against other people. The battles between us would start to become personal, rather than simply a battle over fruit or a cave that in their natural condition could be easily remedied by simply getting another apple or moving on to another cave. Battles would be about social standing and no attack could be left unavenged, as the injury would no longer be just to the person but also to one's sense of self-esteem. It is in this condition that man appears nasty and cruel, the type of condition that Hobbes ascribed to the state of nature. But this, for Rousseau, is not man's natural condition, it is social man. He makes this point in a thinly veiled attack on Hobbes:

Thus, as every man punished the contempt shown him by others, in proportion to his opinion of himself, revenge became terrible, and men bloody and cruel. This is precisely the state reached by most of the savage nations known to us: and it is for want of having made a proper distinction in our ideas, and seen how very far they already are from the state of nature, that so many writers have hastily concluded that man is naturally cruel, and requires civil institutions to make him more mild; whereas nothing is more gentle than man in his primitive state, as he is placed by nature at an equal distance from the stupidity of brutes, and the fatal ingenuity of civilized man. (Rousseau, 1993: 90-1)

So Rousseau suggests that Hobbes is probably right when he ascribes negative characteristics to the men he sees around him; however, he is wrong in ascribing this to the natural man. Dependence upon others and vanity is unnatural to man and enslaves him. It is not only the poor that are enslaved by society, despite their domination by the rich. The rich are equally enslaved by the 'multiplicity of new wants' that meant that 'they stood in need of the services of others' (Rousseau, 1993: 95). Having property, people working for then, and domination over other people boosts another person's self-esteem, making the rich enslaved by the poor.

Rousseau is building a novel concept of freedom here, a concept which simply living without interference will not provide, which we will discuss in a later chapter.

Friedrich Nietzsche

Nietzsche will, broadly speaking, reject all of the discussions we have had so far about whether we are naturally nice or nasty. He will argue that we are not consistently anything, and that what is considered good or bad is a societal construct rather than anything based in nature. In particular, he states that the

Friedrich Nietzsche

Friedrich Nietzsche was born in Röcken in Saxony (modern-day Germany) in October 1844.

Nietzsche studied at the University of Bonn, and later at the University of Leipzig where he specialized in philology (the study of texts).

After a brief spell in the army (where he was injured), he became Professor of Classical Philology at the University of Basel when he was just 24 years old. He became friends with Richard Wagner.

Ill health started to plague Nietzsche and he left Basel whilst still in his mid-thirties and moved around in an attempt to convalesce. However, he continued to write, including perhaps his most famous work *Thus Spoke Zarathustra*.

In January 1889 Nietzsche's mental health declined, and this illness, combined with a number of strokes, led to his death in 1900 at just 55 years of age.

good/evil distinction generally comes from a position of weakness and is life-destroying; however, he also think that this way of thinking dominates Western philosophy.

Nietzsche writes very differently from the other thinkers we have examined so far. He writes often in stories and aphorisms and he certainly does not have a systematic account of the state of nature that we have seen thus far in Hobbes, Locke and Rousseau.

In *Beyond Good and Evil*, Nietzsche outlines what he sees as the genealogy of the concepts of good/bad and good/evil. It is worth pausing here to outline what Nietzsche means by genealogy and how important it is to our purpose in this chapter. The way in which we would standardly use this term in everyday use is perhaps when we discuss family trees and our relationship to one another. An elderly relation might talk of how you have your grandfather's eyes or your uncle's nose or some such, or you or a family member may have joined a website that allows you to work on your family's history by accessing historical records. Family genealogy is about showing relationships with one another and trying to unpick how we got from one person to another. It is showing us how we became the person we are today. So it is in Nietzsche's thought; except rather than talking about people he is talking about how ideas, philosophies and concepts have changed and adapted. He suggests that the way we think about the world has changed over time and his genealogy is an attempt to chart that change by examining changes to key concepts that we use.

Consequently, when we use a concept, for Nietzsche, even though we might be using the same words as someone from the past, this doesn't mean to say that we are talking about exactly the same thing. This method in and of itself is quite radical, as it assumes that people and ideas are not static over time. Indeed, in *Twilight of the Idols*, Nietzsche argues that philosophers have a tendency to create 'conceptual mummies' by removing ideas from their historical environments (Nietzsche, 1990: 45). Likewise, he thinks philosophers have a tendency to do this with their study of humanity, assuming that they remain the same, suggesting in *Ecce Homo* that philosophers 'involuntarily think of "man" ... as something that remains constant in the midst of all flux' despite the fact that, actually, 'everything the philosopher has declared about man is ... no more than a testimony as to the man of a *very limited* period of time' (Nietzsche, 1977: 29). Men and concepts change over time for Nietzsche.

> Concepts such as good, bad and evil had a sociological history, for Nietzsche, and were not constant definitions. Much Western thinking around the nature of good and evil, he thought, came from a position of weakness.

So, definitions of concepts like good and bad, nasty and nice, are not fixed but change over time. Consequently, Nietzsche would have had no time for asking whether humanity is naturally nasty or nice as those concepts by which we are judging humanity change over time. In particular, Nietzsche thinks that the concepts of good and evil, rewarding certain behaviours and chastising others, have a tendency to be dictated from a position of weakness and therefore to be life-denying.

In *Beyond Good and Evil* Nietzsche outlines how sociologically these concepts have changed over time. He argues that originally people in power believed that they, and the manner in which they led their life, were 'good'. They defined people who were not like themselves, less powerful people from the lower classes, as being 'bad'. Powerless people, however, often using religious concepts, argued that it was they who were 'good'. But rather than defining their oppressors as 'bad', they defined them as 'evil'. Consequently, Nietzsche argues that concepts such as good and evil (similar to our concepts here of nasty and nice) were (a) concepts with a history and therefore changeable, and (b) formulated from a position of weakness. Even though much Western philosophy had, by the time Nietzsche was writing, dropped religion in favour of rationality, most philosophers' ideas still had 'theological blood in its veins' (Nietzsche, 1990: 313). It was this struggle to adapt our thinking to a post-religious world, or one in which God was dead, that was the crucial problem for Nietzsche, and one for which humanity had to make way for its successors, the supermen, who would dictate morality from a position of strength rather than weakness.

Activity 5. Outline the difference between good/bad and good/evil. What problems does this pose for us in determining whether humanity is naturally nasty or nice?

Conclusion

Above we have seen a variety of responses from thinkers in the history of political thought that could help us answer the question about whether humanity is by nature nasty or nice (presuming we think that they are not making the question harder to answer).

Hobbes argues that humanity in its natural condition is competitive, greedy and inclined to violence. This is not, however, because they suffer from some ethical or psychological flaw, but rather because in our natural condition there are no police, courts or governments to protect us, and we will work out using our reason that we should use whatever means possible to defend ourselves.

Locke argues that there are natural laws that govern us even without a state above us, so naturally we are rule-abiding and peaceable with an entitlement to be left unharmed, and life would not be as bad as Hobbes makes out. That said, some would not respect the laws of nature, and this would create inconveniences that are less than ideal.

Rousseau argues that the life of competition and greed that Hobbes outlines is not of natural man at all, but rather that of social man. In his natural state man is solitary, content, amoral but with no desire to harm other people. Society makes us dependent upon one another psychologically, each wanting to look good in the eyes of others. This dependence and vanity makes life competitive, not natural tendencies. So, for Rousseau, humanity is naturally good, content and happy (if not moral), and it is society that has made us competitive and acquisitive (albeit moral).

Nietzsche argues that concepts around morality are not set in stone, that is to say they are changeable over time; what is considered nasty or nice in one context would not necessarily be considered likewise in another. So the question as to whether humanity is nasty or nice would be moot as what is considered nasty or nice changes from time to time. What is more, a lot of what is considered good in contemporary philosophy, for Nietzsche, is defined from a position of weakness and should be overcome.

Works cited

Hobbes, T. (1985) *Leviathan*. Harmondsworth: Penguin.
James VI and I (1986) 'A Speech to the Lords and Commons of the Parliament at White-Hall'. In D. Wootton (ed.) *Divine Right and Democracy: An Anthology of Political Writing in Stuart England*. Penguin: Harmondsworth.
Nietzsche, F. (1977) *A Nietzsche Reader*. Harmondsworth: Penguin.
Nietzsche, F. (1990) *Twilight of the Idols/The Anti-Christ*. Harmondsworth: Penguin.
Rousseau, J.J. (1993) *The Social Contract and Discourses*. London: Everyman.

Text reading activity

Hobbes on the state of nature, from Hobbes, T. (1985) *Leviathan*, London: Penguin, p.186.

In such condition, there is no place for Industry; because the fruit thereof is uncertain: and consequently no Culture of the Earth; no Navigation, nor use of the commodities that may be imported by Sea; no commodious Building; no Instruments of moving, and removing such things as require much force; no Knowledge of the face of the Earth; no account of Time; no Arts; no Letters; no Society; and which is worst of all, continuall feare, and danger of violent death; And the life of man, solitary, poore, nasty, brutish, and short.

Rousseau on natural goodness, from 'A Discourse on the Origin and Foundation of the Inequality of Mankind', available at https://www.constitution.org/jjr/ineq03.htm

It is then certain that compassion is a natural feeling, which, by moderating the violence of love of self in each individual, contributes to the preservation of the whole species. It is this compassion that hurries us without reflection to the relief of those who are in distress: it is this which in a state of nature supplies the place of laws, morals and virtues, with the advantage that none are tempted to disobey its gentle voice: it is this which will always prevent a sturdy savage from robbing a weak child or a feeble old man of the sustenance they may have with pain and difficulty acquired, if he sees a possibility of providing for himself by other means: it is this which, instead of inculcating that sublime maxim of rational justice. *Do to others as you would have them do unto you*, inspires all men with that other maxim of natural goodness, much less perfect indeed, but perhaps more useful; *Do good to yourself with as little evil as possible to others*. In a word, it is rather in this natural feeling than in any subtle arguments that we must look for the cause of that repugnance, which every man would experience in doing evil, even independently of the maxims of education. Although it might belong to Socrates and other minds of the like craft to acquire virtue by reason, the human race would long since have ceased to be, had its preservation depended only on the reasonings of the individuals composing it.

Nietzsche on the difference between good and evil, from *Human, all too Human* available at http://nietzsche.holtof.com/ reader/friedrich-nietzsche/human-all-too-human/aphorism-45- quote1c6dca923.html

Double prehistory of good and evil. The concept of good and evil has a double prehistory: namely, first of all, in the soul of the ruling clans and castes. The man who has the power to requite goodness with goodness, evil with evil, and really does practise requital by being grateful and vengeful, is called 'good'. The man who is unpowerful and cannot requite is taken for bad. As a good man, one belongs to the 'good', a community that has a communal feeling, because all the individuals are entwined together by their feeling for requital. As a bad man, one belongs to the 'bad', to a mass of abject, powerless men who have no communal feeling. The good men are a caste; the bad men are a multitude, like particles of dust. Good and bad are for a time equivalent to noble and base, master and slave. Conversely, one does not regard the enemy as evil: he can requite. In Homer, both the Trojan and the Greek are good. Not the man who inflicts harm on us, but the man who is contemptible, is bad. In the community of the good, goodness is hereditary; it is impossible for a bad man to grow out of such good soil. Should one of the good men nevertheless do something unworthy of good men, one resorts to excuses; one blames God, for example, saying that he struck the good man with blindness and madness.

Then, in the souls of oppressed, powerless men, every other man is taken for hostile, inconsiderate, exploitative, cruel, sly, whether he be noble or base. Evil is their epithet for man, indeed for every possible living being, even, for example, for a god; 'human', 'divine' mean the same as 'devilish', 'evil'. Signs of goodness, helpfulness, pity are taken anxiously for malice, the prelude to a terrible outcome, bewilderment, and deception, in short, for refined evil. With such a state of mind in the individual, a community can scarcely come about at all – or at most in the crudest form; so that wherever this concept of good and evil predominates, the downfall of individuals, their clans and races, is near at hand.

Our present morality has grown up on the ground of the ruling clans and castes.

Question 1: Why would life in the state of nature be so bad according to Hobbes?
Question 2: How does Rousseau's account differ from Hobbes's view of natural man?
Question 3: What does Nietzsche have to say about the *concepts* of good and evil?

4
Why should I obey the state?

KEY QUESTIONS

(1) Is all legitimate government based upon a social contract?

(2) What is the nature of that social contract?

(3) Does consent have to be explicit, or is tacit consent sufficient?

(4) Is extensive participation in politics necessary to ensure consent to be governed?

In 2016 just before a preseason game, the San Francisco 49ers quarterback Colin Kaepernick refused to observe the convention of standing for the national anthem, preferring instead to remain seated in protest against racial injustice. In the next game he knelt, a symbolic gesture he persisted with throughout the season, and a number of players throughout the NFL followed his example, taking the knee during the national anthem. This led to intense debate about the appropriateness of this protest, with the President of the United States suggesting that players refusing to stand during the playing of the national anthem should be sacked. Whereas Kaepernick faced no civil penalty for his actions, at the time of writing this book he is without an NFL team, so his career has stalled. He has suffered for his protest. Kaepernick's actions join those of a line of people who have refused to obey laws and/or customs based upon what they think is right.

In 1860 the prominent American author and philosopher Henry Thoreau was arrested and sent to jail for not paying his taxes. Thoreau's failure to pay tax did not involve an accountant's sleight of hand, or under-reporting of income; it was a deliberate political act. Thoreau was known for his reflections on the individual in society; the previous year he had spent living in a wooden hut on his own, experiencing self-sufficiency and solitude, in order to understand how much we needed the society of others. Thoreau was deeply opposed to slavery, and when the United States, unjustly he thought, declared war on Mexico, he stopped paying taxes. He thought that it would be wrong of him to simply pay for a war which he thought was contrary to justice; also, he thought that it was insufficient for people to just say they were opposed to the war; people should do something about it. Thus the modern notion of civil disobedience was born. If there was an unjust law, one should break it.

Likewise, in 1960 a group of students from the local college in Greensboro, North Carolina, decided that it was necessary to take a stand against an unjust policy. The local Woolworths had a segregated lunch counter, where service was only given to white diners, and on 1 February 1960 four African American students, Joseph McNeil, Franklin McCain, Ezell Blair Jr, and David Richmond, sat at that lunch counter and requested service. When they were refused service the sit-in began, as the Greensboro Four, supported by friends and well-wishers from the community, refused to leave. The Greensboro Four and their friends faced arrest and abuse for their civil disobedience, but their actions led to policy changes that ensured that segregation would end so that African Americans could enjoy their rights.

Civil disobedience suggests that there are some times when one should not obey the law. If a law is unjust, it should be disobeyed, but it should be disobeyed peacefully and the consequences of breaking the law should be accepted. Civil disobedience rests upon the premise that by breaking the law peacefully, overall one is respecting law and order; one is just registering protest against certain laws or policies.

Numerous political theorists have addressed a broader concern here, namely why should we obey anything that the state tells us to do? Precisely what authority should the state have over us on any issue? Very few of us have ever specifically agreed to obey the state and yet our obligation remains the same, and this is especially problematic when authority depends upon consent.

Chapter overview

This chapter introduces us to social contract theory, the theory that suggests that all legitimate government is based upon consent, and when a legitimate law is passed we should obey it because of our consent to be governed. We shall see, however, that there is considerable disagreement between thinkers on the nature of consent, and the obligation that we owe to government.

The discussion will begin with Thomas Hobbes, the seventeenth-century English political philosopher. We saw in the last chapter that man in the state of nature was equal and free, but competition, scarcity and uncertainty would ensure that life was nasty, brutish and short for all. This is a situation that all reasonable people would want to escape from, and it is the social contract and the creation of the sovereign power that rescues us from this. We will see here that although the government is based upon consent, when the government is formed, our obligation to obey it is total. Hobbes outlines many reasons why the rational individual would *always* obey the state. We will then go on to compare Hobbes with his near contemporary John Locke. Locke's view of the state of nature was less apocalyptic than Hobbes's, and we will see that although using similar philosophical concepts to Hobbes, he uses social contract theory to build a limited government that can be overthrown if it oversteps its powers. Locke also introduces the notion of tacit consent; how we can consent to government even if we have not directly contracted with it.

The problems with the notion that government is based upon consent will then be discussed. This will begin with David Hume's empiricist critique, that realistically there is not a single government in the world that has been based upon consent, and that tacit consent is not consent at all. For Hume, there are a number of reasons why we as individuals obey the state and consent is not one of them.

We will then outline two thinkers who argue that in order for consent to be meaningful, we need to increase the political role of the citizen from merely consenting to be governed to that of being active participants in the affairs of state. The first of these thinkers will be Jean-Jacques Rousseau, who argues that no one can really be said to be obliged to obey the state if they have not explicitly consented to its formation. Rousseau will outline that a legitimate state should be comprised of a direct democracy in which citizens act as creators of the laws which they then obey. The chapter concludes with a brief overview of Carole Pateman's critique of political obligation and call for greater participation in politics.

Hobbes and obedience

Hobbes does not give one reason why we should obey the sovereign power; he rather gives several reasons why the rational individual should obey the state. It is not necessary to believe all of them (although there is no real contradiction between them) for the individual to conclude that the state has legitimate authority. Writing at a time when people who had previously fought for the royalists in the English Civil War were being asked to engage (promise to obey) the Cromwellian regime, Hobbes, originally a royalist himself, gives them several reasons why they should do this. They are:

1 That if we do not obey the state, we will be thrust back into the nasty and brutish state of nature in which life will be short. It is in our self-interests to obey the sovereign therefore.
2 The state will keep the peace and allow us to get on with the things we want to do in life by enforcing laws, protecting property, etc.
3 We have contracted with one another to obey the sovereign, and to break contracts freely entered into is unjust.

4 The sovereign power uses our powers in the state, so when the state acts it is us acting, and therefore we should not complain about what we are doing. We are the authors of the sovereign's actions.

Hobbes will show how the power of this sovereign is unlimited (with one noticeable, if pretty meaningless, exception). So whereas much social contract thinking will seek to limit power, written as they were when monarchs supposedly held unlimited power directly from God, Hobbes's theory does not do this. Hobbes's view of power is intended to show why we should obey anything that the state tells us to do.

Hobbes's contract

For Hobbes, the state is formed when all men say to all other men:

> I Authorise and give up my Right of Governing my selfe, to this Man, or to this Assembly of men, on this condition, that thou give up thy Right to him, and Authorise all his Actions in like manner. (Hobbes, 1985: 227)

I want to return to the incredible importance of a couple of words and phrases in this sentence in a second, but before we do this, it is important to note that this contract does two things at precisely the same time. Firstly, it unifies a previously disparate and warring people into one body and, secondly, it creates the sovereign power over us. That these two things happen at the same time is exceptionally important for Hobbes, and it will be seen later in this chapter, this element is central to John Locke's critique of Hobbes. For Hobbes, we have a simple choice: create and obey a sovereign power, or live (and probably die) in the state of nature. Disobeying and/or overthrowing the sovereign power puts us back into the state of nature – there is no midpoint.

Going back to the precise words of the contract we make with one another, note that Hobbes does not say that 'I promise to obey the sovereign' or even 'I promise to obey you', but rather that 'I Authorise' and 'give up my Right of Governing my selfe, to this man'.

Hobbes's contract

Hobbes's contract does two things; it unites its signees into one body, and creates the obligation for that body to obey the sovereign.

Think of the word 'Authorise' for a moment. We know that this means to give official approval to something, but Hobbes is using this word in a slightly more specific manner. If one is the author of something, we have to take responsibility for what it is we have written as we have written the words. I have to take responsibility for the content of this book as I am its author. You have to take responsibility for the contents of your last essay as you wrote it. Thus, for Hobbes, authorizing the actions of the sovereign means literally that you, I, and our fellow citizens need to take responsibility for what the state does. We are the authors of the state's actions. The sovereign power has not received its powers from God, nor from natural law (although the impetus to create the sovereign came from natural law); the sovereign has received its powers from us in the contract. We are, for Hobbes, to give up our right to govern ourselves to the sovereign and it is this power that the state needs to govern. Therefore the state uses our powers when it acts so, again, we need to take responsibility for the actions of the state and crucially, obey them.

Another thing worth examining in the contract printed above is precisely who is named in the contract. All men are contracting with all other men to transfer their rights of governing themselves to the sovereign, and promising to authorise the actions of the sovereign. Note, therefore, that the contract is between the *people* to *create the sovereign*. It is not between you and the sovereign or between me and the sovereign, it is between you and me to create the sovereign. The sovereign is mentioned in the contract as an interested party but it is manifestly not a contract between us and the sovereign. I have an obligation via this contract to obey the sovereign, but that obligation is owed to you and our fellow citizens. If I disobey the sovereign, I am breaking a contract I have with you.

Crucially, however, the sovereign has no contractual link with those who have created him. If we have a contract with someone or something, it is normal that all parties in the contract have some obligations. Lebron James cannot leave the LA Lakers mid-season as he has a contract to play for them; likewise the Lakers cannot stop paying him as they have a contract to pay him. Both sides have obligations in the contract. As the sovereign is not actually a party to the contract, it follows for Hobbes that we cannot complain that the state has broken the contract and try to change the regime. The state has no contractual obligations; the only contractual obligations are between the citizens to create and obey the sovereign.

Powers of the sovereign

The power of the state, or sovereignty as Hobbes calls it, is absolute, and our obligation to obey it is likewise absolute. In the state of nature each individual had a right to everything; via the contract we transfer this right to everything, and as a consequence the state has a right to do anything. It can decide which

---

Stop complaining!

For Hobbes, we should not complain about what the state is doing for we have authorized its actions; so it is us doing it. Also we should not think that the sovereign can ever break the contract; it was not named in the contract so cannot break it. We have a contractual agreement *with one another* to obey the sovereign – it has no obligation to us.

religions can be followed and which should be banned. **Hobbes does not think that the sovereign has any special theological powers or access to religious truth any more than you or I do.** Indeed, Hobbes is almost certainly an atheist, or would have been regarded as one at the time (which is astonishing in the seventeenth century). When the sovereign decides which religions should be taught and which banned, **it is decided purely on the grounds of maintaining the peace.** In Hobbes's later work *Behemoth*, for example, Hobbes blames the civil war on the fact that Aristotle's ideas on politics and ethics dominated the universities, so it is possible that *The Politics* might have been banned by a Hobbesian sovereign.

> The sovereign has the power to do *anything* it judges necessary to keep the peace. The only exception is that it cannot expect us to allow it to kill us without a fight; so you are entitled to resist the executioner.

The sovereign has a right to anything it wants, and we have no right to dispute this as if the sovereign does it, using our powers that we have transferred, it follows that we are doing it. Hobbes has already made it clear that the first law of nature is to protect ourselves, and it would make little sense for us to harm ourselves, so it follows that nothing that the state does can actually harm us.

There is one, albeit slight, exception to this. Although we transfer all our rights to the sovereign – as there is a benefit to us in so doing in avoiding the calamities of the state of nature – there is one right we cannot transfer:

> [A] man cannot lay down the right of resisting them, that assault him by force, to take away his life; because he cannot be understood to ayme thereby, at Good to himselfe. (Hobbes, 1985: 192)

So if the sovereign power decides that it is necessary to have you killed for the sake of the peace, you do not have to go quietly. You may resist. This does not mean that the sovereign may not put people to death, nor does it mean that by doing this human rights are broken; it means simply that you can fight the police officer or the executioner. It is the only form of resistance to the state that is perfectly rational.

The contemporary state

So far, perhaps, you may be struggling to see why Hobbes is regarded by historians of political thought as such an important figure. Sure enough, his reasoning about the natural freedom and equality of mankind is an argument that would be built upon by liberal thinkers, but Hobbes himself is no liberal thinker. Likewise, the notion that the ruler gains his power from the consent of the governed, which will become a central tenet of democratic thinking, stems from Hobbes, but he was no democrat. His view of the nature of man is bleak and unappealing, and the absolutist powers of the sovereign he outlines sound terrifying to modern ears. Perhaps his greatest enduring notion is the description of the state; perhaps a description that we still hold to this day.

Activity 1. Outline four reasons why Hobbes says you should obey the state; on what occasion can you resist the state?

Reason I should obey the state no. 1	
Reason I should obey the state no. 2	
Reason I should obey the state no. 3	
Reason I should obey the state no. 4	
The one time I can resist the state is	

Monarchs throughout the ages always thought that they and the state were indivisible; that they personally received power directly from God, and therefore their person and their post as monarch were one and the same thing. As Louis XIV of France is alleged to have said, 'L'Etat, c'est moi' – I am the state. Democratic republicans like Rousseau would later suggest that the state is all citizens – the democratic will perhaps. The state maintains a human face for Rousseau; it is just the people who comprise it that change. Hobbes cuts through both of these arguments, and proposes a definition of the state that has endured to this day.

When one transfers one's powers to the sovereign, it is not a natural person to whom we transfer our powers. Hobbes is not asking his readers to transfer their political powers to Oliver Cromwell, or Charles II, or to himself for that matter.

Hobbes and the modern state

Hobbes sees the state as conceptually different from both the person operating the powers of the state and from the people comprising it. In this way his definitions of the state have endured to the modern world, as we do not regard Donald Trump as the US state, nor do we regard US citizens as the state; we see the state as a set of institutions that Trump uses to which the US citizens have consented to give their power.

He is asking people to transfer their powers to the ***artificial person of the state***. When the actual person who governs uses these powers, he is a bit like an actor in a role; it is not his personal powers he is using but rather he is acting the role of the artificial person of the state. When we are watching a TV programme and one character kills another, we do not call the police and report a murder as we know that the actors are playing a role. No one reported Bryan Cranston to the police for drug dealing after watching *Breaking Bad*, nor do students at Caltech demand their tuition fees back when they realize they will not be lectured by Jim Parsons from *The Big Bang Theory*. We know that they are playing characters rather than being the persons depicted themselves. So it is with the state; the state is an artificial person who the person in power acts, the power does not belong to that actual person.

Nor does it reside with the people of the state. It did once, of course, in the state of nature, but this was prior to sovereignty and the unity of people through the contract. In this contract people transferred their powers to the artificial person of the state. They are authors (scriptwriters if you will) of the state's actions; but they are not actually the state.

This notion of the state being a set of powers that are logically separate from both the person operating those powers, and from the people comprising the state, endures today, and is perhaps Hobbes's greatest innovation. We do not think that Donald Trump is the state, any more than we think that the citizens of the United States are the state. The state is a set of institutions that will be used by another natural person in the future, and although they are said to represent the people, they are not actually the people. The state will exist when there is a new president, and when new generations of people are living.

John Locke's critique

The historical purpose of Hobbes's account of the obligation to obey was to show why, after the civil war, those people who had fought for the royalists should obey Cromwell's government. The purpose behind Locke's *Second Treatise of Government* is quite the opposite. **He wants to show how it is possible to remove a government and replace it with another and how this is justifiable**. Locke was a leading exclusionist, that is to say he thought that James II of England, a Catholic, should be excluded from the throne. His writings can be seen as a philosophical defence of the Glorious Revolution, the successful removal of James II and his replacement with the Protestant William of Orange. That his account is based upon a right to revolution should prepare us for the fact that his account will differ from that of Hobbes.

Just as he had in his account of the state of nature, however, structurally John Locke agrees with a lot of the broad thrust of Hobbes's argument. There can be no just government without consent via a contract, and we should obey government because we have agreed to it. This, however, is where they part company, as Locke is certain that man cannot 'by Compact, or his own Consent, *enslave himself* to any one, nor put himself under the Absolute, Arbitrary Power of another, to take away his Life, when he pleases' (Locke, 1988: 284). The type of government Hobbes proposes simply won't do for Locke, and he tries to show how the nature of the contract, and the transferral of power to the state, will limit the power of government.

Firstly, you may remember from the previous chapter that the state of nature that Locke describes is not as calamitous a condition as Hobbes thinks it is. **The laws of nature compel us not to injure another in their life, liberty and property, and most people will follow this**. The problem is of course that not all will all the time, and punishing those people who break the laws of nature is left in the hands of everyone. This is inconvenient to all, and might lead to conflict as people might punish people too harshly for relatively minor offences. For Locke, when we contract, we transfer to the state not our rights to everything, but rather the right to interpret the laws of nature – a far more limited transferral of powers.

> For Locke, the social contract is a two-stage affair. The first stage unites us as a people and takes us out of the state of nature, the second is with a specific government. This means there is a contractual link with our governors and we can replace them without returning to the state of nature.

Locke thinks that the contract to form the sovereign takes place in two stages. **Firstly, we contract with one another to form what he calls civil society**; this joins us together into a people. **The second stage is between us and a particular person or group of people who will form the government**; this need only be a majority decision (i.e. if there is a dispute about who precisely should form the government, the decision of the majority will hold sway). This two-stage process is important for Locke as it illustrates that one can remove a government without going back into the state of nature. Should we remove a government, civil society will still remain; we just need to contract with another to form a replacement government.

Locke recognizes the fact that after the foundation of a government there is little opportunity to participate in the contract. You and I have probably had no opportunity to say that we consent to be governed. For this problem Locke invokes the notion of **tacit consent**. By living under the government, enjoying its benefits, being able to inherit property that has been protected by the state, we have shown that tacitly we consent to being governed by it. It is not necessary, therefore, to explicitly give our consent to government. If we were really that unhappy with the manner in which we were governed, we could always leave.

Locke thinks that the state must be limited in its powers. Man in the state of nature, you may remember, is limited in his powers as he cannot infringe upon the laws of nature, nor harm another person in his life, liberty or property without penalty. As man did not have the power over another's life, liberty and property in the state of nature, it follows for Locke that the state cannot have these powers either as the state is only comprised of rights transferred to it by us. We form the state purely and simply to enforce the laws of nature, and our lives, liberty and property are none of its business. Property is a pre-political right, that is to say it existed prior to the formation of government rather than being given to us by the government, and the government has no basis whatsoever to interfere with this (more on Locke's justification of a pre-political right to property later in this book).

Government is limited to the role of protecting our lives, liberty and property, and should it try to infringe upon other areas of our life, we can simply remove it and institute another without being plunged into the inconveniences of the state of nature. So long as government sticks to its brief, we should obey it as its powers rest upon our consent; and consent is the only place governments can gain power from. We would be foolish, he thinks, to give too much power to the state, stating that we should not consent to be devoured by a lion to protect oneself from a fox or a polecat.

Locke, we can see, is a far more obvious liberal thinker (although for historical accuracy, we should note that he never described himself as such, as the word 'liberal' in this ideological context was not used until the nineteenth century). Government is limited, based upon consent, and can be removed if it overreaches its powers. Locke does not talk of human rights, or perhaps more accurately the rights of man, however; the idea that there are areas of life which government has no business interfering in is a kind of negative version of human rights. Thomas Paine, as we shall see later in this book, is greatly influenced by Locke in his account of the rights of man.

Activity 2. Define the concepts listed below and suggest why Locke uses them

Concept	Definition	Why he uses them
Two-stage contract		
Tacit consent		
Limited powers of government		

Critics of social contract theory

In the English Civil War a political movement developed called the Levellers who argued, among other things, for the abolition of the Monarchy and the House of Lords, an end to conscription, and the institution of a written constitution. This constitution, a document called *An Agreement of the People*, which asserted the sovereignty of the people, was to be taken around the country for all people to sign as a show of consent to government. Without this, Leveller leader Thomas Rainsborough suggests, 'I do think that the poorest man in England is not bound in a strict sense to that government that he hath not had a voice to put himself under' (Rainsborough in Woodhouse, 1938: 53). The *Agreement of the People* itself provides a clear notion of a social contract – that political power was only permissible if people had consented to it – but the Levellers also argue that people should agree to this. So the contract was a literal thing as well as a philosophical construct.

This example raises an interesting criticism of social contract theory; namely that few of us have ever explicitly consented to being governed by any authority. Laws are made by an authority that we have to obey. Indeed, many laws might even be made before we are born, and yet we have to obey them. Perhaps if you have changed your citizenship and participated in a naturalization process and/or a pledge of allegiance, one might call that consent; but most of us haven't.

This is an argument that the philosopher David Hume takes up in his essay entitled 'Of the original contract'. His purpose in it is neither to say that there *should* be explicit consent to all government via a contract, nor that sometimes there *is* consent, but rather to argue that the idea that the only legitimate basis for the power of government is consent is highly problematic.

Hume's main argument against social contract theory is an empirical one, that is to say one based upon observation, and that is that when one looks around the world most governments 'have been founded originally either on usurpation or conquest, or both, without any pretense of a fair consent, or voluntary subjection of the people' (Hume, 2000: 164). **That is to say, if all legitimate government is based upon consent, why are most governments not based upon consent?** This argument, made as it was in the eighteenth century, has lost a little of its power due to the revolutions and rise in democratic states that have followed it, but it does not make it completely redundant. There are still states in the world that are either undemocratic or less democratic than we would like them to be, and even if the state is democratic that does not mean to say that we have had the opportunity to consent to it. Crucially, however, this argument is a descriptive one rather than a moral one. If one

> Hume points out that there has not been a social contract – that is to say that a literal document does not exist. His point is not that we should sign one, but more to show that we do not obey government because of something that has not happened.

thinks that the only just government is one where power rests upon consent, the presence of one, two or many states where power is exercised without consent does not dent the view that just power is consensual. It just makes a number of states unjust.

Hume also argues against Locke's notion of **tacit consent**; the notion that we can consent to government by enjoying the benefits that it brings. Hume's objection to this argument is that this **cannot really be meaningfully called consent**. His purpose is not really to defend consent here, but rather to continue his attack on the notion that all legitimate government can be said to be based upon consent. He says:

> Can we seriously say, that a poor peasant or artisan has a free choice to leave his country, when he knows no foreign language or manners, and lives from day to day, by the small wages which he acquires? We may as well assert, that a man, by remaining in a vessel, freely consents to the dominion of the master; though he was carried on board while asleep, and must leap into the ocean, and perish, the moment he leaves her. (Hume, 2000: 166–7)

It is nonsense to suppose, Hume is saying here, that by simply continuing to reside in a country under a particular government, one is consenting to that government when there is nothing that one could reasonably do to get away from the government. This seems a plausible argument against social contract theory in the contemporary world. Suppose you or I decided that we did not like the state that we lived in: what choices do we actually have to change the situation? If one is a citizen of the European Union then one can move about relatively freely supposing one has the money, so we could move elsewhere. Indeed, if one was a member of the economic elite, then borders mean precious little. More broadly, however, countries prevent immigration, and unless one qualifies for refugee or asylum status (more serious perhaps

---

David Hume

David Hume was born in Edinburgh in Scotland in 1711 and wrote extensively on political and ethical issues. Along with thinkers such as the economist Adam Smith and the philosopher Adam Ferguson, Hume is regarded as a leading light of the Scottish Enlightenment. Also, like John Locke before him, Hume was regarded as a crucial contributor to empiricist philosophy.

Perhaps Hume is best known for the philosophical device 'Hume's Fork' – that one cannot get an ought statement from an is statement: that the world of enquiry into matters of fact are different in type from those of ethics, and these two realms of enquiry should not be confused.

Hume worked as a librarian at the University of Edinburgh before becoming a tutor and secretary to noted society figures. Whilst working in the British embassy in France, he befriended Rousseau, although the two later fell out.

than just not liking a government), then the opportunities to move are slim. What, however, if we wanted to escape our obligation to obey any government at all? Where could we go then? Short of establishing our own microstate, few realistic opportunities exist for us. So consent, tacit or otherwise, could be said to be meaningless.

Also look at Hume's critique of tacit consent above as being a critique of Hobbes's social contract. Hobbes argues that we should consent to the state and authorize all of its powers because the alternative is death in the state of nature. Is this really a free choice? Is it not like Hume's pressed man who has to choose between the dominion of the ship's captain or death in the ocean? Hobbes's response to this would likely be that the rational person would choose life however hard sovereignty might be, as there is a utility to it.

We should not overstate Hume's critique of Hobbes here though, as he generally agrees with his point about the multifaceted nature of consent to government. There are in fact a number of reasons why we obey government, and consent is only one of them. Generally, we obey government because there are advantages to us in so doing and we get into the habit of obeying; however, he refuses to call this consent.

Activity 3. How does Hume critique the following ideas?

Idea	Hume's critique
Social contract theory (that all legitimate government is based upon consent)	
Locke's notion of tacit consent (that consent need not be explicit – enjoying the benefits of society is sufficient)	

Rousseau and Patemen: obligation and participation

For Rousseau, the social contract is a way to regain some measure of freedom that has been robbed from natural man, as well as the formation of a just government. You maybe remember from the previous chapter that man in society is vain and selfish, and enslaved by his passions and dependence on others. This state of being is not natural to man, but natural freedom can never be regained fully; a type of freedom is achievable, though, with a proper set of political institutions and attitudes. First and foremost, **Rousseau is absolutely adamant that the only legitimate contract is one which all men explicitly consent to**. There can be no tacit consent. However, the contract is not simply a way of legitimating a distant government, but Rousseau's contract also sets up a set of political arrangements which guarantee continuing political participation for all citizens.

The sovereign that is created by the social contract is all of the citizens, as is all of the subjects; so people are sovereign when making laws, and subjects when obeying. So all citizens should play a part in making laws as well as having the obligation to obey legitimate laws. Rousseau, however, says that all citizens should literally play a part in making laws. Rousseau was a proponent of direct democracy like that in ancient Athens or Geneva (where he was born) whereby all citizens would attend an assembly and debate and vote on laws. Representatives (such as Senators, Congressmen, MPs, etc.) were out of the question for Rousseau as citizens had to represent themselves. We who live in representative democracies, Rousseau would argue, are only really free at the moment we cast our ballot in an election; the rest of the time we are enslaved as we cannot represent ourselves.

Indeed, so important is the need to represent ourselves that political parties or factions should have no role in politics. If we are members of the Republican Party or the Democratic Party and form a faction in the assembly with like-minded citizens, we will end up representing the party as opposed to ourselves.

There is still more for legitimate government for Rousseau: the chief cause of our dependence on others are our passions, which make us want more and more money, power and property. It was important for Rousseau that we do not

Rousseau on representation

Rousseau thought that in order for government to be legitimate one must first explicitly consent to it, and secondly one must represent oneself in a democracy. This meant no representatives (a direct democracy) and no political parties; one must always represent oneself.

make decisions and debate purely out of self-interest (or our particular wills as he puts it). Instead, he argues that when a bill or law is debated, rather than us deciding what we would want or how this law will affect us, we should ask what is in the interests of the state (and remember the state for Rousseau means all the citizens). We should always make our decisions on what is in the interests of everyone rather than any group of people, be it our class, party, faction or indeed just us. This Rousseau calls the general will.

When law is made in this manner, we are obliged to obey it; however, the way in which he explains this is perhaps the most debated and controversial passage in the history of political thought:

> In order then that the social compact may not be an empty formula, it tacitly includes the undertaking, which alone can give force to the rest, that whoever refuses to obey the general will shall be compelled to do so by the whole body. This means nothing less than that he will be forced to be free. (Rousseau, 1993: 195)

Being forced to be free seems on the face of it patently absurd; however, we must remember that for Rousseau freedom is not simply doing what you want, as that is the following of the passions which has led to our vanity and dependence on one another. Rousseau's view of freedom is obeying laws which you have made yourself that limit your passions, and the social contract does this as it forms a direct democracy (us making laws which apply to ourselves), which makes us think of the good of everyone when making those laws (limiting our passions). Even if you do not concur with Rousseau's view of freedom (and we shall explore freedom as a concept later in this book), one should not be too shocked by Rousseau's concept of being forced to be free. Under his view of obligation, a citizen is entitled to take part in the making of all laws, does not have his views mediated by a representative or a party, and whose interests (along with everyone else's) people should consider when making a law. When all this is followed and a legitimate law is made, Rousseau thinks we are obliged to obey it, but calls it freedom. This is hardly tyrannical. As Plamenatz writes:

> Rousseau calls making laws for oneself that one then obeys freedom; those who refuse to do so will be forced to be free.

> Rousseau tells us that the citizen who is not excluded from the sovereign assembly, nor exposed inside it to pressures and intrigues which make his opinions and his votes count for nothing, is bound to obey the laws made by the assembly. Whatever the defects of this doctrine, it is not dangerous to liberty. (2006, 106)

Rousseau's critique of Hobbes and Locke's view of political obligation and consent and call for more participation remains prescient hundreds of years after he wrote. Carole Pateman sees the reliance on the voluntary nature of the contract in Hobbes and Locke and liberal democratic theory in general to be a crucial weakness, as that obligation stems from a contract, but the nature of the voluntarism of that contract is ambiguous. As she points out:

> It is frequently argued that even if citizens cannot, with any plausibility, be said to have promised or consented, they are, nevertheless, politically obligated in the liberal democratic state. (Pateman, 1979: 3)

Rousseau's contract is different for Pateman, as rather than agreeing to obey the government in order to be protected (from death in Hobbes's theory, from theft perhaps in Locke's), it is **'a voluntary agreement, or promise, between individuals to create a political association that will give expression to, and maintain,**

their substantive freedom and equality' (Pateman, 1979: 170). Participation in politics, with free and equal individuals making promises with one another rather than creating obligations with contracts, is the way to build a state that would be legitimate for Pateman.

Activity 4.

(1) Outline the ways in which Hume and Rousseau critique Hobbes and Locke's contractarianism.

(2) Why is participation in politics so important to Rousseau and Pateman?

(3) Do you feel that you are obliged to obey government? Explain your answer.

Conclusion

In this chapter, we have outlined the classic 'liberal' social contract argument for why we should obey the state and some of its critics. We have seen how Hobbes argues why the rational person should obey any government that exists, and how Locke tempers this by showing why we should obey any government that protects our life, liberty and property; but that we did not have to directly consent to this government.

We have also seen how Hume rejects the social contract, arguing that, although self-interest is central to why we obey government, we certainly have not consented to government and that tacit consent is no consent at all.

Rousseau and Pateman go a step further by explicitly rejecting self-interest and Hobbes and Locke's contract as being the basis of consent. Rousseau argues that only explicit consent is acceptable to form an obligation, and that political society should be comprised of a direct democracy in order for government to be considered legitimate.

Works cited

Hobbes, T. (1985) *Leviathan*. Harmondsworth: Penguin.

Hume, D. (2000) 'Of the original contract'. In N. Warburton et al. (eds) *Reading Political Philosophy: Machiavelli to Mill*. London: Routledge, pp. 162–7.

Locke, J. (1988) *Two Treatises of Government*. Cambridge: Cambridge University Press.

Pateman, C. (1979) *The Problem of Political Obligation: A Critique of Liberal Theory*. Cambridge: Polity.

Plamenatz, J. (2006) 'Ce qui ne signifie autre chose sinon qu'on le forcera d'être libre'. In J. Scott (ed.) *Jean-Jacques Rousseau: Critical Assessments of Leading Political Philosophers*. Oxford: Routledge, pp. 106–16.

Woodhouse, A.S.P. (1938) *Puritanism and Liberty*. London: J.M. Dent.

Text reading activity

James VI and I *A Speech to the Lords and Commons* in Wootton, D. ed (1986) *Divine Right and Democracy: An Anthology of Political Writing in Stuart England*, London: Penguin, pp. 107–8.

The state of Monarchy is the supremest thing upon earth; for kings are not only God's lieutenants upon earth and sit upon God's throne, but even by God himself they are called gods. There be three principal similitudes that illustrate the state of Monarchy: one taken out of the word of God and the two other out of the grounds of policy and philosophy. In the Scriptures kings are called gods, and so their power after a certain relation compared to the divine power. Kings are also compared to the fathers of families, for a king is truly *parens patriae*, the politic father of his people. And lastly, kings are compared to the head of this microcosm of the body of man.

Kings are justly called gods for that they exercise a manner or resemblance of divine power upon earth; for if you will consider the attributes to God you shall see how they agree in the person of a king. God hath power to create or destroy, make or unmake at his pleasure, to give life, or send death, to judge all, and to be judged nor accountable to none; to raise low things and to make high things low at his pleasure, and to God are both soul and body due. And the like power have kings: they make and unmake their subjects; they have power of raising and casting down, of life and death; judges over all their subjects and in all causes, and yet accountable to none but God only. They have power to exalt low things and abase high things, and make of their subjects like men at the chess: a pawn to take a bishop or a knight, and to cry up or down any of their subjects as they do their money. And to the King is due both the affection of the soul and the service of the body of his subjects …

As for the father of a family, they had of old under the Law of Nature *patriam potestatem*, which was *potestatem vitae et necis*, [power of life and death] over their children or family. I mean such fathers of families as were the lineal heirs of those families whereof kings did originally come, for kings had their first original from them who planted and spread themselves in colonies through the world. Now a father may dispose of his inheritance to his children at his pleasure: yea, even disinherit the eldest upon just occasions, and prefer the youngest, according to his liking; make them beggars or rich at his pleasure; restrain or banish out of his presence, as he finds them give cause of offence, or restore them in favour again with the penitent sinner. So may the King deal with his subjects.

Hobbes on the push to a contract, from Hobbes, T. (1985) *Leviathan*, London: Penguin, pp. 189–91.

And because the condition of man, ... is a condition of Warre of every one against every one; in which case every one is governed by his own Reason; and there is nothing he can make use of, that may not be a help unto him, in preserving his life against his enemyes; it followeth, that in such a condition, every man has a Right to every thing; even to one anothers body. And therefore, as long as this naturall Right of every man to every thing endureth, there can be no security to any man, (how strong or wise soever he be,) of living out the time, which Nature ordinarily alloweth men to live. And consequently it is a precept, or generall rule of Reason, *That every man, ought to endeavour Peace, as far as he has hope of obtaining it; and when he cannot obtain it, that he may seek, and use, all helps and advantages of Warre.* The first branch of which Rule, containeth the first, and Fundamentall Law of Nature; which is, *to seek peace and follow it.* The Second, the summe of the Right of Nature; which is, *By all means we can, to defend ourselves.*

From this fundamentall Law of Nature, by which men are commanded to endeavour Peace, is derived this Second Law; *That a man be willing, when others are so too, as farre-forth, as for Peace, and defence of himselfe he shall think it necessary, to lay down this right to all things; and be contented with so much liberty against other men, as he would allow other men against himselfe.* For as long as every man holdeth this Right, of doing anything he liketh; so long are all men in the condition of Warre. But if other men will not lay down their Right, as well as he; then there is no Reason for any one, to divest himselfe of his: For that were to expose himselfe to Prey, (which no man is bound to) rather than to dispose himselfe to Peace. This is that Law of the Gospell: *Whatsoever you require that others should do to you, that do ye to them.* And that Law of all men, *quod tibi fieri non vis, alteri ne feceris.*

To lay downe a mans Right to any thing, is to devest himselfe of the Liberty, of hindring another of the benefit of his own Right to the same. For he that renounceth, or passeth away his Right giveth not to any other man a Right which he had not before; because there is nothing to which every man had not Right by Nature: but onely standeth out of his way, that he may enjoy his own originall Right, without hindrance from him; not without hindrance from another. So that the effect which redoundeth to one man by another man's defect of Right, is but so much diminution of impediments to the use of his own Right originall.

Right is layd aside, either by simply Renouncing it; or by Transferring it to another. By simply RENOUNCING; when he cares not to whom the benefit thereof redoundeth. By TRANSFERRING; when he intendeth the benefit thereof to some certain person, or persons. And when a man hath in either manner abandoned, or granted away his Right; then is he said to be OBLIGED, or BOUND, not to hinder those, to whom such Right is granted, or abandoned, from the benefit of it: and that he ought, and it is DUTY, not to make voyd that voluntary act of his own: and that such hindrance is INJUSTICE, and INJURY, as being *Sine Jure*; the Right being before renounced, or transferred.

Question 1: Where does political power come for James VI? Are there any problems with this?

Question 2: How does social contract theory differ from divine right theory on political obligation?

5
Is democracy the best form of government?

KEY QUESTIONS

(1) What are the key differences between democracy in ancient Athens and the contemporary world?

(2) How did republican theorists conceptualize democracy?

(3) Is democracy best exercised by representatives or by citizens?

(4) What role did democracy play in the founding fathers' ideals?

(5) Does democracy present a problem with the potential 'tyranny of the majority', and if so how can it best be avoided?

In *The Simpsons* episode 'Bart's Comet', Bart Simpson discovers a comet that is on a collision course with Springfield. Amid a scene of impending doom, congress attempts to pass a bill evacuating Springfield, only for it to be defeated after a politician attempts to attach a rider to the bill giving public funding to the pornographic arts, leaving Springfield to its fate. This leads an exasperated Kent Brockman to declare on TV, 'I've said it before and I'll say it again, democracy simply doesn't work.'

Many would argue that democracy works very well. If you live in a democracy, you are less likely to be involved in wars as democracies tend not to go to war with one another. Democracies are also less likely to have civil wars as, if you do not like the president/prime minister, you know you will have an opportunity in a few years to vote them out of power so you do not have to resort to overthrowing the government by force. You are less likely to die in a famine as the government has a vested interest in ensuring you are fed in times of scarcity, and you are far more likely to have your rights respected. From a purely utilitarian perspective, life is much better in a democracy, so it works very well.

Democracy, after the fall of the Berlin Wall and the breakup of the Soviet Union, seemed on an unstoppable path to become the only form of government in the world. So much so, in fact, that political scientist Francis Fukuyama stated in 1992 that we were close to the end of history with liberal democratic states being victorious. Recent history, Arab Spring notwithstanding, has been more challenging for democracy. The pressure group Freedom House's *Freedom in the World 2019* report argued that democracy was on the retreat following 13 consecutive years of reduction in overall freedom around the world.

Democracy contains its own problems as well, with specific methods of arranging elections often leading to surprising results. Of the five US presidential elections of the twenty-first century so far, two have been won by candidates who got fewer votes than their opponent, with Gore winning the popular vote in 2000 and Clinton doing likewise in 2016, but both losing to candidates with more electoral college votes. In the 2015 UK general election, the Scottish National Party (SNP) received 1,454,436 votes and gained fifty-six seats in the House of Commons, whereas the Liberal Democrats received almost a million more votes (2,415,916) but won only eight seats. The UK Independence Party received 3,881,099 votes, more than the Liberal Democrats and the SNP combined, but won only one seat. In addition to this, millions of people around the world can vote, but do not. In 2016 the UK held a referendum on its continued membership of the European Union, the fallout of which still dominates European politics to this day, with the British exit from the EU (Brexit) causing shockwaves around the world. The turnout seemed high – 72.21% – but another way of looking at this is that in a poll that was unprecedented in its consequences for UK politics, more than a quarter of voters chose not to vote.

These discussions around voting and election results presuppose that democracy is about these elections, and this is something that is disputed in the history of political thought. Democracy, many would argue, is far too important to be left to politicians, political parties and the like. Democracy is about people ruling, not electing people to rule. This chapter will attempt to unpick some of these arguments about the nature of democracy.

Chapter overview

Winston Churchill famously declared 'Indeed it has been said that democracy is the worst form of Government except for all those other forms that have been tried from time to time' (Churchill in Jay, 1996: 93). Whereas this is hardly a ringing endorsement of the idea, it does recognize that for most of the twentieth century it has been considered the baseline for political legitimacy and the type of system of government that most regimes claim to be. As Linz and Stepan assert, democracy is often 'the only game in town' (1996: 15).

The problem with answering the question 'Is democracy the best form of government?' is that democracy is not really a form of government. Instead, it is a legitimating principle for a variety of systems of government. The governments of the United States, the UK, France, Australia and so on are all (or at least claim to be) democratic, but their systems of government are very different.

The idea originates, as we shall see in a minute, from ancient Athens, and the word comes from the Greek *Demos*, meaning people, and *Kratos*, meaning rule of; so literally the rule of the people (as opposed to, say, Aristocracy – rule of the best). But again, this does not really tell us how things will be organized to allow the people to rule, and indeed, who exactly the people are. This chapter will show us that there have been considerable disputes concerning the definitions of these terms in the history of political thought.

We will begin at the beginning, and examine the first iteration of democracy, the political practice in existence in ancient Athens. We will see that Athenian democracy was very different from that which is practised today. It was practised by a small group of citizens whose leisure to discuss political affairs was allowed by their owning of slaves, so political participation was not a right afforded to the whole population. It was a direct democracy, meaning that there were no representatives, citizens attended the assembly, discussed issues, and voted themselves; this was not delegated to a professional political class. It was also all-encompassing, meaning that it did not cover simply 'political' issues – citizens decided on legal issues as well. Consequently, Athenian democracy looked very different from the way in which we practise it today.

After the discussion of ancient Athens, we will move on to a discussion of republican theory inspired by the ancients, and in particular we will look at the ideas of Montesquieu and Rousseau. We will see here how these two republican theorists differed in their ideas of how to achieve a similar goal, that of a government that acted in the interests of all. Montesquieu supported the separation of powers, the notion that the executive, the legislature and the judiciary should be separate in order to balance the state and ensure that no one person or group of people could amass overwhelming power. Consequently, no person or group of people could govern in their own interests. Whereas this does not seem on the face of it to be obviously democratic, it was an attempt to limit the power of monarchs (particularly the French monarchs) and bring other people into the process of governing. Rousseau, we shall see, is more obviously democratic, promoting a direct democracy similar to that of ancient Athens, but one in which all men (and I use the word men here deliberately) should participate in making laws. This would be modified by the notion of the general will, to which all citizens should pay heed when making their decisions in a democracy. The general will is that which is in the interests of the republic (or to put it another way, all the people), so participants in democracy should never simply vote for what would benefit them.

After this discussion of direct democracy, we will move on to the thought of Edmund Burke, who will argue in favour of representative democracy. Allowing your representative to participate in discussions in Parliament unhindered, Burke thought, would ensure that politics did not descend into local infighting, with each constituency attempting to achieve what was in their best interests, and representatives could try to find what was in the national interest. We will then go on to examine Burke's broader thought, in which he argues that politics should not be based upon abstract principles but rather local prejudices; so democracy is not necessarily the only form of legitimate government. This will be contrasted to his contemporary Thomas Paine, who sees democracy as an inevitable conclusion of liberal notions of limited government and rights.

The chapter will then proceed to examine the role of democracy in the founding of the United States. In particular, it will look at the claims made around democracy in the US Declaration of Independence, before examining why James Madison thought that individual and minority rights would be safe under the proposed federal constitution of the United States. He will argue that within a large federal republic, individual liberties are far safer than within a small democracy.

We will then conclude this discussion of democracy by examining the notion of the tyranny of the majority; a fear held, most noticeably by John Stuart Mill and Alexis de Tocqueville, that increasing democracy would increase the powers of the government over individuals and minorities.

Athenian beginnings

Democracy as a form of government was first introduced in ancient Athens. However, its manner of operation and the assumptions it was built upon were very different from what we would understand as democracy in the contemporary world.

Firstly, whereas Athenian democracy was certainly the government of all the *citizens* of Athens, this did not imply that it was the government of all the *people* of Athens, as citizenship belonged to a small elite group. To be a citizen you had to be male, and not only did you have to be born in Athens, but your parents also had to be born in Athens. Women were automatically excluded from citizenship, as were immigrants (which you could be even if you were born in Athens) and slaves. Indeed, the life of deliberation and public discourse that being a citizen required was largely built on the labour of slaves. When slaves, women, and resident aliens were taken out of the equation, the citizens probably equated to around 10 per cent of the total population of Athens (Dunn, 2005: 35).

We assume in the contemporary age that citizenship is universal, in that it applies to all people of a certain country over a certain age. There are a few restrictions: few contemporary countries allow immigrants to vote or stand for elected office, although generally countries will allow for a process of naturalization to gain the rights to participation. It would definitely not exclude, or indeed permit, the existence of slaves, nor do we exclude women. As such, David Held questions how democratic we should find ancient Athens, stating that the 'legendary democracy was intimately connected to what one might call the "tyranny of citizens"' (Held, 2006: 19).

Secondly, Athens was a direct democracy. The role of the citizen was not to participate in elections for their representative (senator, MP, etc.), but rather to attend meetings, to discuss with their fellow citizens, and to vote on proposals themselves. Indeed, all citizens, no matter their background, wealth or education, were entitled to attend assembly meetings, to speak and vote on any issue. So the day-to-day running of the state and making laws was not left to a group of professional politicians who acted on behalf of the citizens; it was carried out by the citizens. As Pericles outlined when discussing the nature of Athenian democracy, 'we do not say that a man who takes no interest in politics is a man who minds his own business; we say that he has no business here at all' (Pericles, quoted in Held, 1987: 17). Politics was an activity that all men had to participate in.

Thirdly, Athens did not make a distinction between legal and political issues like we tend to do in the contemporary world, in that just as citizens made laws, they also comprised the juries to condemn or acquit those accused of crimes. Of course this is not entirely different from the contemporary world where juries are drawn from the citizenry, but where it does differ is in terms of scale, with Athenian juries tending to be around 500 citizens chosen by lot. Also there was little in the way of human rights in Athens, with trials being fought and lost on oratory and argument as opposed to an examination of the law.

Once such Athenian charged with corrupting the young men of the city and failing to acknowledge the city's Gods was Socrates. Socrates was not always popular amongst the democrats, not simply because of his outspokenness, although he certainly had not, by his own admission, 'lived an ordinary quiet life' (Plato, 1993: 61), but also because many considered him a supporter of aristocratic government. Socrates was condemned by the poet Meletus, the prominent politician Anytus, and the orator Lycon, and the trial was conducted in front of any citizen that cared to attend. He was found guilty of the charges by a margin of around 60 votes, and his accusers sought the death penalty. It was normal in Athens after a verdict had been reached for the accused to offer an alternative punishment to that put forward by their accusers; to accept banishment, for example, or jail time. Instead, Socrates offered the willingness to pay the derisory amount of 100 drachma as a fine. His reasoning was that he thought living in Athens and discussing the nature of justice and the good life was what people should do, and he did not want to cease, nor did he imagine that anyone would believe him if he said that he would stop. As Socrates outlines in *The Apology*:

> Socrates was put to death by the ancient Athenian democracy. All citizens were entitled to vote on whether he was guilty of the charge of corrupting the young men of Athens.

> Perhaps someone may say, 'but surely, Socrates, after you have left us you can spend the rest of your life in quietly minding your own business'. This is the hardest thing of all to make some of you understand. If I say that this would be disobedient to God, and that is why I cannot 'mind my own business', you will not believe me – you'll think I'm pulling your leg. If on the other hand I tell you **that to let no day pass without discussing goodness and all the other subjects about which you hear me talking and examining both myself and others is**

really the very best thing that a man can do, and that life without this sort of examination is not worth living, you will be less inclined to believe me. Nevertheless that is how it is gentlemen. (Plato, 1993: 63, my emphasis)

So ancient Athens was where the idea of democracy was born, but it was a different type of democracy to what we are accustomed to today. It was based upon a limited citizenry, direct participation, and a more all-encompassing role for public deliberation. In addition to this, it was practised in a relatively small city state with a small number of citizens (perhaps around 30,000 in total). Think of the practicalities of this. If one is to say that all citizens should have the right to participate and debate the key issues of the day, in ancient Athens this was physically and practically possible. In the United States, with a population of around 325 million people, it becomes harder. Geographically, people live further apart, and even if this was not the case, the biggest stadium in the United States, Michigan Stadium in Ann Arbor, holds 107,000; impressive for a sports stadium, but it would only hold around 0.03% of the population, so how could the citizens meet to discuss things collectively?

Despite the differences between ancient Athenian democracy and the contemporary world, there were certainly elements of it that would become attractive throughout the development of democracy, as we shall see. Firstly, the notion that despite their differences in terms of education, wealth and background (or whatever), citizens should be seen to be equal and have their voices treated as such. Secondly, there is also the notion that democracy is self-improving, that there is something central to the human condition that makes discussing political, social and moral issues inherently worthwhile. And thirdly, that democracy breeds solidarity amongst citizens.

Activity 1. Attempt the following questions about ancient Athens:

(1) Outline the way in which the practice of democracy differs in the modern world to that of ancient Athens.

(2) Could direct democracy be practised in the contemporary world? Explain your answer.

(3) If direct democracy was practical, would it be desirable?

Rousseau and Montesquieu

Rousseau and Montesquieu were both republicans, in that they thought that government should always be conducted in the interests of everybody rather than just a just a few, but they differed in precisely how this idea should be implemented in practice.

Rousseau

Rousseau, in his work *The Social Contract*, was heavily influenced by Athenian direct democracy and the arrangements in small city states such as Geneva (where he was born), and as a consequence he argues that only in a direct democracy can one really represent oneself. Government in the interests of everyone is achieved, for Rousseau, only when all citizens represent themselves and make decisions based upon the general will, therefore making truly autonomous decisions. Autonomy, or to put it another way freedom, can only be achieved if and when citizens make laws that apply to themselves. This means that no group of people such as the aristocracy can make laws for us if we are to be considered free. So freedom for Rousseau is inextricably linked to democracy. In Rousseau's direct democracy there would be no place for political parties, factions or, most importantly of all, representatives.

We have seen how in his work the *Discourse on the Origin of Inequality*, Rousseau argues that men are by nature free and good. Society, although it has brought us good things such as morality, has largely corrupted our nature. We have become dependent upon others not just in the literal sense, but also in the psychological sense of craving people's approval, and this desire for other people's approval has made us vain. This vanity leads to competition between men, and this vanity and competition is both, for Rousseau, enslaving and unnatural to us. We can never regain this type of natural freedom, Rousseau thinks, but by direct democracy we can regain some freedom.

The general will

We should never ask ourselves the question 'Does this proposal benefit me?' when discussing potential laws, according to Rousseau. We should always ask ourselves 'Is this proposal in the interests of the republic?' This is the general will, and that which should guide all decision making in a democracy.

However, simply having a direct democracy and citizenship participation in all aspects of politics is insufficient to make us free, according to Rousseau. This is because our lack of freedom is caused not simply by other people, be they kings, aristocrats or representatives governing on our behalf, but also by our vanity, which makes us want to compete with other men, and live our lives through the eyes of others. Rousseau is concerned that, when we are all in a position to govern ourselves in a democracy, we will end up fuelling this vanity by arguing for, and legislating in favour of, proposals that benefit us as individuals. This would not help subdue our vanity and selfishness. So more is needed, in a democracy, to attempt to regain at least some of our original freedom and lack of dependence on others.

Rousseau's solution to this is the notion of the general will. He is clear that it would be unsatisfactory for people in a direct democracy to simply vote in what they consider to be their own interests, as what would come out of this is an aggregate of people's particular wills as opposed to a general will. Instead, Rousseau suggests that when voting on a proposal we should always consider what is in the interests of the Republic, by which he means what is in the interests of everybody as opposed to what is in my own interests. So let us suppose that we are Rousseau's citizens and we were debating and voting on a proposal to cut income tax. Some people might say 'I am going to vote for this proposal because if it is introduced I would end up keeping more of my income and be better off as a result.' Other people might counterargue that they don't think the tax cuts should pass, as if they did benefits and services that they currently receive would be reduced, leaving them worse off. For Rousseau, even if both these arguments are true, they are irrelevant, and not the kind of debate one needs in a democracy. Instead, the nature of the debate should always be 'are these tax cuts in the interests of the Republic?' The reason why this is so important for Rousseau is because by limiting our wishes and desires by considering what is in the interests of everyone, we subdue our vanity, and in so doing increase our freedom. So, whereas a democracy is the only legitimate type of government for Rousseau, democracy in and of itself is insufficient to make us free. Also, it is worth noting that perhaps **none of the systems in the contemporary world that we call democracies would be regarded as such by Rousseau**. It is a high bar to jump.

Montesquieu

In his work *The Spirit of the Laws*, Montesquieu focuses more on the institutions of governance and how this will bring about more political liberty, than on the nature of freedom itself. Like many other republicans, Montesquieu thinks that the best way to guard liberty is through careful design of political institutions. In order to be free, he argues, one needs to live in a free state. Montesquieu was concerned about the condition of France under the reign of the Sun King Louis XIV. In particular, he thought that the concentration of power in one man's hands could lead to tyranny. Whilst visiting England, he thought that the constitutional framework that existed there balanced power better so that no one person or group of people could have absolute power over society as a whole. It was this that led him to come up with the theory of The Separation of Powers which has become so influential in the contemporary world and in particular in the design of the Constitution of the United States.

Montesquieu was concerned about the concentration of power in any person or group of people. He looked to the British separation of powers to design a theory of dividing the central powers of government into different bodies to ensure this did not happen.

Montesquieu argued that there were three separate powers that government possessed, namely executive, judicial and legislative power. **The legislature makes laws, the executive implements them, and the judiciary interprets them**. If these powers existed in one person or one body, political liberty was impossible. So one needed to ensure that these three powers were placed in three separate institutions; hence the notion of the separation of powers. Montesquieu thought that if you separated these three elements of governance, the bodies tasked with a particular power would balance one another out, ensuring that no one particular body became too powerful to threaten liberty.

It is perhaps ironic that this system is based on Montesquieu's interpretation of the English constitution, as the British political system manifestly does not have a separation of powers. For instance, in order for a person to become part of the government (the executive) in England one must be either in the House of Commons or the House of Lords. As a consequence, the powers of the executive and the legislature heavily overlap. Montesquieu probably thought that the powers of the nobility in England were much greater than their counterparts in France, which meant that they were much more able to provide a check and balance on the power of the monarch.

Having read the above, it might seem strange that Montesquieu is included in a chapter on democracy, as, unlike Rousseau, he is not making an out and out argument in favour of popular sovereignty, nor is he proposing a system of government in which the main part is directly elected. He is, however, proposing an argument that was quite radical for its day and age, which was dominated politically by monarchies and aristocracies. What Montesquieu is arguing is that in order to preserve freedom, one should always ensure that power is checked and dependent on other bodies. The European absolute monarchies of the time, especially the Sun King in France, would not have been able to accept this as they argued that their power, and their right to govern, came from God alone, and only God could judge them. So Montesquieu's republican division of political authority is an attempt to wrestle some political power away from the governing elites at the time.

The role of the representative: Edmund Burke

Whereas Rousseau and the ancient Greeks thought that democracy entailed individuals representing themselves, Edmund Burke provides us with a staunch defence of representative democracy, with the emphasis on the representation. Indeed, Edmund Burke will argue that not only should representatives govern on our behalf, but also they would do well not to pay too much attention to the wishes of their constituents in between elections. Edmund Burke does not

Activity 2.

(1) Define the following with regard to Montesquieu:

Executive	Legislature	Judiciary

(2) Why is it so important for Montesquieu that they be kept separate?

(3) What did Rousseau mean by the general will?

so much say that representatives have any special knowledge that makes their ability to legislate better than their constituents, but rather that, if left to the constituents to dictate how the representative should vote, it would lead to poorer decisions being made at national level.

In his *Speech to the Electors of Bristol*, Burke was arguing against the proposition that a Member of Parliament should be seen as the delegate of his constituents, that is to say he was suggesting that Members of Parliament should be elected, allowed to continue their role at Parliament unhindered by those that elected them, and then backed or sacked at the next election based upon their record. It was not the job of a representative to go back and forth between Parliament and their constituency to canvass the opinion of their electors on each issue that arose. Burke argued that the lot of the individual constituent was limited, generally speaking, to elections. As Burke suggests:

> Your representative owes you, not his industry only, but his judgment; and he betrays, instead of serving you, if he sacrifices it to your opinion. (Burke, 1999)

The problem that Edmund Burke saw with constituents mandating their MPs to vote this way or that on any particular issue was not so much that they did not

Edmund Burke

Burke was born in Dublin in Ireland in 1830 (at this time still governed from London). He was educated at Trinity College Dublin, and then moved to London to follow a career in the law at his father's insistence, despite wishing to be a writer. He gave up the law shortly after arriving in London. He wrote a philosophical piece on aesthetics entitled *A Philosophical Enquiry into the Origin of Our Ideas of the Sublime and Beautiful*, which got him noticed by the leading thinkers in Europe.

He entered Parliament in 1865 in a pocket borough, and was later elected as MP for Bristol. He attracted criticism from those in Bristol for the position he took on trade with Ireland, which many argued endangered the livelihoods of his constituents. Burke argued that he should be judged on his record and that his constituents could get rid of him at the next election if they wished. He was friends with the London intellectuals of his time such as Samuel Johnson and Oliver Goldsmith.

have the ability to do so; Burke is not claiming that politicians are like Plato's philosopher kings. Instead, if each individual constituency mandated their MP based upon what was in the local interest, who then would look after the good of the country as a whole? Or as Burke puts it:

> Parliament is not a congress of ambassadors from different and hostile inter-
> ests; which interests each must maintain, as an agent and advocate, against
> other agents and advocates; but parliament is a deliberative assembly of one
> nation, with one interest, that of the whole; where, not local purposes, not
> local prejudices, ought to guide, but the general good, resulting from the gen-
> eral reason of the whole. You choose a member indeed; but when you have
> chosen him, he is not member of Bristol, but he is a member of parliament.
> (Burke, 1999)

So for Burke, too much democracy can interfere with sensible and responsible government as electors might often let local concerns and priorities trump national policy making and so disrupt the sense of unity within the country. Deliberation around policy issues is important, but this deliberation is best left to politicians at Parliament. So Burke can be seen as an example of minimalist democracy; government should be elected and broadly responsive to the electors' opinion; however, the citizens' role in democracy is limited to election time rather than being an ongoing vocation. Compare this to the Periclean view of democracy outlined in our discussion of Athenian democracy above; the role of the citizen is very different in the two counts, and yet both can be considered democratic.

This only highlights still further the broad range of political ideas that can be considered democratic in the sense of how we understand what the people ruling might mean.

Activity 3. Attempt the following questions:

(1) What role does Burke suggest a representative should play in a democracy? What should they not do?

(2) Why is it important that representatives act in this way for Burke?

(3) What type of relationship do **you** think **you** should have with your representative(s)?

All men created equal?

Thomas Jefferson, lead author of the Declaration of Independence, wrote that it was 'self-evident' that 'all men were created equal' and yet he was a slave owner.

Democracy in America

The Declaration of Independence of July 1776 was written by Thomas Jefferson and his colleagues for the Second Continental Congress with the purpose of the thirteen states represented breaking their links with George III and Great Britain, and starting to govern themselves. It is perhaps the most famous political passage written in the English language, and of the texts that we have examined thus far in this volume, it is perhaps the one that has had the most obvious political impact. *The Declaration* was the end result of a process of democratic authorship as well as being a text promoting democracy, with many authors, hands and committees having a role in shaping the ideas that would be the basis of the newly formed nation. Its opening salvo presents a strong case for the liberty of the individual, equality and democratic control. It does also, however, present us with a number of problems to discuss.

> We hold these truths to be self-evident, that all men are created equal, that they are endowed by their Creator with certain unalienable Rights, that among these are Life, Liberty and the pursuit of Happiness. That to secure these rights, Governments are instituted among Men, deriving their just powers from the consent of the governed, That whenever any Form of Government becomes destructive of these ends, it is the Right of the People to alter or to abolish it, and to institute new Government, laying its foundation on such principles and organizing its powers in such form, as to them shall seem most likely to effect their Safety and Happiness. (Quoted in Allen, 2014: 27)

Firstly, *The Declaration* claims that the **truths** which it presents are **self-evident**; that they need no proof to assure us that they are true. This is problematic as, if there are certain truths which all can see, then why are these truths not already in place? Why does one need to assert one's rights to certain truths if they are self-evident to all? Secondly, it states that all **men** are created equal. Aside from the issue that this ignores women, Jefferson, the chief author of *The Declaration*, owned slaves, so it was clear that 'all men' meant only a certain type of man. Thirdly, it claims that we have certain unalienable rights, and that we received these from our **creator**. This is problematic as most Western societies are characterized by a plurality of religious beliefs, including atheism. Even if you do feel that it was God who endowed you and your fellow citizens with rights, it is problematic to use this to appeal to those who would rid people of rights if they did not believe in God. Then followed a Thomas Paine-inspired argument that government could be removed if it threatened people's life, liberty and pursuit of happiness.

Here there is little mention of democracy *per se*, but rather a claim about liberty and equality and the right to revolution – perhaps unsurprising from a document justifying a revolution. Perhaps the strongest claim that America was founded on democratic principles was made by Abraham Lincoln some time later. 'Four score and seven years ago', stated Lincoln in his Gettysburg Address of 1863, 'our fathers brought forth on this continent, a new nation, conceived in Liberty, and dedicated to the proposition that all men are created equal.' This liberty entailed 'government of the people, by the people, for the people' (Lincoln, 2013). Lincoln's statement here is that the United States was founded to ensure three complementary ideas: equality, freedom and democracy.

James Madison, author of *The Federalist Paper Number 10*, wrestled with a similar problem to Rousseau; in a democracy, what can be done to prevent faction? *The Federalist Papers* were a collection of 85 articles published in a variety of newspapers under the *nom de plume* Publius in support of the proposed American Constitution in the hope of gaining popular support for its ratification. They were written by James Madison, Alexander Hamilton and John Jay, and later assembled into the collection of essays we know today.

Madison thinks that different opinions on social and political issues is an inevitable consequence of liberty, stating that 'as long as the reason of man continues fallible, and he is at liberty to exercise it, different opinions will be formed' (Madison, 1987: 123). As long as there are differences of opinion, there will be faction; so faction and division are an unavoidable consequence of a free citizenry. This being the case, one can, for Madison, either remove the liberty which leads to faction, or attempt to plan institutions that manage it. 'Pure democracies' (by which Madison means city states such as ancient Athens) are very bad at managing this, he argues, as if the faction became the majority, then the minority or an individual might lose out as there would be no check on the power of the faction (Madison, 1987: 126). So just as liberty makes faction inevitable, faction in a democracy could result in the minority of individuals losing their liberties should the majority take against them.

> Humanity in a state of liberty will always lead to a difference in opinion on social and political matters. Denying that liberty is a non-starter, so one needs a set of political institutions robust enough to ensure that faction does not lead to the denial of rights to individuals and minorities.

Herein lies the advantage of the large republic as promoted by the authors of the constitution. Whereas the 'influence of factious leaders may kindle a flame within their particular States', Madison concedes, it 'will be unable to spread a general conflagration through the other States' (Madison, 1987: 128). The size and complexity of the proposed federal constitution would ensure that faction would remain limited in a way that could not be achieved by a smaller democracy.

So, like Montesquieu before him, Madison argued that by constitutional design, albeit here represented by size, one could prevent any group of people dominating in the state, and allowing therefore for individuals and minorities to enjoy the rights promised to them in the US Constitution.

Activity 4. Attempt the tasks below:

(1) Do you think there are any problems with stating that one's political rights come from God? If so what?

(2) Why does Madison say that the US government would prevent the worst problems of faction due to its size? What does this say about democracy?

The tyranny of the majority

When one thinks of those who have critiqued democracy in the history of political thought, our minds first go to people at the extremes of the political spectrum such as fascists like Adolf Hitler or communist dictators such as Joseph Stalin, who destroyed democracy in their respective countries, or perhaps to thinkers such as Plato and Marx who were highly critical of what we would think of as democratic ideas. However, there is also a strand of uneasiness of the effect of democracy on individual liberty that emanates from mainstream liberal thinking. Thinkers such as John Stuart Mill and Alexis de Tocqueville were concerned that with the advancement of democracy, individual eccentricity and the liberty to live life how one felt best might be threatened if government sought to outlaw behaviour that the majority did not like. In this, they were engaged in a similar endeavour to that which Madison addresses in our discussion above. They called this notion the tyranny of the majority. Put simply, this meant that one should be wary of the powers of *any* government however constituted, and that just because a government was democratic and legitimate did not wholly safeguard you from your rights and liberties being infringed upon.

> The restriction of the minorities' way of life, or simply the eccentricities of a group of people, can be threatened just as much by a democracy as it can a more repressive regime for Mill and de Tocqueville.

Alexis de Tocqueville was a French sociologist who visited the United States to study its prison system. Whilst he was there he became interested in the fledgling democracy and how it operated and in particular the spirit of the citizenry that kept it going. Unlike Montesquieu in our discussion above, de Tocqueville thought that when we discuss democracy, we should spend less time discussing institutions, and more time emphasizing the virtues of the citizens that comprise the democratic state. Institutions don't make democracies; citizens do.

In one discussion in his work *Democracy in America*, de Tocqueville asks the question why, if there is liberty of conscience in America, are there so few atheists? He suggests the reason for this is not because of specific laws or persecution that will come from the state, but rather from the values held by the citizens. If one publicly stated that one was an atheist, one might not receive any penalty from the state, but people might not visit your shop, you may not be invited to join local clubs and societies, and one might fail to live life in a happy and prosperous manner. Consequently, there might be a civil and social benefit to conformity in a democracy, and de Tocqueville did not think that this was a good thing.

John Stuart Mill also argues that democracy contained within it the potential for conformity which was damaging to freedom, democracy and society in general. It was for this reason that Mill outlined the Harm Principle, which we will discuss in the next chapter, as he thought that limits should be placed on the powers of any government, however legitimate and democratic it might be. Indeed, Mill's general attitude towards democracy is slightly ambivalent; for example, Mill is a utilitarian – he didn't think we had a natural right *per se* to participate in government or to have rights, as rights imply a deontological moral framework. Instead, Mill argues that we would be happier if we have liberty and democracy as this will ensure that we don't end up holding the opinions that we have simply because there are none others available for us to consider.

When he was an MP, Mill championed women's right to vote by tabling an amendment on the Representation of the People Act of 1867, suggesting that the word 'man' should be replaced with the word 'person', thereby allowing women to vote for the first time in the UK. Although this amendment failed, it illustrates Mill's commitment to everybody getting the vote. Despite this, Mill was not in favour of democratic equality at the ballot box, for although he thought that everybody should get one vote, he also thought that some people should get more than one vote. Mill did not think this was inconsistent with democracy, as he thought that the claim that everybody's voice should be heard in a democracy is not the same as saying that everybody's voice is equal. Some people know more about the political and economic world and, as a consequence, should have more of a say in the election of representatives. Mill also thought that voting should take place in public and as such opposed the secret ballot. We did not have a right to vote, according to Mill, as no one has a right to power over other people, and this is what the vote represents. Instead, the vote was a trust, and as such it should take place in public and due discussion should take place about the issues at hand in the election. These are **safeguards to attempt to ensure that democracy would not end up as mob rule and the rights of minorities and eccentrics would be protected**.

To overview Mill's proposal for an inequality of votes, he argued that all people should have at least one vote, but also that certain people should receive more than one vote. A labourer should get one, but people who 'labour with ... [their] head, and not solely with ... [their] hands' should get more than one vote (Mill, 1993: 308–9). So, by getting a degree one should get more votes, by working successfully in certain professional jobs you should get more votes, by working in the liberal professions you should get more votes, and so on. Nobody should be ignored, but this does not mean to say that everyone's voice is equal. He thought that allowing the more intelligent more votes, but ensuring that everyone got at least one, would mean that government was responsive, but that it was more reasoned.

Conclusion

Virtually every state in the world claims to be democratic, even those that are patently undemocratic. In the contemporary world, being democratic is often seen as the very minimum requirement in order to be seen as legitimate. But it is very hard to pin down precisely what is meant by democracy as it is an

Activity 5. Don't you think it is absurd that I, who teach politics at a university and have written this book, have the same number of votes at election time as one of my students? Write a case for and against this proposition.

For	Against

umbrella term for a wide range of ideas and practices that attempt to allow the people to rule.

Burke, for example, thought that it was sufficient in a democracy that MPs are elected by the people, but then broadly left alone to do their job to legislate in the national interest and then have to face the electorate again at the next election. Rousseau and those in ancient Athens, on the other hand, thought that in democracies all citizens should participate directly in the making of laws. So rule of the people can be interpreted in many different ways by different thinkers.

Many people who could broadly be defined as democrats, were still concerned about the effects that untrammelled democracy could have on individual rights and minorities in society should the majority turn against someone or a group of people. Various ideas have been proposed to combat this. Montesquieu thought institutions should be balanced in order to prevent any group of people getting too much power. Mill argued that whereas everyone should get the vote (a radical suggestion for the time in which he was writing), in order to achieve enlightened government, the more intelligent in society should get more than one vote. Madison thought the size and complexity of the then fledgling constitution of the United States would prevent faction from becoming too serious.

Rousseau's concern was that when we could all participate in politics, we would always vote the way that would benefit us, and that would mean that participation would not quash our vanity. His way around this was philosophical as opposed to institutional, suggesting that legitimate laws in a democratic society were always made with an eye on the general will.

So democracy has prompted quite a spectrum of theory to emerge; so we should use the term advisedly, aware of the fact that behind a relatively simple term, there is much debate. We should not, however, fall into the mistake of thinking that the problems created by defining democracy makes the term ambiguous. Ambiguity implies that someone has not made something clear, and that they ought to have made it clear. What the nature of democracy is cannot be anything other than contested. It is more of an area of discussion than a concept.

Works cited

Allen, D. (2014) *Our Declaration: A Reading of the Declaration of Independence in Defense of Equality*. New York/London: Liveright.

Burke, E. (1999) *Selected Works of Edmund Burke*, vol. 4, *Miscellaneous Writings*, Indianapolis, IN: Liberty Fund. Available at https://oll.libertyfund.org/titles/burke-select-works-of-edmund-burke-vol-4

Dunn, J. (2005) *Setting the People Free*. London: Atlantic.

Held, D. (2006) *Models of Democracy*. Cambridge: Polity.

Jay, A. (ed.) (1996) *The Oxford Dictionary of Political Quotations*. Oxford: Oxford University Press.

Lincoln, A. (2013) *The Gettysburg Address*. Ithaca, NY: Cornel University, available at http://rmc.library.cornell.edu/gettysburg/good_cause/transcript.htm

Linz, J. and Stepan, A. (1996) 'Towards consolidated democracies', *Journal of Democracy*, 7(2), 14–33.

Madison, J., Hamilton, A. and Jay, J. (1987) *The Federalist Papers*. London: Penguin.

Mill, J.S. (1993) 'Representative government'. In *Utilitarianism, On Liberty, Considerations on Representative Government*. London: Everyman, pp. 187–428.

Plato (1993) *The Last Days of Socrates*. London: Penguin.

Text reading activity

Mill on plurality voting. From 'Considerations on representative government', in Mill, J.S. (1993) *Utilitarianism, On Liberty, Considerations on Representative Government.* London: Everyman, pp. 308–9.

I do not deny that property is a kind of test; education, in most countries, though any thing but proportional to riches, is on the average better in the richer half of society than in the poorer. But the criterion is so imperfect; accident has so much more to do than merit with enabling men to rise in the world; and it is so impossible for any one, by acquiring any amount of instruction, to make sure of the corresponding rise in station, that this foundation of electoral privilege is always, and will continue to be, supremely odious. To connect plurality of votes with any pecuniary qualification would be not only objectionable in itself, but a sure mode of compromising the principle, and making its permanent maintenance impracticable. The democracy, at least of this country, are not at present jealous of personal superiority, but they are naturally and must justly so of that which is grounded on mere pecuniary circumstances. The only thing which can justify reckoning one person's opinion as equivalent to more than one is individual mental superiority, and what is wanted is some approximate means of ascertaining that. If there existed such a thing as a really national education or a trustworthy system of general examination, education might be tested directly. In the absence of these, the nature of a person's occupation is some test. An employer of labour is on the average more intelligent than a labourer; for he must labour with his head, and not solely with his hands. A foreman is generally more intelligent than an ordinary labourer, and a labourer in the skilled trades than in the unskilled. A banker, merchant, or manufacturer is likely to be more intelligent than a tradesman, because he has larger and more complicated interests to manage. In all these cases it is not the having merely undertaken the superior function, but the successful performance of it, that tests the qualifications; for which reason, as well as to prevent persons from engaging nominally in an occupation for the sake of the vote, it would be proper to require that the occupation should have been persevered in for some length of time (say three years). Subject to some such condition, two or more votes might be allowed to every person who exercises any of these superior functions. The liberal professions, when really and not nominally practised, imply, of course, a still higher degree of instruction; and wherever a sufficient examination, or any serious conditions of education, are required before entering on a profession, its members could be admitted at once to a plurality of votes. The same rule might be applied to graduates of universities; and even to those who bring satisfactory certificates of having passed through the course of study required by any school at which the higher branches of knowledge are taught, under proper securities that the teaching is real, and not a mere pretense. The 'local' or 'middle class' examination for the degree of associate, so laudably and public-spiritedly established by the University of Oxford, and any similar ones which may be instituted by other competent bodies (provided they are fairly open to all comers), afford a ground on which plurality of votes might with great advantage be accorded to those who have passed the test. All these suggestions are open to much discussion in the detail, and to objections which it is of no use to anticipate. The time is not come for giving to such plans a practical shape, nor should I wish to be bound by the particular proposals which I have made. But it is to me evident that in this direction lies the true ideal of representative government; and that to work towards it by the best practical contrivances which can be found is the path of real political improvement.

Question 1: Upon what grounds does Mill justify voters having more than one vote in elections?

Question 2: What do you think of this argument?

6

When can my freedom be restricted?

KEY QUESTIONS

(1) Should we understand freedom as the absence of constraints (negative liberty), or the freedom to be able to do something (positive freedom)?

(2) Should we be able to do anything that does not harm another person? If so, what constitutes harm?

(3) Can the state prevent us from doing something that is obviously harmful to ourselves?

(4) Is there a useful distinction between freedom as non-interference and freedom as non-domination?

Stephen Gough is a British rambler and ex-marine who set himself the challenge of walking from Land's End to John o' Groats. This arduous walk of 874 miles, which takes some 60 days to complete, commences in the most south-westerly point of mainland Britain and ends at its most northerly tip, and is the quintessential British hike as it takes in most of the country and follows some beautiful countryside. It is impossible for anyone other than the most experienced and dedicated hiker to finish, but Gough made the task harder still for himself by planning to undertake it completely naked, save for some sturdy hiking boots and socks (worn on the feet).

Gough has suffered for his desire to hike naked; he has been arrested numerous times and spent years in prison over the past couple of decades. Often he would be released from prison, then immediately remove his clothing, only to be arrested and sent back to jail shortly thereafter. He has been arrested for removing his clothes on a plane, then in court immediately after a hearing, as well as being naked on the street. He has been arrested for disturbing the peace, for breaching anti-social behaviour orders, and on suspicion of outraging public decency. Although he does not seem to have an overtly political agenda, Stephen Gough (or the 'naked rambler' as he has become known) clearly feels he has a right to be naked in public, a right that the law seems to deny.

Where, then, is freedom if we cannot do what we want to do? Does Stephen Gough have a right to hike naked, or does our desire to not encounter naked people trump his freedom to be naked in public? And what of other exercises of freedom? Should I have the right to take drugs (even those currently deemed illegal) even if that might be detrimental to my health and wellbeing? Should I be able to ride a motorcycle without a helmet, or a car without a seatbelt, read whatever books I want, and use whatever language I want in public.

Or does doing what I want to do actually restrict my freedom? Overall, I will be happier and more free when I finish writing this book; but *The Big Bang Theory* has just come on the TV and right now I want to watch that. Is there something about prioritizing higher goals that leads to greater freedom and, if so, might the state be able to restrict access to lower goals?

Chapter overview

This chapter aims to get you to examine the potential justifications (or lack thereof) for restricting your individual freedoms; whilst at the same time probing how we define freedom. This chapter will show that whereas the intuitive definition that freedom is the ability to do that which you want to do is widely held in the history of political thought, many authors disagree that this is what freedom means.

It will begin with a recap of Hobbes's view of freedom, and how the sovereign state can curtail our liberty pretty much however it chooses if it thinks that this is the best way to keep the peace. It will then go on to examine Isaiah Berlin's famous distinction between positive and negative liberty, and show why he favoured negative liberty and the potential problems he saw with positive liberty. We will continue on the theme of defences of negative liberty then with a discussion of John Stuart Mill's Harm Principle; the notion that the only way in which anyone is entitled to infringe upon our liberty is to prevent harm to others. Neither the state nor anyone else is entitled to make us do something we do not want to do, nor stop us from doing something we want to do simply because it would be better for us, that people were offended by it, or to protect public morals. It will be outlined how Mill's account of liberty is utilitarian in nature, that is to say that we have liberty because overall it will make us happier (indeed, we tolerate other's actions if we don't like them as even this displeasure will make us happier overall).

Finally, we will examine some more radical critiques of this negative view of freedom. We will examine Rousseau's notion of freedom being about obeying laws that we have made ourselves, and Marx's notion that bourgeois discussions of freedom mask the power of the capitalist class, and that real freedom can only be achieved by a communist revolution and society.

Activity 1. Freedom is perhaps the most widely discussed political concept. Before the chapter begins, define what freedom means to you in a couple of lines.

Thomas Hobbes and freedom

According to Thomas Hobbes, **people are free to the extent that they remain unimpeded by external bodies**. Freedom is the realm of being able to do that which you want to do, and lack of freedom is when someone or something prevents you from doing something; this is a classic view of freedom to which, perhaps, the majority of people would adhere when asked what freedom meant. So freedom here means literal physical freedom; if you tie me to a chair then I am unable to get up and walk out of the room. Politically, Hobbes thought that man in the state of nature was radically free as there were no laws, police forces or governments (the external bodies that could impede on this freedom) that could prevent him from doing what he wanted to do. The problem with this is that everyone else was free likewise, resources would be scare, and as everyone would fear they would be attacked, or their property stolen, they might act pre-emptively out of fear; everyone would constantly be on edge, and this would lead to bloodshed and war. Freedom is not necessarily a good thing for Hobbes, and we trade our right to everything by transferring it to the sovereign. The sovereign, then, can do whatever it likes as it is its job to keep the peace. It can ban books and religions, create any type of laws it likes, and even put us to death (although we can resist this latter command). **The sovereign becomes the external body that hinders our freedom, and it is entitled to prevent you from doing anything it likes if it calculates that it will disturb the peace.**

Hobbes on freedom

Hobbes's views on freedom are what might be called the classic negative liberty position. Freedom consists of being able to do whatever you like without any constraints. Hobbes's sovereign would almost certainly curtail your freedom, but freedom is conceptualized as the absence of constraints.

Despite the potential lack of freedom in a Hobbesian state, **freedom as a concept is still conceived as an absence of constraints, and we would still be free to do whatever the sovereign did not actually prevent us from doing.** Not everyone shares this conception of freedom, however, so we need to examine the concept in more depth. A good place to start is the distinction between positive and negative liberty made by Isaiah Berlin in 1958; a distinction that has dominated political theory ever since.

Two concepts of liberty

It is worth noting by way of introduction that although Berlin was an Oxford Don, his distinction between positive and negative freedom was not simply an academic one. **His purpose was to defend negative liberty against positive liberty**; the latter he thought was a threat to pluralism and being able to choose one's way of life. Berlin was born in Riga (modern-day Latvia) and spent much of his childhood in St Petersburg; he witnessed the Russian Revolution as a child before moving to the UK with his family in 1921. Between this time and his 1958 address on liberty, he had seen the rise of fascism and communism in Europe, two ideologies that denied the individual the ability to make their own choices about the nature of the good life. It is for this reason, as we shall see, that he thought negative liberty was the best way to define freedom (indeed he thought that positive liberty was not liberty at all).

> Berlin wanted to defend a specific way of thinking about the nature of freedom, namely negative freedom, as exemplified by Hobbes and Mill. He thought positive freedom, as exemplified by Rousseau and others, provided a licence to tyranny.

Negative liberty is about the absence of constraints; **one is free 'to the degree to which no man or body of men interferes with my activity'** (Berlin, 1969: 122). Negative freedom is, therefore, pretty much the definition espoused by Hobbes (although most adherents would baulk at the powers the sovereign would have over the individual in Hobbes's view). **Positive freedom**, on the other hand, **is about the ability to do something**, to 'be one's own master' even if there is no one to prevent you from doing so (Berlin, 1969: 131). Freedom is about the ability to overcome an impediment and achieve something, and those impediments need not necessarily be physical or legal constraints; the constraints might be abilities, addictions, or lack of money or opportunities to do something. Positive freedom is therefore about what are you able to actually achieve, rather than about what constraints are placed upon you (or the lack thereof). So, for example, I enjoy a weekly game of basketball with my colleagues at university. I am an average player and getting old, but is my freedom restricted by the fact that I will never be drafted into the NBA? A proponent of negative freedom would say no, of course not. There is no law preventing middle-aged British academics from playing in the NBA, nor would an armed gang prevent me from doing so should a team be suitably foolish enough to put me in the squad. It is my ability that prevents me from playing in the NBA rather than any external constraints, so I am free to play professional basketball even though I never will.

Proponents of positive freedom might think it absurd to think of myself as being free to play in the NBA despite my lack of talent to do so. This is not to say that proponents of positive liberty would start a political campaign to force the Golden State Warriors to pick me as power forward; but they would think it strange to talk of me being free to do so.

Isaiah Berlin

Sir Isaiah Berlin was born in Riga (present-day Latvia) in 1909, but moved to England with his family when he was a teenager. He was educated at Oxford and then became a fellow there, before working for the British government in the Second World War.

When he returned to academia in Oxford after the war, he wrote a lot supporting value pluralism; that we should see society as comprised of lots of ways of life rather than one. Indeed, he thought that philosophies that argued that there was one 'truth' were dangerous.

In addition to *Two Concepts of Liberty*, he is famous for writing an essay, again defending pluralism, entitled *The Hedgehog and the Fox*. In this, he argues that there are some thinkers who view the world through a single idea (hedgehogs), and some who draw on various experiences who think the world cannot be boiled down to one thing (foxes).

Berlin was knighted in 1957.

A more serious example might revolve around people in poverty. **If someone is starving and living on the street, are they really free?** A proponent of negative freedom might conclude that they are so long as their poverty has not been caused by someone stealing their possessions or money or some other criminal activity, or that they are not in poverty because there is some law preventing them from working due to their ethnicity, gender or social status. This is not to say that proponents of negative liberty are necessarily indifferent to poverty or social injustice, it's just that this should not be confused with liberty. A proponent of positive liberty again would think it is not possible to think of someone in poverty as being free.

Perhaps the most controversial element of positive freedom is that the restraints to our freedom can often be internal as well as external. We often have higher and lower selves: the actions of our lower selves might prevent what our higher selves really want. We may want to spend the evening working on our political theory essay, but then notice that it is *Shark Week* on TV and spend the evening watching that instead. Our higher selves might want to make a really good job of the essay to work towards a degree and the career and life that that brings, but the pull of *Shark Week* might be too great.

Rousseau, for example, thought that our natural freedom was ruined by our vanity, which made us dependent on our passions and others' opinions of us. Our lower selves enslave us, therefore, whereas our higher selves would follow the dictates of the general will. Plato thought that reason should always dominate over spirit and appetite. Marx thought that often our thought was dominated by ideologies that justified the capitalist state and the politics therein; real freedom consisted in recognizing this for what is was and participating in class struggle.

Psychologically, it seems pretty unproblematic that often we prove our own worst enemy and that we often want instant gratification rather than delaying it for a bigger, longer-term goal. To return to the basketball analogy, even if we had the innate talent, many of us would baulk at the endless training and healthy living that would be required to become a professional athlete. However, we might put this down to a lack of discipline and give ourselves a stern talking to in order to focus more tightly on our longer-term goals in the future. Politically it could be more problematic. What if a government decided it knew what our higher selves really wanted and, in the name of freedom, banned us from doing things that we appeared to want at the time? This is what proponents of negative liberty would find problematic: that it might be damaging to liberty in denying us that which we wanted to do.

Activity 2. Provide a definition of:

Negative liberty	Positive liberty

Which view do you find preferable and why?

Berlin's critics

Not everyone agrees that viewing freedom as a competition between positive and negative freedom is a helpful way of understanding the concept. Gerald MacCallum, for example, thought that 'the distinction between them has never been made sufficiently clear', and attempt to make a distinction 'is based in part upon a serious confusion', and that it will stifle serious discussion on the nature of freedom (MacCallum, 1967: 312). Rather than seeing freedom in positive and negative terms, MacCallum sees it as being triadic in nature:

> [F]reedom is thus always **of** something (an agent or agents), **from** something, **to** do, not do, become, or not become something; it is a triadic relation. (MacCallum, 1967: 314)

Or to put it another way, freedom is always of x, from y, to do (or not do) z. What is at dispute in different views of freedom, for MacCallum, should not be the nature of freedom itself, but rather simply the nature of the variable y (from something).

Take these two examples. (1) Karen's freedom from the agents of the state to attend school. (2) Billy's freedom from his addiction to alcohol to lead a more productive life. (1) appeals to a negative view of freedom in Berlin's dichotomy, whereas (2) appeals to a positive view. Both, for MacCallum, however, take the same form, Karen's/Billy's freedom to do something, which is impeded by an obstacle; one just turns out to be an external constraint, and the other an internal one. Logically, they are the same.

> Freedom for MacCallum, whether positive or negative, is always triadic in nature. It is always the freedom of x, from y, to do (or not do) z. All that is in dispute between positive and negative liberty is the nature of the variables.

So, for MacCallum, there are not two forms of liberty; there is just one – with no useful distinction between positive and negative liberty. Berlin's other main critique comes from the recently resurrected republican view of freedom espoused (amongst others) by Quentin Skinner and Philip Pettit. They argue that there is in fact a third view of freedom which they call 'Freedom as Non-Domination' which is neither negative nor positive by nature.

To introduce the notion of freedom as non-domination, imagine the following hypothetical situation: imagine that tomorrow I became the totalitarian dictator in your country with unlimited political powers, and no democratic checks and balances. I can do anything I want. But then, either because I am basically a pleasant chap, or because I somehow forget I have powers, I let everyone get on with their everyday lives without interference, and only enforce the laws as they stand. Are you free according to the negative and positive views of freedom? It is doubtful that a proponent of positive freedom, linked as they are with democratic ideas, that they could conceive of this as being freedom. On the face of it, adherents of negative freedom would not like it either, but this is not necessarily the case as I am actually not interfering with anyone's day-to-day life; in a negative freedom sense, someone living in this situation might be said to be free.

Freedom as non-domination

Proponents of freedom as non-domination argue that if your freedom rests on the will of another, you may as well not have it. Being dominated will alter your behaviour in an attempt to ensure your freedoms are kept. In order to be free, it is insufficient to not be interfered with; you must also live in a free state whereby your freedoms are protected.

It is this kind of situation that freedom as non-domination (or republican freedom) can be seen to differ from negative freedom. There is a difference between interfering with someone's actions, and someone being dominated. Being dominated is when one's freedom depends upon another. In the situation above, everyone would be dominated in the sense that their freedom would depend upon me keeping my pleasant disposition, and/or not remembering that I could interfere with people. So for this republican view of freedom, two problems exist in the situation outlined above. Firstly, although people's actions are not actually interfered with, this situation could easily change and, secondly, people would start to act differently, perhaps flattering me, perhaps altering their actions slightly so as not to make me change my mind about non-interference. English poet and republican writer John Milton, for example, wrote against censorship not necessarily because censors would start changing people's writing, but more because writers would start self-censoring, writing not what they wanted but rather producing works they knew would get around the censor. Writing would become worse, and people would not be able to be themselves, and would flatter the rulers.

So, one can be dominated without actually having one's actions interfered with, and freedom as non-domination suggests that the situation in which we can be dominated should be negated. This makes it distinct from negative liberty, which is concerned with interference. The way republicans tend to do this is talk of living in a free state with political institutions that ensure that domination does not occur. Negative freedom could logically occur under any form of government, whereas positive freedom tends to be linked to democratic politics, which republican freedom need not be.

Is it the case that negative freedom could be achieved under any form of government? Or to put the question slightly differently, isn't it far more likely that certain types of government are more likely to interfere with our individual liberty. Suppose you and I listed the sets of institutions that we thought would most likely lead to freedom as non-domination. We might argue for a state with a bill of rights that is upheld by an independent judiciary, perhaps also a bicameral system of representation to ensure one chamber does not ride roughshod over the will of everyone else, and perhaps a form of election that ensures that the will of the majority does not destroy the rights of the minority. Whatever we did imagine would be the best way to preserve our freedom of non-domination, might we not also think that the very same set of institutions would also be best to protect our freedom from interference? Whereas logically non-interference might be protected by a dictatorship proving that it is not dependent upon a particular form of government, do we have any example of a dictatorship in the history of humanity that has actually done this?

Activity 3. So far in this chapter we have seen arguments for there being one, two and three concepts of liberty. Defend the case that there is:

one concept of liberty:

two concepts of liberty:

three concepts of liberty:

> **J.S. Mill**
>
> Mill was born in London in 1806. His father was James Mill, who was a utilitarian philosopher. Mill was something of a child prodigy. He was taught Greek when he was 3 years old, and Latin when he was 8. By the time he was a teenager he became interested in economics, philosophy and politics and would write on these topics at a very young age. This childhood took its toll though and he suffered from depression when he was 20, but found the poetry of William Wordsworth helped him back to health.
>
> Mill became a Member of Parliament and in this role he became one of the first to champion women's right to vote. His views on women's rights were thought to be shaped by his long-term friend, and eventual wife, Harriet Taylor, to whom his most famous work *On Liberty* is dedicated.
>
> Mill worked in the administration of India, and wrote extensively on political and economic issues from a utilitarian ethical position.

Mill's Harm Principle

Mill's Harm Principle, as outlined in *On Liberty*, is as influential as it is simple. It is a classic defence of what Berlin called negative liberty and was put forward to ensure that everyone could live as they saw fit, and provide protection 'against the tyranny of the prevailing opinion and feeling' (Mill, 1993: 73). It deserves quoting in full:

> That principle is, that the sole end for which mankind are warranted, individually or collectively, in interfering with the liberty of action of any of their number, is self-protection. That the only purpose for which power can be rightfully exercised over any member of a civilized community, against his will, is to prevent harm to others. His own good, either physical or moral, is not a sufficient warrant. He cannot rightfully be compelled to do or forbear because it will be better for him to do so, because it will make him happier, because, in the opinion of others, to do so would be wise, or even right ... The only part of the conduct of anyone, for which he is amenable to society, is that which concerns others. In the part which merely concerns himself, his independence is, of right, absolute. Over himself, over his own body and mind, the individual is sovereign. (Mill, 1993: 78)

The *only* justification for banning something, for Mill, is if it physically harms someone else.

So, for Mill, the only reason the state (or anyone else for that matter) can take steps to prevent you from doing what you want to do is if it harms another person. It is worth noting here that Mill thinks of harm in a pretty literal sense; that is to say physical harm. Me being offended by what you are doing is not harm; me being outraged is not physical harm. We will see later on that this could be problematic.

So, it is perfectly acceptable for there to be laws against me assaulting you as that would cause harm. Due to the harm that second-hand smoking can do to an individual, it is perfectly plausible that a ban on cigarette smoking in public places would be permissible under Mill's principle. Banning me from smoking on the grounds that it endangers my own health would, however, not be acceptable. Mill makes it clear elsewhere in *On Liberty* that there is no utility in not labelling poison as poison; that is to say that it is not acceptable to sell a substance with people not being made aware of the harm it would cause; so it seems doubtful that Mill would have any quibble with warning labels on cigarette packets, and banning companies from making false health claims. When the facts are made clear, however, it is up to the individual to make a choice.

Mill thought that minors should be exempt from the Harm Principle. This seems reasonable enough; children are often restricted from having the same freedoms as adults, as it is argued that they need to learn about the world, and until they reach a certain age their parents and/or the state are entitled to restrict what they can do. More problematic is that Mill argued that 'primitive peoples' were also exempt from the Harm Principle. At a time in which Britain was a colonial power, he argued that people from around the world could be denied freedoms until such time as they reached Western levels of civilization.

Activity 4. Make a list of things that are currently illegal where you live which, based upon the Harm Principle, you feel should be legal. Is there anything currently legal that you feel should be made illegal if the Harm Principle was applied?

Mill also makes it clear that whereas you and I or the state are not allowed to prevent someone from doing that which they wish unless it is harming someone, that does not mean to say that we have to suffer in silence. People are entitled to the liberty to do as they please, not to live without criticism. If someone is doing something which you feel, for whatever reason, is wrong, then you are entitled to tell that person/those people of your objections. You can publish your objections in a pamphlet, or set up a society to try to prevent something. So if you objected to smoking, you could set up an organization with the aim of persuading people to give up smoking by giving them health or financial information. No one can prevent you from doing this as you are not harming other people by voicing your opinion. There is a big difference, for Mill, in opposing and arguing with people and forcing them not to do something.

So, for Mill, bans on drugs like cocaine and marijuana would be problematic, as they are based upon notions of what we should be doing as opposed to harm to others. So too might laws forcing us to wear seatbelts in cars, helmets on motorbikes, or perhaps even clothing in public places. However, Mill is not necessarily a libertarian. If it is true that exhaust fumes cause asthma in children, is there not a case for banning cars with an internal combustion engine? Asthma is a physical harm, and that is a basis for banning something. Feminists argue that pornography creates an image of women as being sexually available and can therefore lead to increased sexual assaults and rape; is this not then a case to ban it, even if we agree that it does not harm the actual participants? (For an overview of these debates see Cawston, 2019.) This argument does not rest on morality or arguing about what people should like; it rests on harm.

Mill is a utilitarian – that is to say that the purpose of government is about maximizing the amount of happiness we have. We do not have the right to freedom *per se* for Mill – it would make us happier overall, however, if we are free even if some aspects of other people's freedom might occasionally cause us to be unhappy.

In addition, **Mill is a utilitarian, specifically a rule utilitarian**. That is to say he suggests the purpose of government is to promote happiness (as opposed to, say, protecting rights). The way Mill argues that government should do this is by applying certain rules, and the Harm Principle is such a rule. He states that even if we are made unhappy by someone's actions, the overall benefit to society is that we will be happier if we have liberty. Also, we will not hold the opinions we hold simply because they are the only ones available to us. With liberty at play, we will get to hear lots of different opinions, some we may like, others we may not, and some we will find downright offensive. But these opinions will help us to evaluate our own belief system; we may change our minds, or we may not, but without them we might end up believing in certain things because as all dissenting voices had been silenced, we would have no other ideas to hold.

There are a couple of problems with this when one attempts to apply the Harm Principle to the modern world. Firstly, increasingly we are in tune with the notion that mental harm can be as damaging as physical harm. **Receiving abuse and/or bullying based upon our gender, our ethnicity or our sexual orientation may not physically harm us, but we can certainly claim that it harms us mentally.** This is different from being offended, perhaps, but it is not what Mill meant by harm. Someone might direct racist abuse at another person and we can be certain that this in some way harms the recipient. Likewise, someone critical of what you are doing might do so in a way that harms us mentally.

Secondly, states generally seldom actually ban us from doing things which we might want to do, but the state sees as problematic. Smoking is not banned in private places, but smokers do pay a lot of tax on their cigarette purchases. This is intended to put us off smoking. Likewise, in most places in the West, alcohol is not banned but you will pay a lot of tax on it. The State of New York attempted to limit the size of cup that sugary beverages could be sold in. This was not a ban on selling it, but an attempt to dissuade people from drinking too much of it. The attempt failed, but even if it had not, one could still not call it a ban. If one wants to discourage certain behaviour, there are ways of doing this other than banning it.

Activity 5. Which of the following do you feel would be an acceptable infringement on your liberty *based upon Mill's Harm Principle*:

1. The state forces overweight people to join a gym in order to lose weight.

2. The state taxes cigarettes to pay for health services.

3. After you post a tweet outlining your support for a local politician, several people criticize your argument.

4. A local restaurant ceases to serve meat dishes in order to focus on serving vegetarian food as there is a growing market in the area for this cuisine.

5. Supermarkets are forced by the state to label their foods with the amount of sugar and fat contained within their produce.

6. A radio station takes the decision to play a censored version of a song as the original contained several swear words.

7. People under the age of 18 are banned from buying and drinking beer.

8. You are physically stopped from entering a cinema by churchgoers who argue that the film being shown is blasphemous.

9. There are protestors outside a cinema handing out leaflets arguing that you should not see a particular film because it is blasphemous.

10. Police prevent you from strolling down the street naked.

Activity adapted from Warburton (2001: 48).

Conclusion

This chapter has overviewed a number of approaches to freedom in the history of political thought. It began with Thomas Hobbes, who conceptualized freedom as simply that which you can do without someone hindering you. The state, however, was fully entitled to prevent you from doing anything if it judged that the peace was better preserved by doing so.

It then outlined Isaiah Berlin's famous dichotomy of positive and negative liberty, negative liberty being about the absence of constraints, and positive liberty being about the ability to do something. You are free, according to a proponent of negative liberty, insofar as no one (or no law) is actually preventing you from doing something. Consequently, a starving person with no money is free to buy a Tesla as there are no rules actually prohibiting this; the fact that they are unable to do so is an unfortunate irrelevance from the perspective of freedom. Proponents of positive liberty talk of the ability to do things. Often they talk of internal impediments to our freedom such as Rousseau's notion of vanity, which is preventing us from being free by making us live our lives through the eyes of others. Berlin thought that this way of thinking about liberty was potentially dangerous as a government could prevent us from doing things we wanted to do and use the notion of internal barriers to freedom as a justification.

Not everyone concurs that the debate around freedom falls neatly into these two categories. MacCallum argues that there is just one notion of freedom – it is simply the definitions of the things that could prevent our liberty that is in question. Skinner and Pettit argue that there are three concepts of liberty, with freedom as non-domination being the third version.

We then spent the rest of the chapter overviewing John Stuart Mill's Harm Principle from his work *On Liberty*. We saw that the only reason why the state (or anyone else for that matter) could stop adults from doing what they wanted was if it physically harmed someone else. This was justified on a utilitarian basis that although individual expressions of freedom might make us unhappy, overall we are happier and lead fuller, more challenged lives if we are allowed to do as we please.

Works cited

Berlin, I. (1969) 'Two concepts of liberty'. In *Four Essays on Liberty*. Oxford: Oxford University Press, pp. 118–72.

Cawston, A. (2019) 'The feminist case against pornography: a review and re-evaluation', *Inquiry: An Interdisciplinary Journal of Philosophy*, 62(6), 624–58.

MacCallum, G. (1967), 'Negative and positive freedom', *The Philosophical Review*, 76(3), 312–34.

Mill, J.S. (1993) 'On liberty'. In *Utilitarianism, On Liberty, Considerations on Representative Government*. London: Everyman, pp. 69–185.

Warburton, N. (2001) *Freedom: An Introduction with Readings*. London: Routledge.

Text reading activities

Mill's Harm Principle from Mill, J.S. (1993) 'On liberty'. In *Utilitarianism, On Liberty, Considerations on Representative Government.* London: Everyman, p. 78.

The object of this Essay is to assert one very simple principle, as entitled to govern absolutely the dealings of society with the individual in the way of compulsion and control, whether the means used be physical force in the form of legal penalties, or the moral coercion of public opinion. That principle is, that the sole end for which mankind are warranted, individually or collectively in interfering with the liberty of action of any of their number, is self-protection. That the only purpose for which power can be rightfully exercised over any member of a civilized community, against his will, is to prevent harm to others. His own good, either physical or moral, is not a sufficient warrant. He cannot rightfully be compelled to do or forbear because it will be better for him to do so, because it will make him happier, because, in the opinions of others, to do so would be wise, or even right. These are good reasons for remonstrating with him, or reasoning with him, or persuading him, or entreating him, but not for compelling him, or visiting him with any evil, in case he do otherwise. To justify that, the conduct from which it is desired to deter him must be calculated to produce evil to some one else. The only part of the conduct of any one, for which he is amenable to society, is that which concerns others. In the part which merely concerns himself, his independence is, of right, absolute. Over himself, over his own body and mind, the individual is sovereign.

Question 1: What does Mill mean by harm?
Question 2: What is illegal now that should be legal according to Mill's principle?
Question 3: Should the state have the right to force you to do something for your own interests or to protect people from offence?

7

What would a just society look like?

KEY QUESTIONS

(1) Should all citizens be involved in the governance of the state, or is it better left to the most intelligent?

(2) Does the state have any right to take away my property?

(3) Is Rawls correct in suggesting that justice if about a fair 'end game' distribution of goods, or is Nozick's 'historical' justice preferable?

The concept 'justice' is best described as the state of affairs whereby everyone is given that which is due to them. Now this has a number of different applications in politics and ethics. When people first think of justice, they perhaps consider it in its legal/criminal sense of people receiving justice from the courts (which is often referred to as The Justice System), and there is nothing inconsistent with this use of the phrase and the definition given above. People are said to be due fair treatment by the legal system, to be presumed innocent, to not be treated differently to others based upon their ethnicity or religion, and to have their rights respected; to do otherwise would be unjust. This is often referred to as procedural justice. But this is not necessarily the *only* application of justice as 'giving people that which is due to them' in the history of political thought, as we might be due other things rather than procedural justice. We may be due certain types of political rights, we might be due property, we may be due a basic standard of income.

For example, on 17 September 2011 a group of protesters set up camp in Zuccotti Park in the heart of New York's financial district, with the aim of protesting against corporate greed and poverty. This camp became known as the Occupy Wall Street movement, and was the inspiration for a number of similar protests around the world, and received much media attention and comment worldwide. Indeed, 'The Protester', a personification of the movement, was awarded *Time* magazine's prestigious person of the year award in 2011. Occupy's slogan 'we are the 99%' aimed to highlight two interrelated issues. Firstly, it aimed to highlight how the top 1 per cent of earners in the United States received a disproportionate amount of resources in comparison to the remaining 99 per cent. Secondly, in light of the financial crash of 2008 and the impact that this had on public policy, it sought to highlight that, in addition to having the lion's share of resources, the top 1 per cent also had a disproportionate amount of power.

Both of these issues relate to matters of justice. Occupy's claim was that it is unjust that power and wealth be concentrated in the hands of such a small group of people and that in such a situation government would always be to the benefit of that 1 per cent. Power and wealth should be spread, according to this argument, more justly throughout the population. At the time of writing, the wealthiest person in the world, according to *Forbes*, is the founder and CEO of Amazon Jeff Bezos who is worth $131 billion, with Bill Gates, founder of Microsoft, second on $96.5 billion. The President of the United States, the property magnate Donald Trump, is also a member of the billionaires' club, being worth over $3 billion (Forbes, 2019). At the other extreme, billions of the world's population survive on the equivalent of less than $2.60 a day, and it is rare to see people from such a background participate in politics. Is this distribution of wealth in the world just?

All states, with very few exceptions, will tax income to provide services to citizens. These tax rates might in some places be quite low, with likewise the services provided by the state being minimal (law courts, defence, police, for example, to protect the population). Elsewhere, tax rates might be quite high, with the services provided being quite high. European countries generally have higher rates of income tax, which then pays for welfare services, subsidized (or free) healthcare, public education and the like. Citizens in the United States pay far less tax (and in some states no income tax at all) than in Europe, but will have fewer services provided as a result. This is an issue of justice; what is the legitimate role of the state in taxing to provide services? What is an individual due from the state? Are they due protection and little else, or are they due social security and a set of subsidized services?

Chapter overview

This chapter will illustrate that over the history of political thought, justice has been used to describe many different ideas. Essentially, if we take justice to mean that which is fair and reasonable, we will see that the scope of what this means has shifted over time.

We will begin the chapter by going back to the ancient Greeks to look at Plato and his student Aristotle, who take contrasting views on the nature of what would be a fair and reasonable society. Plato argues that harmony is necessary to achieve this, with everyone in society having a role to fulfil, but crucially the precise nature of that role would be different for different groups. He will outline a system whereby the business of governing should be done by those dominated by reason, namely the philosopher kings. He will also show how each individual should be internally governed likewise: our reason should rule over our passions. Achieving this will achieve justice.

Aristotle will critique Plato's notion that there is one 'just' society, and argue rather that balance is necessary in order to achieve justice. There are a variety of good states in the world (good states being those who govern in the interests of all), but these good states are organized in different ways. Likewise, there are lots of bad states, and they are often bad in different ways. Justice means an active citizenry acting in the interests of all, but there are a variety of ways in which this can be achieved.

The debate around justice then begins to shift to become more about 'who should get what', that is to say what is a just distribution of property. We will begin this discussion with an overview of perhaps the most famous defence of private property in the history of political thought, from John Locke. He argues that although God gave the world to all in common, he wanted us to improve the land so if you mix your labour with something you own communally, then that thing becomes your property. This is pre-political, so it follows that the state has no business whatsoever in meddling with your property. Thomas Paine will modify this argument, arguing instead that it was unjust that people took ownership of things given by God to us all, but efficient that people keep private property. It follows for Paine that property owners owe the rest of us rent; and this rent is the justification for the state to tax us.

Our final discussion will take us closer to the current day with the debate in the 1970s between John Rawls and Robert Nozick. Rawls will provide a defence of a tax-and-spend state that attempts to undo injustices caused by the market. He will show that all reasonable people can agree upon a thin concept of political

---

Plato

Plato was born in Athens, then a city state located in modern-day Greece, around 427 BCE into a family with a long history of participation in politics. He did not continue his family's tradition of political service, however, as he was extremely critical of politics in Athens, and provides us with perhaps the strongest philosophical critique on record of Athens's direct democracy.

Plato was taught philosophy by Socrates, and it was Socrates' trial and execution by the state that highlighted the problems with democracy for Plato. He would argue that philosophers, not politicians, should govern.

Plato founded the Academy, perhaps the first university, and taught Aristotle there.

Plato wrote widely, but his best-known work is *The Republic*, which outlines his political and ethical theory.

justice, and that this justice involves equal opportunities and a redistribution of wealth. Nozick disagrees, not only with the substance of this claim as he argues that the state only has the right to tax us to provide for a defence of our property, but also with the basic definition of justice. For Nozick, justice is not about what the ideal distribution of property is, but is simply about the acquisition of property (i.e. have you obtained a thing by buying it or stealing it). So we shall see that Rawls promotes an end game version of justice (is the distribution of property in society just?), whereas Nozick defends a historical version (have you acquired the things you have in a just manner?).

Plato: justice as the harmonious state

A just society, for Plato, is one which is harmonious with all people specializing in their own particular excellence, and one that is governed in the interests of all rather than any one particular group of people. Justice, therefore, is not an economic argument based upon people receiving material goods based upon their desserts (although Plato does touch on issues of income), nor is it a legal concept based upon the correct application of laws. Justice, for Plato, concerns morality and ethics. The just person is one who acts virtuously and consistently, likewise the just society is one which is virtuous and in which people act virtuously and obey the law. Indeed, as we shall see further on in this section, Plato argues that virtue in the individual is analogous with virtue in society.

So, what would the nature of this just society look like for Plato? Firstly, it is one in which everyone has a role to fulfil, but that does not mean to say that this role is the same. Plato is no democrat; his mentor Socrates had been put to death by democratic Athens, and just like Socrates, he thought that the ability to govern was not distributed widely around society. But he did think people had a role to play based upon their own excellence, and ensuring that people were doing the proper thing was what was just.

Plato thought there were three types of people. Those dominated by wisdom, those dominated by spirit, and those dominated by appetite. Which of these governed you determined your place within society. The roles you could fulfil were:

- **Guardians** (also known as philosopher kings) were those governed by reason and able to access the forms (more on what this means later). They were the people who should be in charge and do the governing in society.
- **Auxiliaries** were those governed by spirit, the part of the soul that causes anger and demands honour. These were the soldiers who would protect the people of the state from external attack. They would also be responsible for ensuring that the reasoning of the guardians was implemented and that it was obeyed by all. So they had a protective function, but also a policing function within the state.

- **Producers** were those governed by appetite, probably the vast majority of people within the state. Indeed, this group of people encompassed every other role in society other than guardians and auxiliaries. Producers should concentrate on that task that they excelled at. So, if you were a farmer you should focus on growing crops; if you were an actor you should focus on acting, and so on. Your excellence was the focus of your life, and you should obey the guardians' rule.

> The state is the individual writ large. Just as it is best that we are governed by reason as individuals (rather than spirit or appetite), so too should the state be governed by those who are governed by reason. Reason should always govern.

As I mentioned above, Plato thought that justice in the individual was analogous with justice in society, or to put it another way that the state was the individual writ large. The individual was comprised of three types of desire, **reason** (the desire for wisdom, knowledge and justice), **spirit** (the desire for honour, victory and patriotism), and **appetite** (the desire for money, food, sex and the like). Now each of these desires were necessary and, when kept in balance, good. Appetite was the lowest of the desires admittedly, but it was nevertheless necessary; one needed an appetite for food to ensure one ate and kept alive; one needed a desire for sex to procreate and keep up the population. Unchecked, however, it could lead to money grabbing and chaos. Spirit is a key moderator. Spirit can keep our appetites in order by making us limit what we want in order to protect our honour. It can also help our reason, to make sure that when we have discovered what is right that we do it; to ensure we are consistent with our ethics. So there is a crucial role in the individual to be fulfilled by each of the desires, but Plato is certain that the best desire, and therefore the desire that we should aim to govern us, is reason.

So it is in the individual, so too it is in the state. Those who are governed by reason (guardians) should govern the state, those who are governed by appetite (producers) should be allowed to make the things every society needs (food, furniture, houses, and the like), and those governed by spirit (the auxiliaries) should be a moderating force between those two groups.

Another capability that the guardians have is that of being able to determine the nature of the forms, which necessitates us to have a brief discussion of Plato's metaphysics. For Plato the things we see around us are not really true things, but rather shadows of true things. True things, or forms as Plato calls them, exist in the spiritual realm, and we see shadows of them on earth. The chair I am sitting on at the moment is in fact a shadow of the true form of a chair that exists somewhere in the heavens, and this form comprises the blueprint of all chairs that allows me to recognize all chairs as being capable of being sat on. It is the form which is reality, not the shadows we see on earth; therefore, metaphysically the life we lead on earth is not really real. Just as there are real forms of chairs, and for that matter tables, spoons, knives and so on in the spiritual realm, so too are there forms of government. Therefore, Plato's argument is not just that his outline of the just society is *preferable* to other forms of government, or even that it is the *best* form of government, but rather that it is the only *true* form of government. Other types of government to that which he has outlined, therefore, are false, as opposed to being worse or undesirable. These are different types of political argument.

Plato outlines the link between his political philosophy and moral philosophy in the Allegory of the Cave, perhaps the most famous passage of his work *The Republic*. In this work Plato's narrator Socrates asks his interlocutor Glaucon to imagine a group of people who, since birth, have been prisoners in a cave in the dark. They are chained so they can only look forward at the wall in front of them, and behind them there is a path, and behind that a fire which provides the cave's only light. People walk to and fro on the path behind them with various objects that they are carrying, but the prisoners can see neither the people nor the objects which they are carrying. What they can see, however, are the shadows on the wall that are cast by the other people and the objects they are carrying. Don't you think, Socrates asks of Glaucon 'if they were able to talk to each other, would they not assume that the shadows they saw were real things?' (Plato, 1987: 317). The prisoners would start to regard the shadows as the real world, not the things they cannot see behind them, so their view of what is real and what is not is skewed. This is Plato's metaphysics around the forms, and it is us who are the prisoners in the cave; the shadows that we see around us are not reality, we cannot see the reality, all we see are shadows of the forms that we cannot see.

The allegory of the cave

The allegory of the cave unites Plato's philosophical thinking about the forms, with his view of justice that philosophers should govern. Most of us are prisoners staring at the shadows on the wall; philosopher kings can lead us to the light.

Now imagine, Socrates continues, one of these prisoners was able to break free from his chains and look around. He might notice the path and the fire and the objects on the path and begin to question the reality that he had accepted. He might then also escape from the cave into the daylight. Initially, the exposure to the sun after a lifetime in the gloom of the cave would mean that 'his eyes would be so dazzled by the glare of it that he wouldn't be able to see' (Plato, 1987: 318). But eventually his eyes would become accustomed to the light and he would be able to comprehend the things around him as being real and the things to which he had grown accustomed in the cave as being false. If that person was to go back down to the cave and speak to his former fellow captives and try to explain to them the nature of reality, they would mock him and be unable to comprehend the things he was saying. But this is Plato's politics. Those able to distinguish the true nature of reality are incomprehensible to those who cannot, and might often be mocked by those comfortable by their incorrect understanding of the nature of reality. It is the job of the guardians, in conjunction with the auxiliaries, to ensure that others obey the dictates of reason rather than the dictates of those governed by ignorance and appetite.

> Philosopher kings should always govern in the interests of all – never their own interests. To ensure this would happen Plato says they should be housed by the state and have no private property or families; this way they would have no interests to pursue.

It is worth reflecting for a moment just how undemocratic this proposal is. Not only does Plato posit that there are a group of people better suited to govern than others and outline how their rule is just, but also, as he constructs his argument based upon the governor's access to reason and wisdom, he is effectively saying that if anyone disagrees with that which the guardian is saying, they are just plain wrong. They don't have access to the necessary wisdom to make this judgement. The philosopher Karl Popper warns us of the danger of such an argument, stating that 'personal superiority, whether racial or intellectual or moral or educational, can never establish a claim to political prerogatives, even if such superiority could be ascertained' (Popper, 1966: 49).

One of the requirements of the philosopher kings (guardians) is that they should always govern in the interests of everyone, and never just their own selfish interests. To ensure this happened, Plato discussed the living conditions of the philosopher kings. Their wants would be met by the state, but other than this they would have nothing. They would live in an almost communist manner with no private property and no families, as they would mate with a community of wives which was kept by the state, and their children would be raised by the state. As the guardians did not have anything (nor could they have anything), it followed that nothing they could do could possibly be in their own interests as they had no interests to pursue. They could not legislate to increase their property as they had none; they could not favour their families by their actions as they did not have one.

A couple of problems emerge from this. If Plato's guardians were governed by reason and had access to the forms, surely they would never dream of governing in a manner that was contrary to reason. So why would it be necessary to put safeguards in place to ensure that they would never act in their own interests? Is reason not quite as potent an inducement as Plato suggests? Secondly, if the Guardians are completely immune to the material conditions of the rest of society, how will they gain the knowledge of how the common good will be reached? Although they cannot benefit directly from their actions, their separation from the rest of society might blind them to the effects of their policies.

Activity 1. Consider and answer the following questions:

(1) List the pros and cons of restricting political leadership to the most intelligent in society:

Pros	Cons

(2) What do you think of Plato's suggestion that political leaders should have no possessions to prevent them from acting in their own interests?

(3) Outline the ways in which this critiques democracy.

Aristotle: justice as happiness and the general good

Aristotle was taught by Plato, but is very critical of his philosophical and political proposals. So much so indeed that his philosophy is markedly different from that of Plato. Broadly speaking, whereas Plato favoured the ideal over the real, Aristotle prioritized study of the world around us to reach an understanding. For Plato, there was one form of justice applicable to all people at all times; Aristotle judged that this was unrealistic and saw justice as obtaining a balance, within both the individual and society in general.

> There is not one absolute ideal form of government that is good, for Aristotle – there are different types of good states, and different types of bad states.

Aristotle thought that rather there being one ideal 'correct' form of government and lots of incorrect forms, observation of the world told us that there were lots of types of government, some of which were good, and some of which were bad. Indeed, he also thought that you could not judge whether it was good or bad simply by looking at the people governing, as each type of government had good and bad forms.

If one person governed and it was a good government, Aristotle called this a **monarchy**; if one person governed and it was a bad government then this was called a **tyranny**.

If a small group of people governed and it was a good government, Aristotle called this an **aristocracy**; if a group of people governed and it was a bad form of government then this was an **oligarchy**.

If lots of people governed and it was a good government, Aristotle called this a **polity**; if lots of people governed and it was a bad form of government then this was a **democracy**.

The difference between a good and a bad form of government was whether or not it governed in the interests of the people ruling or in the interests of everyone. Therefore, a government of one person could be good so long as it governed in the interests of all. Indeed, he thought that if lots of people governed, it could still be bad if individuals sought out only their own interests; admittedly, he thought that democracy was the best of the bad forms of government as the more people involved, the closer one was likely to get to the interests of all.

Citizenship was also important for Aristotle, but it was challenged by his views on good and bad government. For Aristotle, citizenship was about what you did rather than what you were. In the modern world, citizenship has a rather legalistic basis, one which originated as the Roman Empire spread and there was a need to form a basis of citizenship around a large area when people could not meet. We are a citizen of a certain state in the modern world, which can be proved by a passport or some other documentation, and we have rights from that state irrespective of whether we use them or not. Someone who did not vote in the last election will not have their citizenship revoked (although some states may punish those that do not vote), as being a citizen in the contemporary world is something we *are* rather than something we *do*.

Social animal

Man is by nature a social animal, for Aristotle, meaning that the state is an entirely natural entity. In situations when the demands of citizenship and one's moral code clashed, for Aristotle our sociability meant that our demands as citizens should always win out.

Aristotle does not see it this way. For him, citizenship is an activity, about participating in the affairs of state, and it is something that we are obliged to do. Man is by nature, for Aristotle, 'a social animal' (Aristotle, 1981: 59). Aristotle would have no time for Locke or Hobbes or any other theorist who suggested that societies were, or could be, founded on a contract. Rather, he thought, whenever you see people, you see some manner of social coordination and this was entirely natural. Just as fish often swim in shoals, or birds fly in formations, human being have always lived together in some form of society. Taking part in your society is, likewise, entirely natural for Aristotle. If you don't want to participate socially then you were either a god or a beast; you were either above society or below it. So participating in your society is very important for Aristotle.

> **Aristotle**
> Aristotle was born in Macedonia in 384 BCE and studied under Plato at the Academy in Athens until Plato's death. He then became the tutor to Alexander the Great, before returning to Athens to set up his own school for philosophers which he called the Lyceum.
> Aristotle differed greatly from his teacher Plato in ethics, philosophy and politics, preferring a search for balance as opposed to absolute truth.
> Such was Aristotle's dominance in medieval and early modern Europe after the recovery of his works that he was referred to as simply 'the philosopher'. After Thomas Aquinas fused Aristotelian philosophy with Christian theology, his work became used by many thinkers such as Marsilius of Padua to justify removing monarchs. Indeed, Thomas Hobbes blamed the civil war on the dominance of his teachings in universities.

But there are problems with this. Aristotle has already noted that there exists more than one form of government, some of them good, some of them bad, and each with different expectations of what the citizen should do. If one lived in a polity, then one might expect to be quite active and influential in the administration of affairs in the state. If one lived in an oligarchy, your role might be extremely limited; perhaps restricted to simply obeying the law.

Aristotle also thought that there was a distinction between a good citizen on the one hand, and a good man on the other. The former carried out the role that was expected of him as a citizen within his state; the latter followed a moral code. Now if one lived in a good state, there was no necessary distinction between a good man and a good citizen; but one did not necessarily live in a good state. So what would you do if you were a good man in a bad state, and your role as a citizen entailed you doing things that you did not want to due to your moral code (or not doing things that were in your moral code)? Aristotle is unequivocal about this. Citizenship is intrinsically linked with being human, being a social animal, and as a result the demands of citizenship trump the demands of morality.

This leaves the citizen in a tricky situation. What if one was a good man who lived in Nazi Germany whereby the law entailed that one informed the authorities of Jewish people in hiding, or in the Soviet Union and you are expected to inform on friends and neighbours who were opposed to the ruling regime? Are we seriously expected to make our citizenship demands trump those of our conscience? Aristotle's response to this appears to be, yes you do, but encourages us to persuade, discuss and cajole behind the scenes to try to effect change and turn a bad state into a good one.

Activity 2. Attempt the following questions:

(1) Do you think humanity is naturally social? What would Hobbes say about this?

(2) Do you agree with Aristotle that the distinction between a good and a bad state is whether or not it governs in everyone's interests?

(3) Do you agree with Aristotle that the demands of citizenship should trump those of one's moral code?

Locke: natural rights and property

For Locke, all of us have natural inalienable rights which must be respected by all types of government. Justice is, for Locke, individuals living according to the dictates of natural law, respecting one another in their life, liberty and property, and the state doing likewise. All legitimate government, as we have seen in our discussion on Locke on the social contract earlier on, is based upon consent, and we transfer to the government our right to *interpret* the natural laws and develop a system of punishment for their transgressors. But just as individuals should be punished should they transgress the natural laws, it also follows that the state has no right to transgress them either. For Locke, natural rights, rights that all of us have, are inalienable; they cannot be transferred to another person or group of people. The state can only act upon those rights that we have directly transferred to it – we have not transferred to it our natural rights (indeed we cannot transfer them), so it follows they are none of the state's business.

> For Locke, we own our labour and if we mix our labour with something to which we have a right in common with all, and improve it and don't waste it, that thing becomes ours. The state then has no business interfering with this.

For Locke we have the natural right to life, liberty, property and religion. We have no right to take away the life, the freedoms or the property of another person, nor do we have the right to force someone to follow another religion. Just as we have no right over another person, so it follows that the state has no rights over these things either. This sounds a little like a notion of human rights. It is certainly a forerunner of human rights, in that there are certain areas in which no legitimate government can interfere. However, human rights tend to be positive things, for example, 'I have a right to life', as opposed to negative things such as 'no one has the right to take my life away', and Locke's argument is the latter.

Perhaps his argument that we have a natural right to property is the most famous one; it is Locke's attempt to show us that the state has no right to take away our property as our right to own it is pre-political (that is to say, prior to the formation of government), so is not dependent on the permission or will of the government. We are all entitled to the property that we own and no one can take it from us.

Locke argued that all of us own some property; we own ourselves and we own our labour. If we mix our labour with something that we have a common right to with everyone, and we improve that land and make it more productive, it follows that we own the produce of this land and the land itself so long as we continue to improve it. So suppose I come across a piece of land that I have a common right to with everyone else, and on it I grow avocado trees. I own my labour, and have mixed my labour with the land, and as a consequence can be said to own the avocado trees, the avocados, and the land upon which they were grown without having to get the permission of anyone. As Locke suggests

> Thus the grass my horse has bit; the turfs my servant has cut; and the ore I have digg'd in any place, where I have a right to them in common with others, become my property, without the assignation or consent of any body. The labour that was mine, removing them out of that common state they were in, hath fixed my property in them. (Locke, 1988: 288)

Locke does place a caveat on this, that the use of the land does not spoil it or cause waste. Now at first glance this could appear a serious challenge to Locke's theory. If I grew avocado trees on the land I claimed and harvested, say, 100,000 avocados a year, but only had myself to consume them, then some of them would inevitably come to waste. There are only so many avocados a person can eat. But Locke thinks we get around this with the invention of money. People buy my avocados and therefore I turn them into money which cannot spoil. I use that money to buy tacos and sourdough bread to use with the avocados, along with the other necessities of life that other people might be growing/making on their land.

Locke thought that God gave the world to everyone in common initially; however, we are expected to extract efficient productivity from the earth; God expected us to be productive. By allowing us to mix our labour with the earth, produce things, and sell the things we produce, the earth is being used efficiently with minimal waste and everyone will benefit. The state had no right to interfere in this. So this is not only a justification of private property, but also a justification of an early free market.

Thomas Paine, in his work *Agrarian Justice*, begins his argument in a similar

Paine argues that those people who took land that was intended for us all now owe society rent. This rent is a justification of taxation to pay for the state.

fashion to that of Locke, but would take it to different conclusions. He agrees with Locke that the world was given to all in common, but that it was not intended for private property, whilst also recognizing that the population of the world has increased, making current marketized arrangements regarding private property an efficient way to arrange this. He argues that every 'proprietor, therefore, of cultivated lands, owes to the community *groundrent*' (Paine, 1999: 8). This rent is an early form of tax, a tax that can then be used by the state to pay for schemes to support those without property. Paine is keen to stress the difference between the land to which he thinks owners have no right, and the labour that individuals put into the land over which society has no right. Land should be taxed, not labour.

What does this mean for us? Locke was writing at a time in which European settlers were claiming land in North America; indeed, in many ways it can be seen as a justification of taking land away from aboriginal Americans. If you had run out of common land you could cultivate and claim as your own in Europe, you could go to America where there was abundant land that could be claimed. The aboriginal peoples could not claim ownership rights over the land, for Locke, as they lived hunter-gatherer existences rather than cultivating the land. If you went out onto common lands and picked berries and nuts, those berries and nuts were rightfully yours, as you had mixed your labour with them; but you have not mixed your labour with the land so that cannot rightfully be said to be yours. If someone came along to those lands, cultivated them and therefore (in Locke's eyes) improved them and made them more efficient, then they could claim ownership of them. Locke's view was premised on a claim of the efficiency of European cultivation techniques and therefore the superiority of the European way of life. The aboriginal peoples of the world had no cultural claim to ownership of lands; ownership only came about by cultivation and improvement.

But since now there are no areas of land of which it can be said that we have a right in common with all, how can we acquire property? There are no vast tracts of land that are unclaimed upon which we can initiate a programme of avocado growing. Note here that we have to have a common right to that property with everyone else before we can cultivate it and claim it as our own. If we think that our neighbour takes insufficient care of their backyard, we cannot enter it, dig it up and grow avocado plants in an attempt to claim it as our own. Our neighbours' backyards are theirs to do with as they please. Locke would say that we still own our labour, so we can sell our labour, and with the money we acquire we can buy property. And when we have purchased property, then the state has no right to interfere in the money we may accrue from it. So whereas we cannot necessarily acquire property by cultivating it, we can acquire it on the open market. But individuals and the state should respect property ownership and not interfere with it. Obviously the state does tax property and, indeed, labour. It also restricts property in other ways. If I purchase a historic listed building, I cannot tear it down and build a new one, or add an incongruous modern extension to it. Neither could I purchase the *Mona Lisa* and then immediately use it to fuel my fire.

In our discussion below of Robert Nozick, a philosopher heavily influenced by Locke, we shall see the potential implications of basing a claim around justice on the inviolability of property rights, as he will argue that any taxation taken by the state to fund the redistribution of wealth is tantamount to slave labour and misunderstands the nature of justice.

Activity 3. Consider and answer the questions below:

(1) Outline the way in which Locke justifies a pre-political right to property.

(2) How does Paine critique this? Do you prefer Locke or Paine?

Hume

Hume is anti-rationalist in his view of justice in that he does not think (like most other people in this chapter) that virtue can be discovered by the use of our reason alone. For Plato, justice is acquired within both the individual and society as a whole, by the application of reason; the discovery of what is just and the acting upon it are seen as the same things. For Hume, whereas we might be compelled to act upon something because we think it reasonable, it is not reason *alone* that does this; passion acts upon reason to prompt action, but action itself is neither reasonable nor unreasonable in and of itself.

Private property, and the right to hold it, cannot, for Hume, come from any abstract notion such as the natural law or from a social contract. Rather, it comes from artificial conventions that we create in societies in order for us to get what our passions desire. In early societies, Hume posits, humanity generally has desires for things which we cannot by ourselves obtain or defend. These societies try to make up for this individual inability by cooperation with one another and by creating conventions that help foster our self-interest. So early (small) societies develop the convention that those things which we have obtained as individuals by either labour or good fortune

> For Hume, there can be no abstract right to property; but rather it comes from associations and conventions. In smaller societies, we simply associated people with things so thought of them as theirs. As societies grew and became more complex, we developed a more legalistic defence of property.

should not be taken by another person, and in return we will not take things off other people. We come to associate things with people by their proximity (if I see you in a particular house all the time, I associate you with that house), and we develop as a result a convention of private property. It is in our self-interest to respect other people's property as without the convention, we cannot really be said to own any property. Likewise, if people do not respect private property, they are likely to be shunned by the community and as a result not be able to benefit from community membership. So early views on property revolve around group membership and access to cooperative efforts from which one would benefit; so the origins of private property are steeped in self-interest. Hume likens this to two strangers, perhaps not sharing a common language, coming together to row a boat across a river; they would both eventually realize that it is in their self-interest to work together to conform to the way one rows a boat.

As societies become bigger and more complex, respecting private property becomes a moral obligation rather than just a self-interested one. As communities grow, in terms of both area and population, it becomes less obviously the case that we are linking respecting people's property with access to community goods. Money is invented and economies grow as it is in our self-interest to do so, but also we cease to know one another and thereby lose our link with people and 'their' property. This reduces, Hume thinks, our incentive to conform to conventions and, as a consequence, societies at this point start to argue that it is right to protect property, and wrong to take it; therefore, a right is established around property, and breaking it is attributed to justice rather than self-interest.

At this stage we start to lessen the link in our minds between taking someone's property (or having our own property taken from us) and the overall economic good, and start to consider instead the uneasiness that people would feel about having their property taken, and from this start to develop notions of the moral virtue of respecting property.

So Hume does not give us a grand theory of justice; he tries to explain how we associate in our minds what is one person's and what is another's. Property rights do not come from God or any other natural law, for Hume; they come from a piecemeal moral development over time. Justice, for Hume, is about the protection of property rights; but this is based upon custom and association rather than natural law.

Rawls: Justice as fairness

John Rawls argues that all of us, whatever our background or belief system – our concept of the good as Rawls calls it – can agree upon a thin, that is to say limited (based upon political principles rather than a larger religious idea), concept of justice. In attempting to show this, he illustrates how we can arrive at this conception of justice, and what that concept of justice will be. Rawls argues that principles of justice are fair if they can be agreed upon by individuals who do not

John Rawls

Political philosophy had been in the doldrums for decades prior to the publication of John Rawls's *A Theory of Justice* in 1971. The influence of logical positivism, which argued that little meaningful could be said on political or ethical issues, meant that very few attempted normative political theory. Rawls's work was important, therefore, not simply because of its contribution to liberalism and the adherents that it gained, but also because of the critiques that it received which reinvigorated political philosophy.

Rawls was born in Baltimore, United States, in 1921. He studied at Princeton before serving in the army during the Second World War, after which he began an academic career which ended up at Harvard where he wrote *A Theory of Justice*.

Rawls was a very shy man, and also one of the pleasantest people in academia.

know how they will be affected by those principles. For principles of justice to be fair, they need to be impartial; we should not discuss them in an attempt to make ourselves better off. So the social contract is being used here; but rather than using it to justify the state or the rule of government, it is being used to show how agreement can be sought on principles of justice in divided societies. Or perhaps more accurately we can identify a thin set of political principles that all *reasonable* people can agree upon.

In his work *A Theory of Justice*, Rawls asks that we imagine ourselves in the original position behind the veil of ignorance. Here we are not ignorant of society, its divisions and groupings, but we are ignorant of our position within it. So I do not know my class, my profession, my religious views, my ethnicity and so on. We are behind this veil of ignorance so that there is no possible way we can advantage ourselves within the discussions on justice; if we do not know where we are positioned in society, we cannot seek to benefit ourselves. Rawls thinks that in this situation we would seek to maximize our minimum utility (or maximin as it is sometimes referred to), that is to say that we would attempt to ensure that the worst possible outcome for ourselves would be acceptable.

In these discussions we would attempt to ensure that the worst-off person in society was relatively well off. This is not because we are particularly altruistic, but rather because we are self-interested. We have an interest in ensuring that the least well-off person in society is relatively well off as behind the veil of ignorance we do not know whether we are that person or not. Likewise, we would attempt to ensure that all people had equal rights, as we would not want any group in society to have less rights than any other group as, again, we could be in the group we were disadvantaging. As a consequence, Rawls concludes that we would all agree to the following two principles of justice:

> First: each person has an equal right to the most extensive scheme of equal basic liberties compatible with a similar scheme of liberties for all.

Second: social and economic inequalities are to be arranged so that they are both (a) to the greatest benefit of the least advantaged, consistent with the just savings principle, and (b) attached to offices and positions open to all under conditions of fair equality of opportunity. (Rawls, 1999: 266)

Talent is not a good justification for inequalities for Rawls as the reward our particular talent receives in a market economy is nothing to do with us. Likewise, hard work in and of itself is not a good justification as not all that work hard are rewarded.

The first principle is not particularly controversial, arguing that everyone should be equal in terms of the rights that they have. No one group of people can have more or less rights based upon their ethnicity, religion or gender. The second is more so. It argues firstly that when there are inequalities in society, they must be available to all on the basis of equality of opportunity. So it cannot be fair that well-paid jobs are reserved for the sons and daughters of wealthy people, or that they are reserved for people from a particular race or religion. We would not have possibly agreed to this in the original position as we may have been in one of the excluded groups. Secondly, Rawls argues that the only justification for one person being paid more than anyone else is that that disparity is to the advantage of the least well-off person in society; this he calls the **difference principle**. So, we may argue that a surgeon should get paid more than a call centre operative as good healthcare would be more important to the least well-off person than good customer service.

Rawls here appears to be really asking us to focus on the reasons why we justify one person having more money than another; and he thinks that a number of the reasons we commonly use simply don't stack up. For example, working hard is not a particularly good reason to pay one person more than another, as we do not consistently apply that principle. Imagine two workers working side by side who are both creating T-shirts. To one worker this comes easily, and so this worker creates ten T-shirts every hour without ever breaking sweat. To the other worker, not a skilled sewer, it is really hard work, and this worker toils to create just five T-shirts an hour. The latter worker might have actually worked harder than the former worker despite the lower return; but if we argue that hard work should be rewarded, is there not an argument that they should be paid more than the worker who has created more? Likewise, talent is not a very good argument to justify one person being paid more than another, as Rawls argues that talents are morally arbitrary. I cannot really help that I have the talents I have (or indeed the talents I don't have) any more than I can help being tall, white, with curly hair. They are things I have no control over. Rawls points out that we already accept, under the auspices of equal opportunities, that people should not be rewarded (or punished) over things they have no control. I should not be rewarded for being a white male as I had no control over being these things. Likewise, no one should be punished for their ethnicity, religion or gender as these are not under their control. Rawls argues that talents are likewise; we should not be rewarded for them. Suppose you disagree with this and think that you are responsible for your talents; Rawls argues that one must conclude that we are not responsible for the reward our particular talent receives in the market economy. If you are an expert beer pong player, there is little reward for this in a market economy; if you are an expert basketball player, you can do very well out of this.

Rawls is no absolute egalitarian; he does not argue for complete equality of outcome, and whereas talents and/or hard work is not a good argument for inequalities in income, working hard to develop your talents probably is. So if one worked hard to develop your talents, you can get paid more than someone who does not (Stephen Curry, point guard for the Golden State Warriors is known for his intense training sessions that have made him the best in his position in the NBA; this training would make it acceptable for him to be paid more than an average guard, rather than any specific talent he had). But what Rawls asks us to do is reflect on precisely to what extent we are responsible for our skills and the amount of money we have, and conversely if the poorest in society are really responsible for their position. He also asks us to imagine if we would really be happy with the allocation of resources in the contemporary world if we were in the original position behind the veil of ignorance.

Politically speaking, Rawls is defending the postwar social democratic consensus. He would argue that the state should provide benefits, healthcare and the like as a safety net based upon the claims of justice, and that safety net should be paid for through progressive taxation. He also asks us, when we look at our payslip and notice the tax taken off to pay for social security, rather than complain we should ask ourselves if, in the original position behind the veil of ignorance, would we not support such a system. If someone has no talents that are rewarded by a market economy, is it really their fault? And if we do well out of the current society, in that it rewards the talents we have, are we really responsible for this?

Nozick

Robert Nozick provides us with not only a comprehensive critique of Rawls's position; but an entirely different concept of justice. Nozick argues that Rawls's position is an end game view of justice; that is to say that given the money, property and goods that exist in the world today, what is a fair and just distribution of these things? But this does not, for Nozick, take into consideration how we got these things in the first place. Buildings were built by individuals and groups of individuals, money was earned by people, wealth was created. Rawls is wrong, Nozick argued in his *Anarchy, State and Utopia*, to regard wealth as if it had appeared like manna from heaven. Nozick would build a view of justice as historical. Rather than ask ourselves what a just distribution of wealth would be in the current world, we should ask how people have got the money that they have, and indeed why people have no money, to see whether justice is being served or not.

Nozick suggests, therefore, that if a person has a lot of money, more money than someone else, it is only unjust if that person has not acquired that money in a legitimate manner. If someone has earned their money through working, or been given it in a fair exchange, then it is just. It is only unjust if someone has stolen it.

So if someone is starving on the streets, and is not in that condition because they have had their property stolen (which would be unjust), this may be unfortunate, this might be something that we want to do something about, but it is not actually unjust. Crucially, Nozick argues, this is not something that the state should get involved with. If you want to help people who are poor, help them. Start a charity, commence a voluntary insurance scheme, take them into your home, but leave the state out of it.

Justice involves the state protecting property from internal and external threats, and the cost of doing this should rightfully be paid by the taxpayer. But any attempt by the state to take money off one person, and give it to another via distribution of wealth or the provision of services is, for Nozick, unjust and akin to slave labour. The state should limit its activities to protecting people and their property, and legal justice systems to organize restitution of property in the event that it has been taken unjustly from an individual. The only justifiable kind of state for Nozick is a minimalist night-watchman state, one that provides defence, police and legal services to protect people's rights and their property.

Nozick thinks someone starving on the street might be unfortunate, but it is only unjust if they have been robbed or illegally denied access to work. Justice is historical for Nozick, not end game. We shouldn't look at the distribution of things, we should look at each acquisition.

Nozick illustrates one of the key problems of Rawls's theory of justice with his Wilt Chamberlain principle, in which he attempts to show how Rawlsian theory would be upset by just transactions. Suppose you lived in a society which was based upon Rawlsian principles (or any other set of egalitarian principles for that matter), and in this society there was an excellent basketball player who people enjoyed watching. This player was in high demand by various basketball teams due to his skill and popularity, so in order to sign for one, he strikes a deal whereby the team puts a box at the turnstile with his name on it, which anyone attending the game puts an extra 25 cents in. The money from this box would go directly to Wilt Chamberlain. The fans are happy enough to do this as they are excited to see him play, and at the end of the season 1 million people have attended and Wilt Chamberlain gets $250,000. Why has the state any business in interfering with this voluntary transaction? The original distribution of wealth in society was just (D1 Nozick calls it), the transaction was voluntary and people were happy to do it, so must not the new distribution of wealth that arises from this (D2 Nozick calls it) also be just?

Nozick's point here is that every free and fair distribution of property disrupts egalitarian distributions of wealth, and it is not just basketball players that receive money from free and fair distribution of property, but many/most of us do. If you go to the movies a percentage of what you pay will go to the leading actors, if you buy a book a percentage will go to its author, if you buy a shirt some of the money will go to the owners of the store in which you purchased it, and if you buy a burger some of the money will go to the restaurant's proprietors. If we part with some of our property in return for goods and services from someone else we have entered into a voluntary exchange, one which disrupts principles of patterned justice such as Rawls's. If we hold that people should be at liberty to dispose of their property as they see fit, it follows that we cannot hold an egalitarian view of justice for Nozick.

Activity 4.

(1) Make a list of the talents (if any) you feel are over- and under-rewarded in your society:

Over-rewarded	Under-rewarded

(2) What skills do you feel should be paid more in order to be of a positive advantage to the least well-off person in society (i.e. Rawls's 'difference principle')?

(3) Outline how Rawls and Nozick disagree on us deserving the fruits of our talents.

Conclusion

This chapter has attempted to show how a variety of political thinkers have conceptualized how one might achieve justice in the state. Plato regarded justice as being about order, with each member of society doing the task best associated with their abilities. This meant that those governed by reason (the philosopher kings) should rule, but that they should do so in the interests of all rather than their own. This is a comprehensive criticism of democratic ideas which hold that the ability to govern is spread throughout the population (or the citizenry at least in ancient Athens). Aristotle rejected Plato's absolutism, although agreed with him that the main characteristic of 'good' states was that they governed in everybody's interests. This could be achieved, he thought, in a number of different ways.

We then went on to quite a lengthy discussion about property. John Locke argued that property is a pre-political right as, prior to the formation of government, we were entitled to take land out of the common stock, improve and cultivate it, and claim it as our own. This was despite God initially giving it to us all in common as he also gave us ourselves and our labour, and mixing this with something to which we have a right in common with everyone else makes it our own. As a consequence of this, Locke argues that the state has no business whatsoever messing with our property. Paine disputed this, arguing that those who own land owe the rest of us rent; and that rent is the basis of progressive taxation.

We then went on to examine the debate between John Rawls and Robert Nozick and in so doing two stark differences between them became apparent. Firstly, Rawls thought that the just state was a social democratic one that looked after all people regardless of the talents and money they had. Nozick argued that the just state was a night-watchman state that protected property. Secondly, Rawls argued that justice was end game; one examines the wealth present in a given society and considers the fair way to distribute it. Nozick argued that justice should be seen as historical: whether the acquisition of what you had was achieved in a just fashion. Money and goods did not simply fall from the heavens; they were the result of people's efforts.

Works cited

Aristotle (1981) *The Politics*. London: Penguin.
Forbes (2019) 'Billionaires 2019', *Forbes*, available at https://www.forbes.com/billionaires/ #14025ab4251c
Locke, J. (1988) *Two Treatises of Government*. Cambridge: Cambridge University Press.
Paine, T. (1999) *Agrarian Justice*, available at http://piketty.pse.ens.fr/files/Paine1795.pdf
Plato (1987) *The Republic*. London: Penguin.
Popper, K. (1966) *The Open Society and its Enemies: Vol. I, The Spell of Plato*. London: Routledge
Rawls, J. (1999) *A Theory of Justice*. Oxford: Oxford University Press.

Text reading activities

Locke on property from the 'Two treatises of government' in Locke, J. (1988) *Two Treatises of Government*. Cambridge: Cambridge University Press, pp. 286–9.

26. God, who hath given the World to Men in common, hath also given them reason to make use of it to the best advantage of Life, and convenience. The Earth, and all that is therein, is given to Men for the Support and Comfort of their being. And though all the Fruits it naturally produces, and Beasts it feeds, belong to Mankind in common, as they are produced by the spontaneous hand of Nature; and no body has originally a private Dominion, exclusive of the rest of Mankind, in any of them, as they are thus in their natural state: yet being given for the use of Men, there must of necessity be a means *to appropriate* them some way or other, before they can be of any use, or at all beneficial to any particular Man. The Fruit, or Venison, which nourishes the wild Indian, who knows no Inclosure, and is still a Tenant in common, must be his, and so his, i.e. a part of him, that another can no longer have any right to it, before it can do him any good for the support of his Life.

27. Though the Earth, and all inferior Creatures, be common to all Men, yet every Man has a *Property* in his own *Person*: this no Body has any Right to but himself. The *Labour* of his Body, and the *Work* of his Hands, we may say, are properly his. Whatsoever then he removes out of the State that Nature hath provided, and left it in, he hath mixed his *Labour* with, and joined to it something that is his own, and thereby makes it his *Property*. It being by him removed from the common state Nature hath placed it in, it hath by this *labour* something annexed to it, that excludes the common right of other men: for this labour being the unquestionable Property of the Labourer, no Man but he can have a right to what that is once joyned to, at least where there is enough, and as good, left in common for others.

28. He that is nourished by the Acorns he pickt up under an Oak, or the Apples he gathered from the Trees in the Wood, has certainly appropriated them to himself. No Body can deny but the nourishment is his. I ask then, When did they begin to be his? when he digested? Or when he eat? Or when he boiled? Or when he brought them home? Or when he pickt them up? And 'tis plain, if the first gathering made them not his, nothing else could. That *Labour* put a distinction between them and common. That added something to them more than Nature, the common Mother of all, had done; and so they became his private right. And will any one say, he had no right to those Acorns or Apples, he thus appropriated, because he had not the consent of all Mankind to make them his? Was it a Robbery

thus to assume to himself what belonged to all in Common? If such a consent as that was necessary, Man had starved, notwithstanding the Plenty God had given him. We see in *Commons*, which remain so by Compact, that it is the taking any part of what is common, and removing it out of the state Nature leaves it in, which *begins the Property*; without which the Common is of no use. And the taking of this or that part, does not depend on the express consent of all the Commoners. Thus the Grass my Horse has bit; the Turfs my Servant has cut; and the Ore I have digg'd in any place, where I have a right to them in common with others, become my *Property*, without the assignation or consent of any body. The *labour* that was mine, removing them out of that common state they were in, hath *fixed* my *Property* in them.

From Paine's *Agrarian Justice*, available at http://piketty.pse.ens.fr/files/Paine1795.pdf

There could be no such thing as landed property originally. Man did not make the earth, and, though he had a natural right to *occupy* it, he had no right to *locate as his property* in perpetuity any part of it; neither did the Creator of the earth open a land-office, from whence the first title-deeds should issue. Whence then, arose the idea of landed property? I answer as before, that when cultivation began the idea of landed property began with it, from the impossibility of separating the improvement made by cultivation from the earth itself, upon which that improvement was made.

The value of the improvement so far exceeded the value of the natural earth, at that time, as to absorb it; till, in the end, the common right of all became confounded into the cultivated right of the individual. But there are, nevertheless, distinct species of rights, and will continue to be, so long as the earth endures. It is only by tracing things to their origin that we can gain rightful ideas of them, and it is by gaining such ideas that we discover the boundary that divides right from wrong, and teaches every man to know his own. I have entitled this tract 'Agrarian Justice' to distinguish it from 'Agrarian Law'.

Nothing could be more unjust than agrarian law in a country improved by cultivation; for though every man, as an inhabitant of the earth, is a joint proprietor of it in its natural state, it does not follow that he is a joint proprietor of cultivated earth. The additional value made by cultivation, after the system was admitted, became the property of those who did it, or who inherited it from them, or who purchased it. It had originally no owner. While, therefore, I advocate the right, and interest myself in the hard case of all those who have been thrown out of their natural inheritance by the introduction of the system of landed property, I equally defend the right of the possessor to the part which is his.

Cultivation is at least one of the greatest natural improvements ever made by human invention. It has given to created earth a tenfold value. But the landed monopoly that began with it has produced the greatest evil. It has dispossessed more than half the inhabitants of every nation of their natural inheritance, without providing for them, as ought to have been done, an indemnification for that loss, and has thereby created a species of poverty and wretchedness that did not exist before.

In advocating the case of the persons thus dispossessed, it is a right, and not a charity, that I am pleading for. But it is that kind of right which, being neglected at first, could not be brought forward afterwards till heaven had opened the way by a revolution in the system of government. Let us then do honor to revolutions by justice, and give currency to their principles by blessings.

Having thus in a few words, opened the merits of the case, I shall now proceed to the plan I have to propose, which is,

To create a national fund, out of which there shall be paid to every person, when arrived at the age of twenty-one years, the sum of fifteen pounds sterling, as a compensation in part, for the loss of his or her natural inheritance, by the introduction of the system of landed property.

Rawls: Two principles of justice, from Rawls, J. (1999) *A Theory of Justice.* Oxford: Oxford University Press, p. 266.

First Principle: Each person is to have an equal right to the most extensive total system of equal basic liberties compatible with a similar system of liberty for all.

Second Principle: Social and economic inequalities are to be arranged so that they are both

(a) to the greatest benefit of the least advantaged, consistent with the just savings principle, and

(b) attached to offices and positions open to all under conditions of fair equality of opportunity.

Nozick: The Wilt Chamberlain Principle, available at https:// dascolihum.com/uploads/CH_46_Nozick_Justice_and_ Entitlement. pdf

Now suppose that Wilt Chamberlain is greatly in demand by basketball teams, being a great gate attraction. (Also suppose contracts run only for a year, with players being free agents.) He signs the following sort of contract with a team: In each home game, twenty-five cents from the price of each ticket of admission goes to him. (We ignore the question of whether he is 'gouging' the owners, letting them look for themselves.) The season starts, and people cheerfully attend his team's games; they buy their tickets, each time dropping a separate twenty-five cents of their admission price into a special box with Chamberlain's name on it. They are excited about seeing him play; it is worth the total admission price to them. Let us suppose that in one season one million persons attend his home games, and Wilt Chamberlain winds up with $250,000, a much larger sum than the average income and larger even than anyone else has. Is he entitled to this income? Is this new distribution D2 unjust? If so, why? [...] If D1 was a just distribution, and people voluntarily moved from it to D2, transferring parts of their shares they were given under D1 (what was it for if not to do something with?), isn't D2 also just?

Question 1: God gave the world to all in common, according to Locke, but private property was still possible (indeed desirable). Why/how is this possible?

Question 2: Paine doesn't think that everything should be owned by all (unlike, say, Marx). How does he argue in favour of limited distribution?

Question 3: What is the 'Wilt Chamberlain Principle'? What would Rawls have to say about it?

Question 4: Is Nozick correct in suggesting that taxing an individual to redistribute wealth is akin to slave labour? Should we abolish the welfare state?

8

Why have women been ignored in the history of political thought?

KEY QUESTIONS

(1) Is the inequality between men and women best understood as the result of natural processes or of power?

(2) What role has education played in defining gender roles in the history of political thought?

(3) Is the language of contemporary democracy a gendered one that favours male forms of reasoning about ethics?

Each year *Time* magazine designates someone as person of the year. The normal winners are presidents, popes, prominent people and the like. Often the award goes to groups of people, Middle Americans in 1969, 'The Protester' in 2011, and the Ebola Fighters in 2014. In 2018 the award was given to 'The Silence Breakers', a group of (mainly) women who had spoken out about sexual harassment by powerful figures in the entertainment industry, despite the damage it might do to their careers, to highlight endemic abuse and to protect more vulnerable members of their community. Their actions led social media users to post the iconic #metoo describing the harassment they had faced in their lives, highlighting how prevalent sexual harassment was in the workplace. Whereas many men were also victims of the powerful at work, this generally female campaign began to highlight what many knew already but were scared to mention, that the workplace was not an equal place. They argued that until everyone could go to work without the fear of harassment, and that failure to submit to sexual advances would not result in the loss of a job, then equality before the law was meaningless.

The internet has provided a venue for people to document the inequalities that still exist between the genders. In August 2017, Noa Jansma began a month-long Instagram project called 'Dear Catcallers' where she took a selfie with any man who shouted at her in the street. This project was designed to highlight the prevalence of catcalling, and to point out that it is not a compliment. Most men were happy to have their photo taken as they saw nothing wrong in their behaviour; as of June 2019, her Instagram page had over 275,000 followers. Elsewhere, The Everyday Sexism project invites readers to submit stories of sexism that has occurred in their lives. It promotes a call-out culture of sexist behaviour that women face on a daily basis. That this is necessary suggests that calls for equality by men and women in the history of political thought have not resulted in an equal society.

This book thus far has, some might say, been very male. The vast majority of the thinkers have been men, and they have been describing states of affairs which, many might argue, are very male. Take, for example, Hobbes's state of nature, whereby all men will be constantly at war with one another over scant resources in a quest for glory; is this not a very male view of the world? The history of political thought seems like a male club depicting things in a male way, favouring men. This chapter looks at thinkers who have sought to challenge political inequalities between men and women.

Chapter overview

We saw in the chapter on democracy the astonishing contradiction put forward by the authors of the US Declaration of Independence, saying that it was self-evident that all men were created equal; and yet a number of the authors of that document, including perhaps its main author Thomas Jefferson, were slave owners. This seems astonishing to us now; not just that people might own slaves, but that they could put forward a political scheme which would totally ignore them whilst claiming that all men were created equal. Of course, when they said 'man', they meant just that – they weren't misguidedly using the phrase men to mean all of humanity; they meant men. Women were completely ignored. And so it is too in most of the history of political thought. Until Mary Wollstonecraft and John Stuart Mill in the eighteenth and nineteenth centuries, respectively, started to discuss the rights of women, they were largely ignored. There were some exceptions. Plato discussed the role of women in society, and Rousseau cannot be accused of ignoring women as he actively discusses their role in society, but he says that men and women are not equal, and nor should they be.

This chapter will commence by providing a brief overview of the position of women in the history of political thought in general, and this will largely be a story of their omission until we hit Rousseau. Rousseau will argue that women have a role to play in society, but that this role is different, and not equal to that of men. Rousseau, crucially, will assert that women cannot be citizens in the republic; whereas men are capable of being governed by reason by following rules that they have made themselves, women will always be governed by emotion, and whereas this makes them useful in certain aspects of society, citizenship is not one of these.

We will then go on to examine Mary Wollstonecraft's manifesto in favour of the rights of women. Written shortly after the French Revolution, and Thomas Paine's *The Rights of Man*, Wollstonecraft will argue that there are few slaves left in society other than those in the household, namely women. She will show that if women seem less intelligent than men, there was nothing in nature about this, but rather women were denied access to education and the improving professions, and as a consequence did not have the same opportunities to expand their minds as men did. Equality could be brought about by allowing women the same rights as men, not just political rights mind you, but also rights to access education and work so that they could be independent. Wollstonecraft's ideas will then be compared to those of John Stuart Mill, the utilitarian philosopher and lover of liberty who has been discussed previously in this book. We will see that Mill also thought that women should have access to education and employment, and a whole package of political rights. Mill thought it patently absurd that one would argue that women be naturally inclined to certain roles in society whilst simultaneously banning them from all others. If women would naturally take on certain roles in society, why would one need to ban them from others? John Stuart Mill also thought that rights for women would be good for men and society in general too, as the intellectual companionship that men would get in their marriages will make both men and women happier.

The chapter will then conclude by bringing this discussion nearer to our contemporary age, by examining the ideas of Iris Marion Young. Wollstonecraft and Mill are what we could broadly define as liberal feminists in that they feel men and women are essentially the same, so long as they have access to education and a similar package of rights. Young, we shall see, argues but there are differences between men and women, especially in terms of their understandings of ethics and morality. Where the problem lies is that the male form of reasoning about ethics and morality in contemporary liberal democracies is universalized and presented as the only way of conceptualizing society.

Women in the history of political thought

Although the vast majority of the history of political thought involves women being simply ignored, at its inception they were addressed and put on an equal footing with men in some matters. Plato, in his *Republic*, where he outlines that people are not equal, and that people governed by reason (the guardians, or philosopher kings) should rule in society, specifically addresses the issue of women in society. Ancient Athens was a deeply male-dominated society, with only men being able to participate in the much heralded direct democracy. Indeed, in the ancient world, where the dead male ancestors were said to reside in the embers of the household fire, to be tended to by the senior male, women when they married were first separated from their own family prior to the ceremony in preparation for joining a new line of ancestry; their identity was to change completely.

It is from here that our current tradition of carrying a bride over the threshold of a house emanates, symbolizing joining a new family (Siedentop, 2015: 12). Plato, hardly a feminist by any stretch of the imagination, was a radical in suggesting that women had a role to play in Greek society.

For Plato, it was possible that some women were capable of becoming guardians, just as some men were capable; his point is not that all women were capable, but this should not surprise us as neither did he think that all men were capable either. Plato is an elitist; but this elitism does not appear to be based upon gender issues. '[T]he natures of men and women are akin', for Plato, so where women of superior intellect exist, they should be picked to 'share the life and duties of Guardian with men', and also they 'should share [the] intellectual and physical training' (Plato, 1987: 235). So there is nothing by nature different between men and women for Plato; there is no reason to not train women for all roles in society if they show the correct aptitude, and it is possible for women to become guardians. In his scheme, where men and women had differing roles in society was the result of his general demand that we sacrifice our own individual wants and desires for the overall common good. A community of wives, for example, was necessary to breed future generations of guardians, and to break down the family unit that might be so damaging when asking the philosopher kings to govern in the interests of all. So Plato does address women, attacks claims that they are by nature different from men, and ascribes a political role to them even if he is expecting this to be the exception rather than the rule.

> Plato argued that there was very little difference in ability between men and women other than in physical strength. As a result, there was no logic in not picking the best women to take on the role of a guardian and training them for that role alongside men.

Hobbes and Locke when talking about the public sphere, however, talk about it in an exclusively male way. Men are capable of deducing the content of natural law, of entering into contracts with fellow men, and of governing and being governed, but there is no discussion of women doing likewise. Women are seen by them as being 'wives and mothers, weak creatures ... whose interests were bound up with those of their family, and who therefore had no need for independent political rights' (Bryson, 2003: 8).

It was here in the growth of early liberal thought that a distinction between the public and private realms began to grow. The public realm was the stuff of politics; it was here that we were citizens and had to act in conjunction with others. The private realm was posited as what we did outside of the public sphere and was no one's business but our own. This was bound up in claims to religious freedom, natural rights, and life, liberty and the pursuit of happiness. The problem for women was that they, working as they often did in the home, became bound up in notions of the private realm. **The private realm was non-political, it was a private matter, not something for political discussion – and consequently women's subservience to men was regarded**

as a non-political matter, not worthy of discussion in the public realm.
And so it was that women became ignored in political discussion. Until, that is,
Jean-Jacques Rousseau addressed the issue of the difference between men and
women head on.

In 1762, Rousseau published his novel *Émile* in which he addressed the subject
of the education of young men in order to break free from the corrupting influences society has had over their natural state. The theme of the corruption of
society to our natural selves has been addressed in previous chapters, but for
our benefit here, we are naturally good (but amoral), and it is society that takes
away our freedom by making us dependent psychologically on one another,
and consequently vain and selfish. *Émile* was Rousseau's attempt to show how
a child could be raised and educated in a manner designed to recapture one's
natural state. It is perhaps the single most important book in the history of pedagogy, as its impact on how education is run has been immense. It does, however,
show us how one of the thinkers most linked to doctrines of rights, equality and
democracy *amongst men* actively defends a lesser position for women. Women
'do wrong to complain of the inequality of man-made laws', Rousseau asserts,
'this inequality is not of man's making ... but of reason' (Rousseau, 1993: 388).

> **Rousseau**
>
> Men and women are different by nature for Rousseau – and their education should be
> tailored to reveal this nature. We should not treat men and women as equals as they are
> not; the role of citizen was exclusively reserved for men.

Men and women are different by nature for Rousseau, and should therefore
have a different education to reveal this nature, and thereafter differing roles
and responsibilities in society. Men and women are not equal, and therefore we
should not treat them as such, he asserts.

> The man should be strong and active; the woman should be weak and passive;
> the one must have both the power and the will; it is enough that the other should
> offer little resistance.
>
> When this principle is admitted, it follows that woman is specially made for
> man's delight. If man in his turn ought to be pleasing in her eyes, the necessity
> is less urgent, his virtue is in his strength, he pleases because he is strong. I grant
> you this is not the law of love, but it is the law of nature, which is older than love
> itself. (Rousseau, 1993: 385)

Men need women in Rousseau's scheme, but that does not mean to say that
they are equal in any way. There are certain roles that women naturally perform
in society much better than men; indeed, *Émile* was written for an audience of
women whom Rousseau thought made much better educators (of both men and
women) than men did. Men and women were naturally different, but despite this

they should also be educated very differently for the different roles that they were expected to fill in society. It is this assertion that Mary Wollstonecraft, perhaps the first feminist author in the canon of the history of political thought, tackles in her work that we will now go on to examine.

Activity 1. Attempt the tasks below

(1) Outline Rousseau's argument for the natural differences and inequality between men and women.

(2) What is meant by the public/private distinction? Why could it be seen as presenting a problem for women in liberal thought?

Mary Wollstonecraft

In writing *A Vindication of the Rights of Woman*, Mary Wollstonecraft is trying to show how women have been ignored by people calling for the rights of man, and how women are entitled to have rights just as much as men. *A Vindication of the Rights of Woman* was published in 1792, a year after Thomas Paine's *Rights*

Mary Wollstonecraft

Mary Wollstonecraft was born in London in 1759. After leaving home she became a lady's companion in Bath, before returning home to care for her dying mother.

She began writing novels and political tracts before moving to Paris, which was in the midst of the aftermath of the French Revolution. Indeed she witnessed Louis XIV being taken to trial, and despite her being a staunch supporter of the revolution, she was said to be moved by the dignity that he exhibited. It was in France that she wrote A *Vindication of the Rights of Woman* in an effort to apply the principles of the revolution to the position of women in society.

Upon returning to London, she met and fell in love with William Godwin, the political philosopher and founding father of anarchism. Whilst giving birth to their daughter (her second child) she fell ill and died a few days later. She was only 38. That daughter was Mary Wollstonecraft, who would later become Mary Shelley who wrote the novel *Frankenstein*.

of Man and just after the French and American revolutions. Those revolutions had been based on the Enlightenment principles that **men** were governed by reason, and using that reason they could determine certain laws about politics, specifically that all men were equal and in possession of inalienable rights. The only institutions that were permissible, according to this thinking, were those that could be justified by reason; political institutions based upon traditional history, and perhaps even religion, were no longer valid. Consequently, new political systems based upon rights, written constitutions and democratic thinking were being instituted in places such as America and France, and the monarchies and aristocracies that had previously dominated society were being removed.

Wollstonecraft certainly fits into this way of thinking about the world – she is an Enlightenment thinker; but she also strongly criticizes this body of thought for the fact that it largely ignored women. **If men should have rights, which she thinks that they should, why shouldn't women also have rights?** Women have, she asserts, been largely ignored by political thinkers, or when they are addressed, they have been patronized by men. Men use condescending 'pretty feminine phrases' to 'soften our slavish dependence' when they do address women, referring to their grace, charm, looks and similar qualities, when Wollstonecraft thinks that they should be praised for the same qualities that men are given credit: character, reason, judgement and the like (Wollstonecraft, 1995: 76). As long as women are judged by a set of feminine characteristics, and not those prized by the social and political world, they will never be able to achieve equality. Broadly speaking, Wollstonecraft's argument is that men and women are easily capable of equality, but that through education and society's attitude towards them, women become inferior. **They are not allowed to be educated, take improving work, and are only prized for charm and looks, and then told they are insufficiently intelligent for the role of a full citizen**. There is nothing in nature about the role women play in society; it is a creation of society. Wollstonecraft begins *A Vindication of the Rights of Woman* by addressing women about her message:

> Wollstonecraft thought it unjust that women were forced to become mothers and wives due to lack of access to education and employment. If one did choose to become this by free will, then this was your role in society.

> My own sex, I hope they will excuse me, if I treat them like rational creatures, instead of flattering their *fascinating* graces, and viewing them as if they were in a perpetual childhood, unable stand alone. I earnestly wish to point out in what true dignity human happiness consists – I wish to persuade women to endeavour to acquire strength, both of mind and body, and to convince them that the soft phrases, susceptibility of heart, delicacy of sentiment, and refinement of taste, are almost synonymous with epithets of weakness, and that those beings who are only the objects of pity and that kind of love, which has been termed its sister, will soon become objects of contempt. (Wollstonecraft, 1995: 76)

Education is the key to this for Wollstonecraft, as education at its best will 'enable the individual to attain such habits of virtue as will render [them] independent' (Wollstonecraft, 1995: 89–90). Young men and young women, however, received very different types of education, with the former achieving independence, and the latter degraded by an incoherent curriculum that focused on the supposed feminine graces and their use to men. Indeed, Wollstonecraft does not think that men have accidentally fallen into this way of thinking, but rather they deliberately educate women in this way of thinking so that they can keep them in a position of slavishness:

> Strengthen the female mind by enlarging it, and there will be an end to blind obedience; but, as blind obedience is ever sought for by power, tyrants and sensualists are in the right when they endeavour to keep women in the dark, because the former only want slaves, and the latter a play-thing. (Wollstonecraft, 1995: 93)

So women are hampered in their ability to become full and rounded citizens by (a) their education, which is inferior to that of men, and (b) society that prizes different attributes in women than it does in men. This then leaves women unable to choose their direction in life; they cannot have a meaningful career of their own as they are denied the education to do so, so the only role that they can perform is that of wife, mother and homemaker. This is forced upon them, and as a consequence they do these things badly. This is perhaps where Wollstonecraft and later feminists depart. Wollstonecraft appears to say that the key problem is that women are forced into a particular role rather than being able to choose it for themselves. If they did then choose it, then that is fine. But Bryson points out that Wollstonecraft 'did not expect that education and freedom of choice would lead most women to reject their traditional role' and that therefore she does not challenge 'the male monopoly of formal political and legal power' (Bryson, 2003: 18). Also, Wollstonecraft's account here fails to challenge the notion, accepted by most contemporary societies, that one does not have to choose between being a partner and/or motherhood and a career, but one should be entitled to do both just as men are not expected to have to choose between being a father and/or partner and a career.

Activity 2. Attempt the tasks below:

(1) Why is the education of women so important to Wollstonecraft?

(2) What do you think of the fact that she did not believe you could be a wife/mother and have a career?

John Stuart Mill

John Stuart Mill's *The Subjection of Women* was published in 1869, some 10 years after the death of Harriet Taylor, Mill's wife, to whom he attributes a number of the key ideas within the work. Two years previously, in 1867, Mill, a Member of Parliament, had presented a motion that in the Representation of the People Bill, a bill that extended the franchise to working-class men, the word 'man' should be replaced with 'woman' in order to give women the vote in Britain for the first time. It lost by 123 votes, and women would not get the vote in Britain for another half a century.

Women and slavery

Mill argued that just like with slavery, the powerful had turned their physical power over women into legal obligation, and then attempted to enslave their minds to make them feel less worthy than men. At the heart of it all was power still.

John Stuart Mill commences *The Subjection of Women* by comparing the position of women in society to that of slavery. Law followed force for Mill in slavery, whereby people physically coerced into something later became legally coerced as well, as slave owners used law as another form of dominance. So slavery 'from being a mere affair of force between the master and the slave, became regularized ... [and] guaranteed by their collective strength the private possessions of each, including his slaves' (Mill, 1970: 7). Likewise, women became dominated by men due to the latter's physical strength, and then that dominance was codified in laws. So, far from men and women's legal and political differences being based upon nature, or justice, it 'has no other source than the law of the strongest' (Mill, 1970: 7). Slavery was abhorred by all, Mill suggests, and yet we have no problem with the slavery of the female sex by the male sex. Mill is not attempting to denigrate slavery here; he accepts that the position of a middle-class woman is better than that of a slave. 'I am far from pretending', he asserts, 'that wives are in general no better treated than slaves; but no slave is a slave to the same lengths, and in so full a sense of the word, as a wife is' (Mill, 1970: 32). It is not the treatment of slaves to which Mill is referring, but rather the position of powerlessness of slavery.

As if it was not enough to turn brute force into legal obligation, Mill then suggests that men have enslaved the minds of women by making them think that their role in society is to be subservient to others:

> All women are brought up from the very earliest years in the belief that their ideal of character is the very opposite to that of men; not self-will, and government by self-control, but submission, and yielding to the control of others. All moralities

tell them that it is the duty of women, and all the current sentimentalities that it is their nature, to live for others; to make complete abnegation of themselves, and to have no life but in their affections. (Mill, 1970: 16)

It is impossible to tell if there are any natural differences between men and women for Mill, as there are so many artificial societal differences, that to formulate a scientific experiment to determine anything in nature would be impossible. So here Mill is making a strong case against Rousseau; how can one possibly tell if there are any natural differences when the sexes have so many different societal and legal differences? 'Most men', he argues, 'have not had the opportunity of studying this way more than a single case', by which he means that many men unscientifically imagine all women to be like his wife (Mill, 1970: 25). Of course, Mill was not interested in scientifically studying the differences between men and women; he did not think that there were any. What he was interested in doing was showing that to claim that things exist as they do due to nature is a scientific claim, and a particular method is necessary to establish this, a method that was not used, nor could it be used. Consequently, the claim that women should be morally and legally subservient to men due to natural differences is just another repackaging of turning physical force into an obligation.

Mill also highlights the absurdity of rules that ban women from certain education, or professions, based upon the notion that they would naturally not want to do that work or that they naturally could not. 'What women by nature cannot do, it is quite superfluous to forbid them from doing' (Mill, 1970: 27). If you are reading this for the purposes of a university degree, or preparing for exams that you hope might allow you to study at a university, have you ever reflected on the award that you will be getting, and why it is called a bachelor's degree? It is called this for the simple reason that in the past in order to be a member of the university community, you needed to be an unmarried man. If you married, you had to leave the community; if you were a woman, you were never allowed to join in the first place. Suppose it was promoted in the contemporary world, that women were not allowed to read for an undergraduate degree upon the basis that they could not do it, or they naturally would not choose to do it. Aside from issues about fairness and equality, Mill would argue that this is an absurd argument. If women could not achieve the level of intelligence to enter a university, then they would not pass their entrance exams; if they would naturally not want to do it then the issue is a moot one as no one would apply in the first place. Why then ban women from entering a university if nature would prevent them from doing so? Likewise, why ban women from certain professions if nature would call them to others? If nature

> Mill thought that it was an absurd argument to say that women were banned from certain occupations or positions of responsibility because it was against their nature. If they were truly against women's natures, they simply would not do those things, so there was no need to ban them.

would call women (or indeed any other classification of people) to certain jobs, it makes no sense to ban them from others as nature will simply take its course. Mill calls this argument out, suggesting that nature has nothing to do with it; it is pure protectionism, with mankind wanting to protect certain societal goods for themselves.

For Mill, the only way out of this situation was to give women full access to education, the same political and social rights as men, and to ensure that women had the same rights in marriage as men (i.e. an independent legal status, ability to keep property, access to divorce). Two similarities with Wollstonecraft persist that would be challenged by later feminist authors. The first is that Mill thinks it is wrong that a woman is forced into marriage by the inability to do anything else; but if she, having had opportunities to do other things, chose that then that is her role. Again, like Wollstonecraft, the notion that a woman could be married, have children, and have a career is not discussed. The second is that Mill places a lot of faith in the law. His argument is that by nature there is probably very little difference between men and women, and it is just that men have codified their brute force into law, and denied women access to things such as education and the professions. His solution, sensibly enough it would seem, is to recognize this, and alter the laws where there is injustice. Many contemporary feminists would argue that laws have (generally) been changed, and yet women still earn less than men, there are fewer women than men in public life, and there are much fewer leaders of public and private bodies who are women. If all that is needed is to change unjust laws, and those laws have been, for the most part, changed, why are men and women still unequal. Perhaps something more than just laws are at play? It is this argument that Iris Marion Young will put forward.

Activity 3. Attempt the questions below:

(1) Why does Mill say that the condition of women when he was writing is like slavery? Do you agree?

(2) Outline Mill's argument that it makes no logical sense to ban women from doing roles that they are naturally not inclined to do.

Iris Marion Young

For Iris Marion Young, it is a mistake firstly to see men and women as being essentially the same, and secondly to think that merely changing unjust laws will end the inequalities between men and women in contemporary society. Young has spent her career writing on the politics of difference, the key idea of this being that modern liberal democracies are based on moral and ethical reasoning that banishes the notion of difference, and attempts to reduce discussions to one format. This format, impartiality reasoning, although it purports to be impartial (by its nature), is actually partial in favour of men and against those different from the dominant ethnic or cultural groups in society.

> Impartial reason aims to adopt a point of view outside concrete situations or actions, a transcendental 'view from nowhere' that carries the perspective, attributes, character, and interests of no particular subject or set of subjects. (Young, 1990: 100)

We see this impartiality reasoning across the history of political thought, but more recently in Rawls's 'original position' and 'veil of ignorance' in his *A Theory of Justice*, and in Habermas's 'ideal speech situation'. They are attempts to take ethical, moral and political discussions out of everyday life and turn them into logical, philosophical arguments; to take away the particularities of any given situation, and to unify them into one philosophical structure; to attempt to find a big theory to explain any given ethical, moral or political situation.

For Young it is insufficient to change laws in order to bring about equality between men and women. That would only work if the democratic system was neutral. Instead, the language of politics pretends to be impartial, but it actually favours men and those in the dominant culture.

For Young, the problem with this is that it favours male ethical reasoning over female ways of thinking. And this is the big departure from the thinking about women in society that we discussed above, as for Young, men and women are not the same; they think about ethics and politics differently. When discussing moral issues, men attempt to abstract situations out of the contexts in which they are placed, and to discuss them in that context. Women, by contrast, are far more likely to attempt to contextualize situations, and think of specific examples of that situation that they have encountered. Men therefore tend to favour more abstract forms of justice such as rights and impartial rule, whereas women are more likely to favour more contextualized forms of justice such as nurture, responsibility and care.

The problem here, for Young, is not in and of itself that men and women feel differently about the nature of justice, but rather that the male form of reasoning is universalized to be the only legitimate form of reasoning about ethics, morality and politics. Men have created a form of democratic discussion that on the one hand purports to be impartial, yet on the other denies a voice to women, and also those who differ from the majority culture in any given society. Consequently, democratic culture in contemporary liberal democracies uses a language of politics that is not neutral between the genders. It is for this reason that there are still inequalities between men and women; changing the laws where there are injustices, and focusing on inequalities in education between men and women, will not in and of itself decrease the inequalities between men and women while we continue to use a language of politics that inevitably favours men. Likewise, arguing that men and women are essentially the same in an attempt to reduce the inequalities between them is problematic as differences do exist. Young is, of course, not making a similar kind of argument about essential differences between the genders that Rousseau was doing earlier on in this chapter; she is referring to a completely different type of difference, but imagining that men and women are exactly the same will end up enforcing patriarchal rule.

Activity 4. Attempt the tasks below:

(1) Outline Young's argument that liberal democracies are based upon male forms of reasoning on ethical and political issues.

(2) Do you think men and women think differently on ethical and political issues? Explain your answer.

Conclusion

This chapter has illustrated a number of different responses in the history of political thought to the differences between men and women. Although perhaps the founding father of political philosophy, Plato, did not see any essential natural differences between men and women, we noted that thinkers such as Hobbes and Locke relegated discussions of women to the private (therefore not political) realm, or they argued, like Rousseau, that men and women were by nature different to one another, and therefore should not be treated equally.

The challenge to Rousseau's way of thinking came first from Wollstonecraft, and then from Mill. Both argued that it was very hard to see any natural differences between men and women, but they did notice numerous social disadvantages, such as access to education and employment, that meant that women could not compete with men. Both saw the dominance of men over women as being unjustified and based upon power rather than nature, arguing that women should have better access to education, and in Mill's case a raft of political and social rights. Changing unjust laws and providing for more equal education was, for Wollstonecraft and Mill's liberal way of thinking on this issue, the way in which we would bring about fairness and equality between the sexes.

Young provides a dissenting voice to this way of thinking about equality between men and women. Changing laws will not in and of itself end gender inequalities as the entire language of politics is not neutral between the genders. In order to bring about equality, we must consider the way in which our public discourse takes place and include more female voices therein.

Works cited

Bryson, V. (2003) *Feminist Political Theory: An Introduction*. Basingstoke: Palgrave Macmillan.

Mill, J.S. (1970) *The Subjection of Women*. Cambridge, MA: MIT Press.

Plato (1987) *The Republic*. London: Penguin.

Rousseau, J.J. (1993) *Émile*. London: Everyman.

Siedentop, L. (2015) *Inventing the Individual: The Origins of Western Liberalism*. London: Allen Lane.

Wollstonecraft, M. (1995) *A Vindication of the Rights of Men*, and *A Vindication of the Rights of Woman*. Cambridge: Cambridge University Press.

Young, I.M. (1990) *Justice and the Politics of Difference*. Princeton, NJ: Princeton University Press.

Text reading activities

From *A Vindication of the Rights of Woman*, in Wollstonecraft, M. (1995) *A Vindication of the Rights of Men*, and *A Vindication of the Rights of Woman*. Cambridge: Cambridge University Press, p. 87.

To account for, and excuse the tyranny of man, many ingenious arguments have been brought forward to prove, that the two sexes, in the acquirement of virtue, ought to aim at attaining a very different character: or, to speak explicitly, women are not allowed to have sufficient strength of mind to acquire what really deserves the name of virtue. Yet it should seem, allowing them to have souls, that there is but one way appointed by Providence to lead *mankind* to either virtue or happiness.

If then women are not a swarm of ephemeron triflers, why should they be kept in ignorance under the specious name of innocence? Men complain, and with reason, of the follies and caprices of our sex, when they do not keenly satirize our headstrong passions and grovelling vices. Behold, I should answer, the natural effect of ignorance! The mind will ever be unstable that has only prejudices to rest on, and the current will run with destructive fury when there are no barriers to break its force. Women are told from their infancy, and taught by the example of their mothers, that a little knowledge of human weakness, justly termed cunning, softness of temper, *outward obedience*, and a scrupulous attention to a puerile kind of propriety, will obtain for them the protection of man; and should they be beautiful, every thing else is needless, for, at least, twenty years of their lives.

From *The Subjection of Women*, by J.S. Mill, available at http://www.digitalhistory.uh.edu/disp_textbook.cfm?smtid=3&psid=3600

The generality of a practice is in some cases a strong presumption that it is, or at all events once was, conducive to laudable ends. This is the case, when the practice was first adopted, or afterwards kept up, as a means to such ends, and was grounded on experience of the mode in which they could be most effectually attained. If the authority of men over women, when first established, had been the result of a conscientious comparison between different modes of constituting the government of society; if, after trying various other modes of social organization – the government of women over men, equality between the two, and such mixed and divided modes of government as might be invented – it had been decided, on the testimony of experience, that the mode in which women are wholly under the rule of men, having no share at all in public concerns, and each in private being under the legal obligation of obedience to the man with whom she has associated her destiny, was the arrangement most conducive to the happiness and well-being of both; its general adoption might then be fairly thought to be some evidence that, at the time when it was adopted, it was the best: though even then the considerations which recommended it may, like so many other primeval social facts of the greatest importance, have subsequently, in the course of ages, ceased to exist. But the state of the case is in every respect the reverse of this. In the first place, the opinion in favour of the present system, which entirely subordinates the weaker sex to the stronger, rests upon theory only; for there never has been trial made of any other: so that experience, in the sense in which it is vulgarly opposed to theory, cannot be pretended to have pronounced any verdict. And in the second place, the adoption of this system of inequality never was the result of deliberation, or forethought, or any social ideas, or any notion whatever of what conduced to the benefit of humanity or the good order of society. It arose simply from the fact that from the very earliest twilight of human society, every woman owing to the value attached to her by men, combined with her inferiority in muscular strength was found in a state of bondage to some man. Laws and systems of polity always begin by recognizing the relations they find already existing between individuals. They convert what was a mere physical fact into a legal right, give it the sanction of society, and principally aim at the substitution of public and organized means of asserting and protecting these rights, instead of the irregular and lawless conflict of physical strength. Those who had already been compelled to obedience became in this manner legally bound to it. Slavery, from being a mere affair of force between the master and the slave, became regularized and a matter of compact among the masters, who, binding themselves to one another for common protection, guaranteed by their collective strength the private possessions of each, including his slaves. In early times, the great majority of the male sex were slaves, as well as the whole of the female. And many ages elapsed, some of them ages of high cultivation, before any thinker was bold enough to question the rightfulness, and the absolute social necessity, either of the one slavery or of the other. By degrees such thinkers did arise; and (the general progress of society assisting) the slavery of the male sex has, in all the countries of Christian Europe at least (though, in one of them, only within the last few years) been at length abolished, and that of the female sex has been gradually changed into a milder form of dependence. But this dependence, as it exists at present, is not an original institution, taking a fresh start from considerations of justice and social expediency – it is the primitive state of slavery lasting on, through successive mitigations and modifications occasioned by the same causes which have softened the general manners, and brought all human relations more under the control of justice and the influence of humanity. It has not lost the taint of its brutal origin. No presumption in its favour, therefore, can be drawn from the fact of its existence. The only such presumption which it could be supposed to have, must be grounded on its having lasted till now, when so many other things which came down from the same odious source have been done away with. And this, indeed, is what makes it strange to ordinary ears, to hear it asserted that the inequality of rights between men and women has no other source than the law of the strongest.

Question 1: Mill and Wollstonecraft argue for equality between the sexes. Why do they think inequality is rife?

Question 2: How does Mill link the situation of women to that of slavery? Is he right to do so?

9

When is revolution against government justified?

KEY QUESTIONS

(1) Does the social contract imply the right of revolution, or does breaking it plunge you back into the state of nature?

(2) Should revolution be based upon principles deduced from reason, or is history and tradition a better guide for political action?

(3) Can a communist society be achieved by electing a socialist government, or is a revolution necessary to overthrow the state?

At 8 a.m. on 17 December 2011, 26-year-old Mohamed Bouazizi began his working day selling fruit from a cart beside the road in Sidi Bouzid in Tunisia, fruit he had got into debt to purchase. During the morning he was approached by an official demanding to see a permit, and when he did not produce one, he had his produce and scales confiscated meaning his only source of income was removed. He went to the Governor's offices demanding that his produce and scales be returned, but no one would see him. At 11.30 he returned to the Governor's offices, doused himself with petrol, shouted 'how do you expect me to make a living' before setting himself on fire. He died two weeks later in hospital. Bouazizi's self-immolation served as a catalyst in the Tunisian Revolution, as the protests that followed led the authoritarian President Ben Ali to flee Tunisia ending his 24-year authoritarian reign. Similar protests followed around the Arab world in what has become known as the Arab Spring.

Change might come from the ballot box, but quite frequently in the history of humanity it has come from the overthrow, often violent, of the government. Ideology plays a key role in this. In the twentieth century, Marxism led to revolutions in Russia, China and Cuba, amongst others, and also near the end of the century revolutions occurred against many communist regimes in the name of freedom.

But on what grounds can we overthrow the government? When Charles I of England was put on trial during the English Civil War, which had removed him from his throne, he asked his prosecutors on what grounds they were prosecuting him, asserting that he was still the rightful king. His rule was ordained by God and the laws of England, none of which had provision for a revolution. Charles I's point here is about legitimacy, and it is an argument that has been used by tyrants put on trial throughout the ages; courts uphold the laws of the land, and they do not (generally) allow for revolution. At what point does a particular political principle (such as freedom, equality and/or democracy) trump the law of the land.

Of course, Marxists would argue that asking what the justifications could be for revolution is asking the wrong question; and that under capitalism, a revolution is the only way to bring about change. The state is part of the apparatus of bourgeois rule, so they may argue, and it is therefore incapable of bring about real justice. Revolution on this account is not just justifiable, but instead a necessary step to bring about change.

Chapter overview

Do citizens have the right to overthrow the state? If so, what principles should guide this revolution, and what kind of action by the state is serious enough to precipitate this kind of action? This chapter is designed to allow us to explore a number of responses in the history of political thought to questions like these, and to examine a thinker who is highly sceptical about the right to revolution.

We will begin this chapter with a sceptic about the right to revolution, namely Edmund Burke, who argues that change in society should never be based upon abstract principles such as the rights of man. If we do this, Burke thinks, we might well end up losing the rights and liberties that we already possess. Instead, any change that occurs in society should always be based upon ideas and traditions that already exist in our society. If one is denied liberties that people have enjoyed in your state for some time, then perhaps one does have a right to overthrow government; but this should always be for the restoration of traditions lost as opposed to being built on novel theorizing. Burke will be contrasted with Thomas Paine, who argues that if a government infringes upon your rights, you can overthrow it, and that the only permissible political institutions in any society are those that are in line with reason.

Finally, this chapter will examine the role revolution, and class revolution in particular, plays in the political thought of Karl Marx. It will show how Marx argues that the only way to change a capitalist society to a communist one is through revolution. Marx will argue that in a capitalist society the state will inevitably act in the interests of the bourgeoisie, and that consequently electing a socialist government to make reforms will never achieve a fair society. Indeed,

Marx will also show how capitalism by its class oppression will create the revolutionary working class that will bring about this revolution.

Burke vs Paine

Edmund Burke's *Reflection on the Revolution in France* gives a case against the French Revolution, and is widely regarded as the classic defence of a conservative political disposition. But the following will outline that Burke is not necessarily against revolution, and he certainly wasn't against change, but rather he was against the type of revolution that had occurred in France. Indeed, elsewhere Burke outlines his support of the American revolutionaries against the British. The difference between these events will help us to understand the circumstances under which Burke sees a revolution against the government as justified, and what type of revolution is allowable.

Burke's chief criticism was of the rationalist Enlightenment thinking that was growing in Europe at the time he was writing. Enlightenment thinkers argued (broadly speaking) that the only political or moral institutions that should exist were those that attuned to reason. Political institutions that rested their authority on history and/or religion were considered relics of the past that should be removed and overthrown. Therefore, monarchies, such as those in France, that argued that they were put in place by, and answerable only to, God should be removed and replaced by institutions that rested their authority on the will of the people and the social contract. The French revolutionaries called for the new system of government to be based on Robespierre's principles of *liberté, égalité, fraternité* (liberty, equality and brotherhood).

Burke was opposed to revolutions based on abstract principles that did not exist in a particular society at that given time. The individual who participated in abstracted reflections on politics and society ignored the stock of wisdom that had accrued in a given society at any one time. As Burke said:

> We are afraid to put men to live and trade each on his own private stock of reason; because we suspect that this stock in each man is small, and that the individuals would do better to avail themselves of the general bank and capital of nations and of ages. (Burke, 1986: 183)

Abstract principles such as liberty, equality, fraternity, and for that matter human rights, were abstract principles that ignored the prejudices of individual societies. Prejudice, for Burke, means something different from how we would use it today. Rather than meaning that we have some preconceived notion about a person or group of people, prejudice for Burke was more about the ways of thinking about politics contained within a society, ways of thinking about politics that have been shaped by tradition and experience as opposed to abstract thinking of principles. Politics should be about preserving these ancient ways of thinking, and using them as guides for our action when making necessary

Change in society should be based on principles that are already present in that society rather than abstract principles. Abstract principles are dogmatic, whereas experience based upon history is pragmatic.

change, rather than implementing any top-down plan based on reason. We should aim to preserve the best of the past for future generations rather than destroy the old and replace it with the new for the sake of it. Basing decision making in politics on abstract principles is a dogmatic approach, whereas basing it on prejudice and experience is pragmatic.

Burke is not a proponent of keeping the past for the sake of it and is not against change, but rather when change is necessary it should be informed by existing prejudices that exist in a particular society. Change should be gradual, incremental, and recognize society as being like a living organism that gradually grows and changes over time. Not only does Burke think that this is sensible, he also thinks it is vital for the success of a particular change. One of the chief problems with the French Revolution, Burke thought, is that by basing the overthrow of an ancient regime on the abstract notion of liberty, one is likely to destroy existing notions of liberty that existed in France at the time, and in so doing end up with less liberty than previously existed. So basing revolutions on abstract principles was self-defeating; it would never work if it did not take into consideration existing ideas and practices that existed in a given society.

Burke supported the revolutionaries in America, or perhaps more accurately he understood why they were driven to take the actions that they did. One of the oldest constitutional principles in the United Kingdom, for Burke, was no taxation without representation; if you were having money taken off you by way of taxes, you should be able to have a system of representation in place to oversee how those taxes were spent. The American colonies were being taxed by the British Crown, but were not allowed to elect representatives to oversee expenditure; therefore, they were being denied their rights. This right was not an abstract right deduced from reason, it was a right that had existed in UK law and custom for some time, and therefore the American colonies could expect this to be honoured.

French versus American revolution

Whereas Burke condemned the French Revolution, he supported the American Revolution. The former was based on the abstract principles of *liberté, égalité, fraternité* that were not present in French society, and would threaten existing liberties. The latter was based on the historical principle of no taxation without representation, which had been denied the American colonists. Burke was not anti-change; he was against changed based on abstract principles.

Here we see a distinction between the revolutions in the two countries, which helps us to understand Burke's thinking on the nature of a just and unjust revolution. Today, we think of a revolution as the tearing down of an old regime, and replacing it with a new one based on a new set of principles. But imagine you laid a bike on its side and put a piece of tape on the wheel and then gave the wheel a full revolution (that is to say one turn): the piece of tape would end up in precisely the same place as it was before. And this is the type of revolution Burke supported; a revolution that resulted in things being as they were before. The American Revolution was not, for Burke, based on new abstract principles: it was based on the restoration of existing rights and privileges that they had been denied. It aimed to return things to how they had been prior to novelty and innovation removing said rights.

So, for Burke, revolution was allowable, or perhaps understandable, if a government removed rights and privileges from people who had enjoyed them before. It was not allowable if it was based on abstract principles; indeed, not only was it not allowable, it was also futile, as you would nearly always end up in a worse position than you were before.

Activity 1. Attempt the following questions:

(1) Outline why Burke opposed the French Revolution, but supported the American Revolution.

(2) Do you feel Burke is being contradictory here?

Paine on rights

Paine takes Locke's argument that we all have areas of our life over which government has no right to act, and turns this into a notion of rights. If government breaks these rights, then we can legitimately overthrow it and replace it with another.

Thomas Paine's *Rights of Man* was written in 1791 in direct response to Burke's *Reflections on the Revolution in France*, and rather than condemning the events in France, he supported them. Paine was Lockean in the sense that he thought government could be removed by the people if it did certain things which it had no right to do. Locke, however, put this in a negative fashion; that is that there were certain areas of life (a man's life, liberty, property or religion) that government had no right to infringe upon. Paine put this in a positive fashion: that men had rights, government had a duty to uphold those rights, and if it did not, revolution was justified. Paine thought we had reason and we could use this reason to deduce fair and reasonable laws. Only those political and social institutions that could stand up to reasoned scrutiny should be permitted.

> Paine rejects Burke's argument that history and tradition can limit our political demands in the present, arguing that every generation must be able to act for itself and cannot be bound by the decisions of the past.

Compare this last viewpoint to those of Burke. Paine thinks that mankind has rights and these are discoverable by reason, and as a consequence all people in all countries should have them. Burke, on the other hand, thinks that our local prejudices provide us with the best guide to the rights and privileges we should have. We are entitled to those rights and privileges that have been provided over time in our society; certainly we can revolt to the restoration of those rights should they be removed (such as the right to a vote if one is taxed), but if a certain right has not been granted over time, then we do not have it. And any revolution is not to set up a new society based on new principles, but rather a society based on those old principles that had been replaced by novelty. Therefore, it follows from this that **Paine looks to reason** to justify any given set of political arrangements, whereas **Burke thinks that history and tradition** provide political legitimacy. Paine thinks that all men have a certain set of rights, whereas Burke thinks that one's rights might vary depending on where you live.

Paine thinks it is patently absurd to think of people and ideas from the past being able to dictate what we in the present want to do with government. 'Every age and generation', he suggests, 'must be free to act for itself' and that 'there can never exist a parliament, or any description of men ... possessed of the power of binding and controlling posterity' (Paine, 1985: 41). He also suggests that if, as Burke does, one cannot tax without consent, then it is contradictory to also suggest that people in the past can remove from us our ability to act politically without our consent. History must not constrain us from our ability to act now.

> A greater absurdity cannot present itself to the understanding of man, than what Mr Burke offers to his readers. He tells them, and he tells the world to come, that a certain body of men, who existed a hundred years ago, made a law; and that there does not now exist in the nation, nor ever will, nor ever can, a power to alter it. Under how many subtleties, or absurdities, has the divine right to govern been imposed on the credulity of mankind! (Paine, 1985: 43)

For Paine, man has natural rights, some of which he keeps, some of which 'he throws into the common stock as a member of society' (Paine, 1985: 68). The ones that he transfers are those which he has no power to execute by himself. So, one has the right to follow the religion of one's choosing and this can be executed by study, contemplation and joining an appropriate congregation of fellow believers; so it is easy to execute and is kept to oneself. Being able to protect oneself is less easy to execute. Certainly if I am attacked on the street, I have a right to defend myself, but a better way to defend myself would be to allow the state to employ police officers to defend me, and institute courts and state-sanctioned punishments to those who harm fellow citizens. So perhaps the right to punish those who break other people's rights is one that is better thrown into the common stock to be better able to institute it. Paine makes a distinction here between natural rights, that all people have, such as the right to religion or the right to not be hurt by another person, and civil rights, which are those provided for by the community, such as the right to fair treatment from the police and the law courts, for example. Civil rights are different from natural rights as they do not exist by nature, but 'every civil right grows out of a natural right; or ... is a natural right exchanged' (Paine, 1985: 69).

So, government is created for the convenience of rights-holding individuals who either retain their natural rights after the creation of government, or they allow them to be executed better by transferring them into the common stock and turned into civil rights. It is the purpose of government to enforce these various rights, and if they do not, they are not fulfilling their purpose and can therefore be removed and replaced by people who will.

> For Paine government is formed by individuals who are possessors of rights, who pool those rights which they have that they are unable to execute by themselves in order to better exercise their rights. If this ceases to happen, then they can remove the government.

Activity 2. Attempt the tasks below.

(1) Outline any similarities **and** differences you can see between Paine and Locke.

Similarities	Differences

(2) To what extent do you agree that each generation is not bound by the decisions of the past?

Capitalism

Before we dive into the thought of Karl Marx and his critique of the capitalist system, it is worth outlining what capitalism means. We have mentioned John

Locke and the notion of pre-political rights to property above, which is certainly an early capitalist idea, and we have outlined Nozick's defence of a night-watchman state. But we haven't really provided a working definition of capitalism, which is necessary if we are to understand Marx's critique of it. Market capitalism is seen as developing in the seventeenth and eighteenth centuries and really coming into force in the Industrial Revolution with notions of private property, individual rights and freedom. Workers were no longer tied to their feudal master, they were able to change employers, and gradually economies in Europe and America moved away from being agricultural in nature and became industrialized. Also wealth and power was taken from the landowning aristocrats by the modern industrialists who owned factories. The wealthiest people in the world now tend not to have inherited their wealth or be massive landowners; they have their wealth through the ownership of companies.

Market capitalism holds that economies are more efficient if property and businesses are privately owned, and the state does not interfere in the market, so the market is free. This, market capitalism posits, will lead to better outcomes for all as it is more efficient to allow markets to determine the provision of services and goods rather than the state. Take this example: I collect cufflinks and have over 50 pairs, but I have no necklaces as I don't like them. Other people might have a number of necklaces but no cufflinks. There is no optimal or fair number of either of these things, as it depends entirely on one's tastes, but market economies allow me to buy cufflinks to my heart's content, whereas it also allows other people to buy necklaces. The efficiency in the market lays in its responsiveness to what people want.

Adam Smith in his *Wealth of Nations* outlined this efficiency especially with regard to the division of labour. Economies work best when one person is a baker, another a dairy farmer, another a butcher and so on. It is because of each of these people's self-interest and desire for profit that we get our daily bread, milk and meat, rather than their altruism. In 2015, Andy George from Minneapolis attempted to make a chicken sandwich from scratch, meaning that he grew the grain to make flour, raised a chicken and so on; he estimated that the overall cost of that sandwich was $1,500. Capitalism and the division of labour is more efficient as it provides economies of scale by people concentrating on their specialisms – a chicken sandwich in the shop is cheaper because people do not need to grow grain, raise chickens, etc., to feed themselves.

This is a rough and ready, and by no means comprehensive, overview of what capitalism is; but the chief points are that it favours free markets (i.e. the government not interfering in the running of the economy), the division of labour, and feels that markets are better placed to respond to what people actually want. The desire for profit is not only good for the individual business owner, capitalism would argue, it is also good for society as a whole as it brings us goods and services that we need more efficiently than other economic systems. The invisible hand of the market (as Adam Smith calls it) will provide what you want in a better manner than the state.

Karl Marx

For Karl Marx, revolution was not only justified against the capitalist class, it was the only way one could change society. But it was not simply a revolt against the government that Marx called for; it was an overthrow of the entire bourgeois system and its replacement with a communist society that he championed. The proletariat, Marx's phrase for the working classes, must rise up against their capitalist oppressors and overthrow the state.

Marx and his collaborator Engels begin *The Communist Manifesto* with the famous phrase that the 'history of all hitherto existing society is the history of class struggle' (1985: 79). For Marx, a different class system develops according to the mode of production (the way in which goods are produced) that exists in society at any one given historical period. The dominant class in any mode of production is the one that owns the means of production (factories, mills and the technologies that drive production). The nature of this class structure changes over time, but the class that owns the means of production dominates society in three key ways.

Firstly, the dominant class, as they own the means of production, control you in the workplace. They get you to labour on their behalf, filling your time with tasks they want doing, and can alter the pay and conditions that come with this work.

Secondly, they dominate you via the state, as the state will always act in the interests of the dominant class in society; they will enact laws and legislation to ensure that their dominance is ensured. The state is not neutral between classes and interests, for Marx; it will always act in the long-term interests of the dominant class in society. It is for this reason that Marx was so sceptical about bourgeois democracy, as it implies that by electing this party or that party to government, you can change society. Any government that you elect in a class-riddled society will always act in the interests of the dominant class as no government can counteract the bias of the state. It is for this reason that Marx calls the state a tool of class oppression; that is its function is to aid the dominant class to rule over the others.

> The class that owns the means of production is always dominant in society; they dominate you in the workplace, via the state, and by creating ideas which support and mask their power.

Thirdly, the class that controls the means of production also, for Marx, controls the means of production of ideas. They will create ideas that valorize their position in society, shield them from criticism, and ensure that subordinate classes remain divided and ignorant of their position.

These three forms of domination ensure the power and position of the dominant class in society, and stave off any potential rebellion against them.

Activity 3. Attempt the tasks below:

(1) How does Marx say that you can identify the dominant class in any epoch?

(2) Outline three ways the dominant class have control over us.

1	
2	
3	

For Marx, the nature of the mode of production, and consequently the composition of the class structure, underwent a major change when the feudal system was replaced with the capitalist system that we live under today. The feudal system, which existed before the Industrial Revolution, was based on oaths of loyalty and service, and a feudal class owned the agricultural land upon which people worked and the pre-industrial machinery that existed at that time. Workers were often required by law to work for their feudal lord, and laws were in place to ensure that servants did not leave their employment to seek a better deal elsewhere. Ordinary workers were tied to the land, and to their master to whom they owed their loyalty and respect. This changed with the fall of feudalism and the rise of capitalism that occurred after the Industrial Revolution, and the invention of more mechanistic forms of production. Power remained with the owners of the means of production, but the class that owned this machinery changed, as the owners of factories and mills were often not feudal lords. As Marx and Engels suggest:

> The modern bourgeois society that has sprouted from the ruins of feudal society has not done away with class antagonisms. It has but established new classes, new conditions of oppression, new forms of struggle. Our epoch, the epoch of the bourgeoisie, possesses, however, this distinctive feature: it has simplified the class antagonisms. (Marx, 1985: 80)

Marx argues that this change to capitalism was in the first instance beneficial to the development of technology, but this does not mean to say that it was advantageous to all of society. Workers started to move from the country to the cities and towns to work in factories and mills, leaving agricultural life behind them, along with their bonds of loyalty to their feudal lords. Indeed, bourgeois philosophers

Karl Marx

When Karl Marx died in 1883, there were just 11 mourners at his funeral (Wheen, 1999: 1). Yet the impact he had on twentieth-century politics, for good or for ill, was massive.

Marx was born in Trier, Prussia (modern-day Germany) in 1818. He commenced his university studies in Bonn where he became interested in poetry, drinking and fighting, before moving to study in Berlin.

After studying he became interested in radical politics and began writing, and lived at various times in Paris, Brussels and Cologne, before settling in London in 1849. In London, he would read and write in the reading room of the British Museum.

He met fellow Prussian Friedrich Engels whilst in Paris and the two of them would collaborate on a number of works. Engels would, as he owned a textiles mill in Salford, often bankroll Marx, who spent most of his life in genteel poverty.

such as John Locke and Adam Smith started to talk of individual liberties and rights, and a notion that government should be based on consent, but they also provided justifications for the ownership of private property and the division of labour. They were no longer owned by their feudal lords, but were at liberty to seek employment in whatever job and location that they chose. These freedoms were, for Marx, entirely illusionary, however, as although they gained their freedom from the feudal system, the oppression that they would face from the bourgeoisie was arguably much worse, and certainly better hidden.

As mentioned in the quote from *The Communist Manifesto* above, the capitalist epoch simplifies the class system. Under feudalism there were numerous different classes of people and workers; under capitalism there were really only two main classes, namely capitalists and proletarians. One small class had all the power, and one very large class had none. The capitalist class, like the dominant feudal class before it, owned the means of production; the proletariat class, on the other hand, owned nothing but their labour. Indeed, for Marx, there is a very simple way of determining which class you are a member of. If you work for a wage, then you are a member of the proletariat class. So we see that Marx here is using class in a simply economic sense, perhaps differently therefore than the way in which we would use it in contemporary society. Signifiers of class in the contemporary world might be the particular job we do, whether, for example, we are in a professional job, or if we are in a more working-class job. So a lawyer will probably argue that they are middle class, whereas a construction worker might suggest that they are working class. Also, there might be more social elements to claims around class in the contemporary world. If one eats quinoa salads for lunch, or listens to classical music, or has a collection of suits, or lives in a McMansion, or drives a BMW, or has a college education, we might take these as being badges of the middle class. This would be missing the point for Karl Marx and his view of class. If one does not own the means of production, and one survives by selling one's labour, then you are a member of the proletariat just like the construction worker, or the person stacking the shelves in a supermarket.

Under a capitalist system, the government will always act in the interests of the bourgeoisie. If you elected a progressive government that instituted a raft of social changes and brought about legislation to increase the minimum wage, or limit working hours, or create safer workplaces, this might make you think that the state is sufficiently pliable to moderate capitalism and bring about a fairer deal for the proletariat. But for Marx you would be wrong in thinking this. The capitalist class will always ensure that the state will act in their long-term interests, but sometimes acting in their long-term interests involves acting against their short-term interests. So the state might make the lot of the working classes better by introducing a number of state benefits; however, all the time the purpose of this would be so that the proletariat feel contented under the capitalist system, and therefore do not have the inclination to revolt against it. For this reason, Marx was opposed to democratic socialism and the trade union movement, not because their goals were in and of themselves bad, but rather they prolonged capitalism by massaging it into something more acceptable. The only way that one could effect real and lasting social change was to revolt against capitalism and overthrow the system.

As capitalists were also in control of creating ideas, they managed to create a number of false beliefs that will prevent us from realizing that revolution was necessary to bring about social change. Nationalism was one such idea, as it divided the proletariat. It made the working class of one country think that their natural enemy was the working classes of other countries, when in actual fact they all had a mutual interest in uniting to overthrow the capitalist class. Likewise, bourgeois democracy was a false belief; it made us think that we were free in that we could choose a government and that that government would do our bidding, but as the state was inherently biased in the favour of the capitalist class, it mattered little as to how we elected our representatives, or what type of government or party we chose. This is another example of capitalist masking their power and preventing revolution. Indeed, most of the discussions we have had in this book so far would be, for Karl Marx, pointless bourgeois ramblings, as they mostly did not discuss class and/or the need for revolution.

I mentioned earlier that Marx thinks that initially capitalism is good for the development of technology, machinery that will prove necessary for a future communist society. Indeed, Marx thinks that one needs capitalism to help develop these things, and therefore the historical march from feudalism to capitalism, and then eventually on to communism, is a necessary set of stages. One cannot jump a step from feudalism straight into communism, as the infrastructure necessary to maintain a classless society would not yet have been developed. Capitalism also creates the very thing that will bring about its downfall, namely a revolutionary working class.

But not only has the bourgeoisie forged the weapons that bring death to itself; it has also called into existence the men who are to wield those weapons – The modern working class – the proletarians. (Marx, 1985: 87)

Marx argues that as capitalism progresses, the exploitation of the proletariat will grow and grow to such an extent that they will develop a political consciousness, see past the false beliefs that the bourgeoisie have created, and recognize them for what they are, and rise up to overthrow the system. The capitalist state will be replaced with a communist society. So for Marx it's not simply a question of whether a revolution is legitimate to overthrow the state in certain circumstances when it exceeds its legitimate boundaries, but rather that revolution is the only way of making the change from a capitalist to a communist state.

How ideas come about

Marx thinks that before man can think he must eat, and the methods we put in place to ensure our economic survival shape the way we think. For this reason, it is impossible to predict what ideas would be like in a communist society.

Marx writes very little about the nature of a communist society, and while you might think this is a bit of a cop-out, it is actually quite consistent with his general thinking on politics. Marx thinks that before man can think, he must be able to eat. The methods and organization around being able to eat, things such as machinery, technology, and the ownership thereof, determine the relations of production, that is to say class structure, that is present in any given society or epoch. It is whoever is dominant in these relations of production that determines the ideas present in that society. To put it in perhaps a simpler fashion, one cannot know the ideas in any one epoch until you are actually in that epoch; it is impossible to predict.

There are a few things that we can determine about the nature of a communist society, however. Firstly, the class system will be simplified still further than it was under capitalism. Rather than there being two classes, the bourgeoisie and the proletariat, there would be just one class, namely humanity. Secondly, as there is only one class, there cannot be any class oppression, and if there is no class oppression, it follows that there will be no need for the state as the state is nothing but a tool of class oppression. The state would, therefore, wither away and die, as its only purpose would have been removed. Thirdly, there would be no private property, with things being owned communally, with each receiving that which they need. It would be at communism, therefore, that history reached its resting point. As the driving force of history for Marx was class struggle, and class struggle would have been removed by a communist society, humanity would have reached its natural conclusion, and the forms of dominance under feudalism and capitalism will have come to an end. Only a revolution could make this possible; it cannot be achieved by gradual change, or by government legislation.

Activity 4. Attempt the following tasks:

(1) Why does Marx think it would be impossible to achieve a communist society via the ballot box?

(2) What would a communist society look like?

Conclusion

This chapter has introduced us to a variety of responses to the question 'when is revolution justified?'

Locke argues that if a government interferes in those areas where man has not transferred their powers of action, so does not stick to simply implementing the laws of nature, it can legitimately be removed. Indeed, he was writing to justify removing a monarch in just such a way, namely the Glorious Revolution. Paine makes a similar argument, again justifying revolutions, specifically those in France and America. Paine's argument starts introducing the language of rights, and so looks more familiar to us than perhaps Locke's did. Paine argues that government is created by rights-holding individuals, and if government breaks those rights, it can (and should) legitimately be removed.

Marx argues that not only is revolution permissible, it is a necessity if one wishes to bring in a communist government. Under capitalism, the bourgeoisie dominate the state, meaning that it would be impossible for an elected government to institute the changes to bring about Marx's vision of a fairer society even if it wanted to. This means that revolution is the only way to change society, and due to the nature of capitalism, it is a perfectly legitimate activity.

Burke issues a note of caution. He is not opposed to revolutions *per se*, but he restricts the areas to which they can legitimately take place, and has a different notion of the nature of a just revolution to the other authors we have examined. Firstly, he is opposed to revolutions (such as those in France) that are based on abstract arguments such as human rights, as opposed to tried and tested principles that have existed in any given society through the ages. When he supports revolutions, they are those based on existing principles that have been denied to people. So the American Revolution, based on the age-old principle of 'no taxation without representation', is acceptable (if slightly regrettable). If you revolt in favour of a set of abstract principles, you will probably never get them, Burke thinks, and you will probably also lose the rights you already possessed. Secondly, Burke argues that a revolution should take you back to where you were before this historic right was taken off you; so a revolution is going backwards in one sense, not forward. It is the novelty that you are revolting against, as opposed to revolting towards a new form of government.

Works cited

Burke, E. (1986) *Reflections on the Revolution in France*. London: Penguin.

Locke, J. (1988) *Two Treatises of Government*. Cambridge: Cambridge University Press.

Marx, K. and Engels, F. (1985) *The Communist Manifesto*. London: Penguin.

Paine, T. (1985) *Rights of Man*. London: Penguin.

Wheen, F. (2000) *Karl Marx*. London: Fourth Estate.

Text reading activities

From the *Communist Manifesto*, available at https://www.marxists. org/archive/marx/works/1848/communist-manifesto/ch02.htm

In what relation do the Communists stand to the proletarians as a whole?

The Communists do not form a separate party opposed to the other working-class parties.

They have no interests separate and apart from those of the proletariat as a whole.

They do not set up any sectarian principles of their own, by which to shape and mould the proletarian movement.

The Communists are distinguished from the other working-class parties by this only: 1. In the national struggles of the proletarians of the different countries, they point out and bring to the front the common interests of the entire proletariat, independently of all nationality. 2. In the various stages of development which the struggle of the working class against the bourgeoisie has to pass through, they always and everywhere represent the interests of the movement as a whole.

The Communists, therefore, are on the one hand, practically, the most advanced and resolute section of the working-class parties of every country, that section which pushes forward all others; on the other hand, theoretically, they have over the great mass of the proletariat the advantage of clearly understanding the line of march, the conditions, and the ultimate general results of the proletarian movement.

The immediate aim of the Communists is the same as that of all other proletarian parties: formation of the proletariat into a class, overthrow of the bourgeois supremacy, conquest of political power by the proletariat.

Question 1: Why, for Marx, will capitalism inevitably fail?

Question 2: Why, then, does it still exist?

10

Conclusion: Ideologies

KEY QUESTIONS

(1) What are the core components of liberalism, conservatism and socialism?

(2) Which thinkers that we have examined in this book so far fall into these categories?

(3) Are ideologies a helpful way of examining the history of political ideas?

Introduction

To conclude this book, it is perhaps worth moving away from the political and moral questions that have framed all discussions chapter by chapter, and attempt to pull what we have examined so far into their respective political ideologies. This concluding chapter, therefore, will give an overview of liberalism, conservatism and socialism, perhaps the major ideologies that exist in the world today, and try to illustrate firstly, where some of the thinkers that we have discussed sit therein, and secondly, how some of the political issues they have discussed have led to the formation of modern ideologies.

Ideologies are an extremely helpful way of learning about political ideas; however, there are some problems with this approach. The first is a contextual concern. Political thinkers that span the centuries have written within specific national and historical contexts, responding to specific political events, and are then pushed (some might say lumped) together into an ideology and assumed to be talking about similar kinds of things. Indeed, some of the thinkers who we will label as 'liberal', 'conservative' and/or 'socialist' might never have referred to themselves in the same manner. Indeed, the terms may have never existed at the time. Take John Locke, for example. The term 'liberal' or 'liberalism' did not exist in its current understanding at the time he was writing; indeed, Locke's thought was never really described as liberal until the nineteenth century, and yet he is regarded as one of the founding fathers of liberal thought. So we must take some pretty large liberties with historical accuracy when we are describing political ideologies.

Another problem is a more practical one, and that is due to the generalizations that we must make when describing political ideologies for the reasons outlined above. We might often find that major thinkers straddle two ideologies, or indeed not fit into any. Edmund Burke is unproblematically a conservative, perhaps, but where does one put Hobbes? He is a methodological individualist and a proponent of social contract theory, which would tend to suggest that he is a liberal, but he shares none of the standard liberal concerns for rights or limited government.

Another problem we face is in the term 'ideology' itself. In this chapter we will take the word 'ideology' to mean a value-free description of bodies of political thought; however, this is not a definition that everyone would agree with. Conservative thinkers tend not to think of conservatism as being an ideology. An ideology for them is a dogmatic set of ideas, to be contrasted with a conservative disposition of judging specific political issues on their merits and acting accordingly. So for conservatives, ideology is not a neutral descriptive word; it is a body of ideas to be avoided. Likewise, Marxists do not see ideology as being a neutral descriptive word, and do not regard Marxism as being an ideology; however, their quibble with the term differs from that of conservatives. For Marxists, an ideology is an idea that has emanated from the dominant class in society, and as a consequence is an element of power and class oppression. So ideology, according to this definition, means a false belief. Marxist ideas, on the other hand, are not loaded with power, and represent the truth.

That said, for the beginner in the history of political ideas, ideologies are a helpful way of understanding the key differences between different bodies of thought, and as long as we are mindful of the methodological challenges outlined above, it is worth examining them. This concluding chapter will, therefore, outline the key modern ideologies liberalism, conservatism and socialism. It will begin with liberalism, the body of thought that argues that society is a collection of free and equal individuals, that government should be based on consent, and that government should respect certain inalienable human rights. We will also see that liberalism is not without its different ways of thinking, and therefore how there are two key strands of liberal thought, one that emerges from Kant and Rousseau that places autonomy at the heart of its argument, and another that emerges from Locke, which regards toleration as being all important.

We will then go on to outline conservative thought, and show how Edmund Burke is regarded as the founding father of modern conservatism, which attempts to show how society should defend and protect traditions and institutions, and preserve the best of the past for future generations.

Finally, we will examine socialist thought, and the myriad of thinkers that can be said to be the founding fathers of socialism. We will also examine the link between Marxist thought, and more mainstream socialist thought.

Activity 1. Link the thinkers on the left with the ideologies on the right

Edmund Burke

Immanuel Kant   Socialism

Karl Marx

Jean-Jacques Rousseau   Liberalism

Thomas Paine

John Locke   Conservatism

Liberalism

Broadly speaking, liberalism is a body of thought emanating from the seventeenth century onwards that views political societies as comprised of free and equal individuals, that government is based on the consent of the people to be legitimate, that government should be limited, and protect a core set of rights that are inalienable from the individual. Any government that fails in its duties to the individual can, and should, be removed, and whereas liberals would always support some manner of democratic state, they would also be wary of the conformity that is possible under it.

For William A. Galston, there are **two key strands of thinking within the liberal tradition**. Firstly, there is the strand he calls **'liberal autonomy'**, which developed as part of the Enlightenment project. Here 'reason is understood as the prime source of authority ... [and] preference is to be given to self-direction over external determination' (1995: 525). Autonomy is the central theme of this strand of liberalism, and in order to be free from external forces, individuals are asked to use their reason to reflect upon morality of political issues and make appropriate choices after their reflection. The second he calls **'liberal diversity'**, which, rather than focusing on an individual's capacity to make free choices, attempts to find ways in which more options and more diversity are available to them. Liberal diversity places toleration at its heart, and attempts to

> Galston argues that there are two strands of thought in liberalism. Liberal autonomy (Kant and Rousseau) on the one hand, and liberal diversity (Locke) on the other.

find a way of 'accepting and managing diversity through liberal toleration ... [w]ithin a framework of civic unity, a plurality of religions could be allowed to coexist' (Galston, 1995: 526).

Both of these traditions of thought have already made an appearance in this book. The crucial thinkers for the 'liberal autonomy' strand of thought would be Immanuel Kant, who we introduced in the chapter on the nature of politics, and Jean-Jacques Rousseau, who has appeared in many of the discussions we have had thus far. For Kant, in order for us to lead free moral lives, we must always make our decisions about how to act based purely on the morality of the act itself; we must never make decisions based on the outcomes of those acts. If we decided to do something because it would make us better off, or increase our happiness, or lead to some other end that we thought was beneficial, then we are failing to act autonomously, and those consequences are acting through us. Therefore, Kant asks us **to act as if our actions should become our maxim; that is to say a universal moral law**. If I lie to you, Kant argues, I am implying that it is acceptable for you to lie to me as well. Freedom for Kant, therefore, is not simply being able to make decisions free from the control of anybody else; we also need to be free from the consequences of actions to ensure that we make decisions that are moral.

Rousseau likewise thinks that it is important to make autonomous decisions in order to be free; however, the potential impediment to us acting in an autonomous fashion is slightly different to that outlined by Kant. For Rousseau, you may remember, one of the things that is really preventing us in contemporary societies from being free is our vanity (our *amour propre*), and this vanity is not natural to us. Whereas we are naturally good, have few desires, and wish no harm to our fellow humans, society has corrupted us and made us vain, competitive and selfish. Like Kant, Rousseau states that even if we make decisions independently from other people, we are still not free if we act selfishly. Consequently, **making autonomous decisions involves mitigating our vanity and making decisions based on what is in the interests of everybody**, within the context of a direct democracy in which one is both sovereign and citizen.

What Kant and Rousseau share is a concern about the influences on the individual when they are making choices; it is worth us spending a little bit of time reflecting on this here, as what they are asserting is that even when somebody is not forcing us to do something and we act, we may not be acting autonomously. Suppose you were having a conversation with your best friend about their concerns that their husband might be seeing another woman, and they asked you the direct question 'Do you think my husband is having an affair?' Now suppose the previous evening you had been out and you had indeed seen your friend's husband having dinner with another woman; what would you tell them? You may consider that it would be prudent not to tell your best friend what you had seen, as (a) perhaps seeing someone with another woman does not directly imply that they are having an affair - it could be a work associate, or a distant cousin, or (b) perhaps you want to shield your friend from their hurt as whatever it was

Liberalism

The term liberal is used in a lot of different contexts. If one is a liberal in American political parlance, one is thought to be on the left of centre of politics (although progressive is more widely used these days). If one is a liberal in Europe, you are more likely to be regarded as a centrist politician. Also, neoliberal is a term used by many political commentators to refer to politicians who want a return to classical minimalistic government and free markets. So its use is contested.

Our understanding of liberalism is the body of thought that places individuals, consent to government, and rights at the heart of its argument. John Locke is regarded as its founding father (although he never used the term himself), and other adherents include Kant, Rousseau, Paine, Rawls, and perhaps even Nozick. Most liberals would regard J.S. Mill as part of their canon, despite his utilitarianism, meaning he had no time for natural rights.

that you had seen may run its course in time, so you might think it best to leave it alone. For Kant, there is no excuse not to tell your friend what you had seen, and what's more, if you made your decision about what to tell and what not to tell your friend based on the consequences of what telling them might bring, you are not acting autonomously. No one here has physically or legally forced you to do one thing over another, nor has power been exerted over you in any way, shape or form, but rather the act is not autonomous as it cannot be universalized, and it is based not on the morality of the act but rather the consequences of the act.

Now imagine that you lived in the kind of direct democracy advocated by Rousseau, and you are asked to consider a proposal to lower the rate of income tax payable by citizens. Suppose one person argues that they think that tax should be lowered as they would end up paying less tax, and be better off as a result. Another person argues against tax being lowered, as they suggest doing so would end up with government services being cut, and their livelihood depends on these very services. These are on the face of it very plausible reasons to either support or reject tax cuts, but Rousseau would not feel that these are autonomous arguments, and as a consequence they are not permissible ones. People should always argue about how tax cuts would affect the republic, that is to say how these tax cuts will affect everyone in society. So arguments that ran along the lines of 'this tax cut would have a positive result in society as it would leave people with more money to spend on goods and services that would increase everyone's livelihood' or 'these tax cuts would result in government services upon which so many people rely being reduced, thus having a detrimental effect on society' would be acceptable as they attempted to focus on the good of all.

The other strand in liberal thought that Galston identified, that of liberal diversity, has also been represented in this book, primarily through the work of John Locke, although perhaps we have not yet fully explored his notion of toleration that is central to this aspect of his work. **Thinkers in this strand**

of thought are less concerned about the nature of decision making, and more concerned that there are a variety of different viewpoints available for people to make decisions about in a manner of their own choosing. In his *A Letter Concerning Toleration* of 1689, Locke gives us a number of different reasons why we should tolerate other people's religious opinions. Chief amongst these is his argument that it is entirely irrational to persecute someone for beliefs that they hold; namely to say persecuting someone in the hope that they would change their mind never works. **Persecution acts upon the will, not upon the mind; so all you will ever get from persecuting someone is outward compliance, never a changed opinion.** Suppose, for example, that I decided to torture an Auburn Tigers football fan, and would only stop if they uttered the phrase 'the Alabama Crimson Tide football team are the best', or likewise torture a Manchester United fan until they declared that 'Liverpool are brilliant'. Eventually they may say it, but they would never believe it; they will only ever say it to make the torture stop. So it was for Locke and religion in the seventeenth century; we might as well tolerate one another, as there is little we can do to change one another's mind.

The word tolerate has come under fire relatively recently, as toleration implies putting up with something that you don't like. Going back to the previous example, it would seem strange linguistically for a supporter of the Alabama Crimson Tide to say that they 'tolerated' the Alabama Crimson Tide football team, or that a Manchester United fan 'tolerated' their team. We don't tolerate things we like; we tolerate things we don't like, as it implies putting up with something. On matters of diversity, whereas toleration is generally regarded as a good thing, it does necessarily imply that one is putting up with people of a different way of life, rather than championing individuals' autonomous choices, or celebrating diversity. Do we not owe our fellow citizens of different backgrounds and different ways of life more than just our grudging acceptance?

> Locke argued that it wasn't only unfair to persecute people because of their beliefs, it was also irrational. Persecution might eventually get outward compliance to another set of ideas, but it would never change anyone's mind.

Liberals from this strand of the ideology are not too concerned with the manner in which individuals make decisions, that is to say whether they are autonomous in the sense that they can be applied as a universal law, or are always tuned towards the good of the republic. Instead, they hope that toleration and limited government, whereby rights are retained by the individual, will allow a number of different ways of life to flourish, and people can make their own decisions based upon which form of life they like best. So whereas liberals often **start** from the position that we are free and equal, that government is an artificial construct that is based on consent, and that we should all have rights even after we have founded government, **liberals' final political blueprints are often very different from one another.** John Rawls is regarded in political theory circles as being emblematic of modern liberal thought; but his thinking is substantially different from that of, say, Locke.

Activity 2. Please attempt the tasks below:

(1) Outline how Galston defines the following:

Liberal autonomy	
Liberal diversity	

(2) Which thinkers fall into these two categories?

Liberal autonomy	
Liberal diversity	

(3) Define liberalism in no more than two sentences:

Conservatism

Conservatism, broadly speaking, is a body of thought that aims to preserve the best of the past for future generations, therefore that institutions and traditions should be preserved, and that change should only occur when absolutely necessary. Traditions and institutions provide us with the best framework to judge our political actions, for conservatives; we should always be suspicious of big plans in politics, especially on changes that come from the top down.

Conservative thought has been represented in this book chiefly through the works of Edmund Burke, who we discussed in the chapters on revolution and

Conservatism

There are conservative parties all over the world, be they called that by name (in the UK), the Christian Democratic Union in Germany, or the Republican Party in the United States. Whereas conservatism, like all other ideologies, exists on a spectrum, with some conservatives more liberal than others, conservatives will generally attempt to defend tradition and institutions over the use of pure reason in society. Tradition represents historical wisdom stored up for our use, and this can come under threat from top-down plans.

The twentieth-century conservative thinker Michael Oakeshott likened conservatism to captaining a ship (an analogy used by many political thinkers). But rather than attempting to take the ship to a particular destination, or steer it in any one direction, the goal always remained to keep the ship afloat. So it is with politics: politicians should not try any grand plans; they should ensure that society 'remains afloat'.

democracy. Conservatism can be seen as a reaction against the Enlightenment (perhaps liberal) principles of the primacy of reason for judging political matters, the social contract as the sole source of legitimacy for the state, and the focus on rights. Crucially, conservative thinkers **do not regard conservatism as an ideology**. Ideologies are rigid dogmatic things; they cause us to attempt to judge all political matters via a set of principles. They are like the baseball slugger who swings hard at every pitch they face, or the singer who bellows out every note they sing at high volume. Whereas sometimes both of these approaches will lead to some success, other times the slugger should bunt, or not play a ball to get ahead in the count, and any singer realizes that some songs should be sung softly and quietly. Politics, likewise, is not about doing the same thing over and over again; it is about judging the situation and doing the best thing for the particular circumstances. Thus conservatism is presented as a disposition, a way of thinking about politics, as opposed to a set of absolute principles to be followed at all times.

Preserving tradition is one of the crucial goals of the conservative disposition. Tradition should not be seen as arbitrary; it is a type of knowledge, of wisdom. Traditions 'contain the residues of many trials and errors, as people attempt to adjust their conduct to the conduct of others' (Scruton, 2014: 21). Conservatives hold that one of the reasons why rational top-down planning is always likely to fail is that it ignores the fact that people find ways of getting on with one another, building bonds and affection, by face-to-face contact as individuals and in local institutions like clubs, charities, churches, bars and similar. These ways of living communally

> Conservatives do not regard conservatism as an ideology; instead, they think of it as a disposition. Ideologies are dogmatic whereas conservatism is pragmatic.

with one another are far better expressed through tradition than they are by rational top-down planning. So we are unwise to ignore the value of tradition in society as it represents a sum of knowledge that past generations wish to pass on to future generations, and it is unjust to both of those groups if we demolish that for our own purposes. It is like someone who has inherited a fortune from their family that was earned through hard work and prudence, frittering it away on booze and fast cars, so that future generations had nothing to inherit. We, the existing generation, should see our position as one of stewardship, preserving traditions, institutions, and ways of life so that future generations can benefit from them. So, if we are to see society as a contract, as Edmund Burke puts it, it is one 'not only between those who are living, but between those who are living, those who are dead, and those who are to be born' (Burke, 1986: 194–5).

Conservatives are not anti-change. Change is sometimes necessary; however, when it is carried out, it should always be informed by traditions and institutions present in that given society, and not on abstract, top-down plans. Society should be seen as an organic institution, gradually changing and growing, but never dramatically changing.

Of course, some of the most wide-ranging changes that have occurred in the last fifty years have occurred in conservative countries. The Republican president Ronald Reagan, and the UK Conservative Party prime minister Margaret Thatcher instituted a raft of social, economic and political changes in the 1980s, all from a conservative standpoint. They both reacted against the postwar consensus that had developed in the United States and the UK, a consensus that saw the state playing a large role in the day-to-day running of the economy. Thatcher, for example, privatized a number of state utilities, substantially reduced the top rate of income tax, and altered conservative thinking away from being about preserving social cohesion in society. The state was no longer to be seen as a body that looked after citizens from the cradle to the grave; it was the individual's responsibility to look after themselves and their families, not society and certainly not the state. So just like with liberalism, there are significant variations within conservative thought.

Activity 3. Attempt the questions below:

(1) Why do conservatives think that preserving traditions is so important?

(2) Does this make conservatives anti-change?

Socialism

Socialism as an ideology stresses the social aspect of life and economic production. Again, broadly speaking, **socialists would point out that wealth is the result of common social effort, and a consequence of this is that that wealth should be distributed more equally amongst society**. So, socialism is *social*, that is to say that it opposes individualism. We should not see, as many liberals do, that society is created by individuals for mutual self-benefit; rather, society is more than this. The bonds of solidarity that we have with our fellow citizens transcend mere self-interests. The problem for socialists is that although liberals believe in **procedural equality** (equality in the eyes of the law), and **equality of opportunity** (that race, ethnicity, gender, etc., should play no part in distributing goods in society), they do not take equality seriously, as massive inequalities in wealth persist in capitalist societies. Likewise, socialists concur with liberals in the importance of freedom, but argue that **inequality of wealth also means an inequality of freedom**. It is for this reason that Fabian Socialists regarded socialism as the natural conclusion to liberalism rather than its opposite; socialism could add meat to the bones of concepts such as freedom and equality and make them more meaningful.

While Thomas Paine, whom we have already discussed in this book, would not have termed himself a socialist, he does, in his work *Agrarian Justice*, tackle the issue of inequality of wealth. He suggests that **the state should not only be involved in protecting rights, but also provide goods and services to make society more equal.** As such, Paine would be regarded as a modern liberal in that the state is not seen just as a necessary evil and something that we need to be protected against in order to bring about freedom, but also that the state, through addressing poverty and inequality, could be a vehicle to increase some people's freedom. He argues that the landed property distribution was unjust, and far from property being a pre-political right that the state has no right over (as Locke did), that people's initial acquisition of private property was unjust, and therefore people can be taxed on land to provide goods and services to people with no land. God gave the world to all in common, thought Paine, and people taking it had no right to do so. Whereas the work they did on the land itself was rightfully theirs (e.g. the tomatoes or courgettes they grew, and the profit they received

> Paine argues that it is unfair and unjust that some people managed to gain land and others didn't. He thinks it is entirely reasonable for landowners to pay the rest of us tax. Rawls takes this one step further, arguing that talents are rewarded in a morally arbitrary fashion in a market economy, and that it is fine to tax the wealthy to support the poor.

from that), the land itself rightfully belonged to everyone and therefore land 'owners' owed us all rent. This rent was taxation. It is unjust, this argument goes, that we all did not get an opportunity to claim land for ourselves at the time of initial acquisition, and this should be compensated by a tax-and-spend government.

Rawls, another liberal, takes this argument one step further. It isn't simply unjust that those without property missed out on the initial acquisition of land through not being born; it is also unjust if we haven't been blessed with talents that can be rewarded in a market economy. Some talents are rewarded in a market economy much more than others. If I am the 100th best baseball player in the United States, then I am almost certainly a multi-millionaire. If I am the 100th best shot putter, then I almost certainly get no remuneration at all for my talent; indeed, I most probably have to pay my own expenses to participate. It is a matter of pure luck, for Rawls, that the person who has the talent for baseball gets so much more money than the person who has the talent for shot putting. So we cannot claim responsibility for our talents as they are morally arbitrary (or at least we cannot claim responsibility for their reward in a market economy); and likewise we cannot be blamed for having no talents at all. So it is entirely just to tax people who have done well financially out of their talents (which are morally arbitrary) to provide goods and services to those who have no talents.

Rousseau also critiqued private property ownership, especially the role it played in the corruption of the naturally good man by society. As he points out in his *Discourse on Inequality in Man*:

The first man who, having enclosed a piece of ground, bethought himself of saying 'This is mine', and found people simple enough to believe him, was the real founder of civil society. From how many crimes, wars, and murders, from how many horrors and misfortunes might not any one have saved mankind, by pulling up the stakes, or filling up the ditch, and crying to his fellows: 'Beware of listening to this impostor; you are undone if you once forget that the fruits of the earth belong to us all, and the earth itself to nobody.' (Rousseau, 1993: 84)

Rousseau is not as anti-property as the quote above would suggest; indeed, he would, in *The Social Contract*, outline how one of the benefits of a properly constituted state would be that we would gain property rights. In his natural state, however, man would have no need for property as he lived a hunter-gatherer existence, rarely coming in contact with his fellow man. It is only when he starts living with other men that he starts to need property, and he needs property to make him look important to other people. So inequality comes about through man's vanity, and so does men's dependence upon one another, which reduces his freedom. When the state is properly constituted via a social contract, one will limit the amount of property one has based on what is in the interests of the republic, that is to say what is in the interests of all; so there would be none with too much or with too little.

But whereas Paine, Rawls and Rousseau are all thinkers we have examined who share the concerns of socialists, or perhaps in Paine and Rousseau's case have influenced socialist thinkers, they are probably not socialists *per se*. The thinker we must examine in this light is, of course, Karl Marx.

Marx's unremitting analysis of the nature of capitalism, of its unfairness and its structural defects, makes him the chief and most influential critic of

Socialism

Socialism is an ideology that calls for greater equality between people in material terms – that is to say a greater equality of wealth in society. Socialists will often advocate a raft of reforms to the economy such as the state intervening in the economy to bring about fairer ends, or taxing rich people to redistribute wealth via goods and services to the poorer in society. Often socialists will also advocate common ownership of the means of production, either through nationalization and state control, worker's cooperatives, or allowing workers a greater say in how industry is managed.

Various different sources have been the inspiration for socialist thought. Some socialism emanates from Christian religious thinking, some from liberal thought, but the central figure in worldwide socialist thought has been Karl Marx who argues for communal ownership of property and an end to class oppression. Equality must be conceived of as equality of outcome if it is to be meaningful.

capitalism. In the workplace capitalism robs us of our **species being**, our very essence and purpose. We are by nature producers who wish to interact with our environment and make things. However, capitalism (and indeed feudalism to a lesser extent) prevents us from being free with our production. We cannot labour in a manner that is true to ourselves, but instead we have to make whatever it is that our employer instructs us to do. As capitalism advances, and technologies such as assembly lines are introduced, we cease to even make whole 'things', but instead make only a very specific part of a thing. So we no longer craft a car or a door from start to finish, which at least would give us some satisfaction, but rather we only work on putting in the car windows, or work on the lock on the door; so our work is dull and unfulfilling. Workers also are exploited as the **surplus value** that they create in a product through their labour is taken by their employers. Workers create a value in an item that is higher than the wages, overheads and raw materials that an employer pays for, and yet is all taken by capitalists for themselves. This is unfair for Marx, as is the decline in conditions he predicted would occur in late-stage capitalism.

> It would be insufficient for Marx to campaign for government legislation to improve workers' pay and conditions – instead, one should aim to overthrow the capitalist system and replace it with a communist society when property would be owned in common, and workers could do meaningful, creative work.

Electing a socialist government, one that would tax and spend (perhaps the type of policies advocated by Rawls and Paine), would be insufficient to remedy this for Marx. The state will always act in the long-term interests of capitalism, even when it appears to be acting in the workers' interests. Progressive policies that we take for granted in the modern world such as minimum wages, health and safety policies at work, paid holidays and the like, perhaps even welfare payments and subsidized health systems are a chimera for Marx. What they do is blind workers to the true nature of socialism and stave off revolution; they are not done to help the working classes; they are done for the benefit of capitalism. It is for this reason that Marx was suspicious of the trade union movement; whereas, by campaigning for better pay and conditions for workers, it sought to aid them, in the long term they were protracting their misery. What they should do instead was support the overthrow of the state and the institution of a communist society.

In a communist society there would be no private property; everything would be owned in common. There would be no classes, and crucially there would be no division of labour. People would be freer to use their labour to create as they saw fit. This, indeed, is one of the least fair things in capitalism for Marx, that the unpleasant and boring, but sometimes necessary tasks are always completed by the poorest in society. Technology would be able to take some of the drudgery away from all when owned in common with all (private ownership of technology hindered its development for Marx), but unpleasant tasks would still need to be done. These tasks would be shared by all, as would the more creative enjoyable tasks. Work would become meaningful again.

Activity 4. Attempt the questions below:

(1) What is meant by equality of outcome? How does it differ from equality of opportunity?

(2) What does Marx mean by surplus value? How is it linked to the exploitation of the workers?

Applying the ideologies

Of course, learning about a variety of political ideologies is of interest to us as it helps us to understand the contested nature of political life. The reason why there is disagreement over policy issues is because people will interpret these issues using their ideological attachment. We should not be too simplistic here, as you will often find that adherents to different ideologies might often agree on certain policy issues, albeit agreeing for entirely different reasons. Take Brexit in the UK for example, and the wave of Euroscepticism that led up to it. Often those on the right of the Conservative Party, and those on the left of the Labour Party are jointly critical of the European Union, and placed sovereignty at the heart of their arguments, but used it in a different manner. Those on the right of the Conservative Party might invoke notions of national sovereignty and suspicion of institutions that water this down. Those on the left of the Labour Party might argue that it is important that the state is able to intervene in the economy to help foster equality, and might be suspicious of the market assumptions of the single market. It is possible for people with differing political beliefs to coalesce around policy issues even if their fundamental belief systems are different.

But this is not always the case as ideologies will often make different interpretations of political events; indeed, perhaps this is the normal state of affairs. For example, in 2008 a financial crisis hit the world economy, and although this was over a decade ago, its impact is still felt in the world economy. In this crisis, caused by excessive risk taking by banks, financial institutions such as Lehman Brothers in the United States and Northern Rock in the UK collapsed, with the latter being taken into public ownership. Several other financial institutions received bailouts from governments who stepped in to ensure that the world financial system remained working. The consequences of this crisis were far-reaching, with a worldwide depression and public spending cuts in order to maintain the amount of debt governments had accrued. The various ideologies may interpret the causes of this crisis differently, and would have proposed different solutions to it.

For **socialists**, the key cause of the financial crisis was states' unwillingness to regulate the banks leading to light-touch regulation, which meant that they were at liberty to take financial risks such as subprime mortgages. The banks were greedy and put profit over anything else, and this illustrates the inherent instability of a free market capitalist economy; it would not have happened had states played a bigger role in managing and/or regulating banks' behaviour. The statement 'managing and/or regulating banks' of course illustrates that there is not *a single socialist* response but rather a variety of socialist responses. Some socialists would argue that banks should be state owned, others that it is fine for them to be privately owned but they should be regulated by the state to ensure their worst excesses are managed. Socialists might also point to states' willingness to bail out banks, when they would not bail out other failed industries, as further proof of the tight link between money and government; of course politicians would argue that had they allowed the banks to fail numerous other industries would have likewise collapsed because of the centrality of their role in economies.

Socialists would also argue that the austerity policies that followed the financial crisis and its subsequent depression should not have focused on the poorest in society. It would posit that it was not the poorest who caused the crisis, and that cuts to public services disproportionately affected the poor, so they were being punished for the excesses of the banking industry and government's inability to rein them in. This is, of course, a moral argument, but socialists would also put forward economic arguments against public spending cuts. By reducing public spending you limit the amount of money in the economy, which then results in economic pressure elsewhere. For example, if you are a librarian who loses their job due to a reduction in public funds to libraries, you will no longer spend your wages in local shops and restaurants and therefore impact on their profits. If a significant amount of the population are in a similar position, then the shops and restaurants may have to let employees go, which in turn creates still less money in the economy. Also these people who have lost their jobs may then claim unemployment benefit, which creates more stresses on public spending. Economically and morally, therefore, socialists would argue that cutting spending in times of depression makes little sense and doing so will end up detrimental to equality.

Conservatives, like socialists, come in different hues and might put forward a variety of responses to the causes of, and solutions to, the global financial crisis. An old style Burkean conservative might argue that the main cause of the financial crisis is governments' focus on providing economic growth. The activity of governance should not be dominated by any one imperative, be it equality, freedom, or in this instance providing year-on-year increase in gross domestic product (GDP). This has encouraged all of us, states and individuals alike, to live beyond our means financially. The best response to this is to recalibrate the economy so that it reinstalls traditional values of frugality and responsible spending and as such government initiatives to reduce public debt are a good thing, as is all of us as individuals reducing our reliance on debt by saving and spending only what we can afford. This type of conservative would, however, most likely oppose any austerity programmes that detrimentally affected the poorest in society; society is one organism and no one part of it should be singled out. It behoves the wealthiest in society to look out for the poorest – rank has its responsibilities.

A more free market-orientated conservative might be concerned that the financial crisis provokes overreaction by states in the regulation of financial organizations, believing that free markets are still the most efficient way to run the global economy. Banks are in a competitive market and the financial crisis shows that certain types of behaviour might lead to their downfall. They might argue that ironically governments bailing out institutions that acted irresponsibly might end up encouraging that very irresponsibility, as they may feel they have a safety net underneath them. Far better to allow the market to deal with these issues. Likewise, they would generally be opposed to much public spending as it is inefficient, so reducing this is what states should be doing anyway. Individual institutions should take responsibility for their actions, as should individual people take responsibility for their actions.

Free market **liberals** would probably share the views of free market conservatives outlined above. More socially minded liberals might be closer to the socialist perspective on the financial crisis. Rawls, for example, calls for enlightened understanding on policy issues; would we be happy if we did not know how we personally would be affected by the untrammelled capitalism of financial institutions and/or austerity cuts to reduce debt, or the policies that led to them? Probably not, he would argue, and therefore we should always bear this in mind when suggesting lack of regulation for banks or austerity cuts on public spending. We might be the ones who are negatively affected by the austerity cuts. What marks out the liberal response here from the socialist one outlined above is the focus on the individual. Socialists would point to the collective endeavour involved in the economic output of a country, which suggests a moral imperative to share the benefits of that endeavour more equally, whereas socially minded liberals would start with the premise of an individual considering what is in their best interests, albeit in a disaggregated manner.

Conclusion

This chapter has sought to conclude the book by drawing some of the thinkers and discussions outlined in the previous chapters into the framework of the three major world ideologies: liberalism, conservatism and socialism.

It commenced with liberalism, which is perhaps the oldest of the ideologies, with the others developing in response to it. It outlined the key elements of the ideology, a belief in human rights, individualism and government by consent, but also attempted to show the variety that exists therein by using Galston's dichotomy of autonomy versus toleration at the hand of competing strands of liberal thought. Kant, Rousseau and Locke were highlighted as key liberal thinkers from those we examined in this book.

We then went onto look at conservative thought, a body of ideas (not an ideology according to conservative thinkers) that shows value in preserving traditions and institutions, and being suspicious of top-down plans that disrupt these. Edmund Burke was identified as the key conservative thinker from earlier in the book.

Following this, we discussed socialism, highlighting its commitment to equality in a fuller sense of the word than is appealed to by liberalism. Equality should be understood as defined in terms of outcomes rather than being procedural or pertaining only to opportunity. Karl Marx was highlighted as the key socialist thinker.

The chapter concluded by applying the principles discussed above to the global economic crisis of 2008 and the austerity cuts that followed, illustrating a range of responses from each ideology.

Works cited

Burke, E. (1986) *Reflections on the Revolution in France*. London: Penguin.

Galston, W.A. (1995) 'Two concepts of liberalism', *Ethics*, 105(3), 516–34.

Rousseau, J.J. (1993) *The Social Contract and Discourses*. London: Everyman.

Scruton, R. (2014) *How to be a Conservative*. London: Bloomsbury.

Index

aboriginal peoples, 116
abstract principles, 147–8, 149, 158
Agathocles, 17, 18
Agrarian Justice (Paine), 116, 126–7, 169
An Agreement of the People (Levellers), 61
alcohol, 100
Allegory of the Cave, 109–10
American Revolution, 134–5, 147, 148–9, 158
Anarchy, State and Utopia (Nozick), 121
appetite, 94, 108, 110
Aquinas, Thomas, 113
Arab Spring, 71, 145
Aristotle, 9, 56
  biography, 113
  citizenship, 28–9
  justice, 8, 105–6, 111–14, 124
atheism, 42, 43, 56, 84
Athens, 12, 64, 106
  democracy, 4, 7, 13, 64, 72, 73–5, 80, 86
  women, 131–2
austerity, 173, 174
Australia, 71–2
autonomy, 161, 162, 163–4, 174–5
auxiliaries, 107, 108, 110

banks, 173, 174
Behemoth (Hobbes), 56
beliefs, 4, 13
  false, 156, 157
  ideologies, 172
Bentham, Jeremy, 12, 19–20, 21–2, 28, 30
Berlin, Isaiah, 7, 91, 92–4, 96, 102

Beyond Good and Evil (Nietzsche), 46, 47
Bezos, Jeff, 105
Blair, Ezell Jr, 52
Borgia, Cesare, 16, 17–18
Bouazizi, Mohamed, 145
bourgeoisie, 146, 153, 154–5, 156–7, 158, 159
Brexit, 71, 172
brotherhood, 147
Bryson, V., 132, 136
Burke, Edmund, 9, 28
  conservatism, 161, 166–7, 175
  democracy, 7, 72–3, 78–81, 86
  Paine compared with, 150
  revolution, 8, 146, 147–9, 158–9

capitalism
  definition of, 151–2
  financial crisis, 173
  inequalities, 168
  Marx, 8, 91, 94, 146–7, 153–7, 158, 170–1
Castiglione, Baldassare, 15
Categorical Imperative, 24
censorship, 97
Chamberlain, Wilt, 122, 127–8
change, 147–8, 166, 167
Charles I of England, 33, 34, 146
children, 99
China, 145
Christian virtues, 15
Churchill, Winston, 22, 25, 71
citizenship, 28–9, 73, 76, 112–13, 130
civil disobedience, 51–2
civil rights, 151

civil society, 59
Civil War, 33–4, 53, 56, 61, 113, 146
civilization, 7, 43, 45
class struggle, 94, 146–7, 153, 154,
    157
communism
  Berlin, 93
  Marx, 8, 91, 146, 153, 157, 159, 171
  Stalin, 84
The Communist Manifesto (Marx and
    Engels), 153, 155, 159
compassion, 43, 44, 48–9
competition, 76
conformity, 84
consent, 7, 114
  Hume, 53, 61–3, 66
  liberalism, 161, 162, 164, 165, 174
  Locke, 53, 59, 60, 66
  Rousseau, 64
consequentialism, 18, 19, 23, 25
conservatism, 160, 161, 166–8, 175
  definition of, 166
  financial crisis, 173–4
  view of humanity, 32
Conservative Party, 3, 168, 172
*Considerations on Representative
    Government* (Mill), 87–9
Constant, Benjamin, 24
contract *see* social contract
contractual obligations, 55
cooperation, 32, 117, 118
Craft Analogy, 13
Cuba, 145

Declaration of Independence (1776), 73,
    81–2, 130
democracy, 3–4, 7, 70–89
  American, 81–3
  Aristotle, 112
  Athenian, 13, 64, 72, 73–5, 80, 86
  bourgeois, 156
  Burke, 78–81
  freedom, 97
  Marx, 153
  Mill, 84–5, 87–9
  Montesquieu, 77–8
  Plato, 123–4
  Rousseau, 53, 64–5, 66, 76–7, 86, 133,
    163
  Socrates, 13–14
  tyranny of the majority, 84–5
  see also voting

Democrats, 3
deontology, 25, 85
desires, 108
dictatorships, 97
Diderot, Denis, 1, 37, 41
difference, politics of, 140, 141
difference principle, 120
Diogenes, 12
direct democracy
  Athens, 4, 72, 73–5
  Rousseau, 53, 64–5, 66, 76–7, 163, 164
dirty hands, 25, 28
Discourse on the Arts and Sciences
    (Rousseau), 1–2, 41
Discourse on the Origin of Inequality
    (Rousseau), 40, 41–2, 76
Discourses on Livy (Machiavelli), 14, 16,
    18
diversity, 162–3, 165
division of labour, 152, 155
dominant class, 153, 155, 161
drugs, 100

Ecce Homo (Nietzsche), 46
education, 131, 133, 135–6, 138–9, 141–2
elections, 71, 79, 86
  see also democracy; voting
Émile (Rousseau), 133
emotion, 130
empiricism, 39, 62
ends and means, 18, 20
Engels, Friedrich, 153, 154, 155, 159
Enlightenment, 37, 41, 135, 147, 162,
    167
equality
  Declaration of Independence, 82, 130
  French Revolution, 147
  gender, 130, 131, 142
  Hobbes, 35, 56
  of opportunity, 120, 127, 168
  Pateman, 65–6
  procedural, 168
  Rawls, 120, 121, 127
  Rousseau, 133
  socialism, 170, 175
  see also inequality
equity, 11
ethical dilemmas, 5, 22
ethnicity, 120
European Union, 71, 172
evil, 33, 38, 45–6, 47, 49–50
executive, 72, 78

Fabian Socialism, 168
fairness, 11, 118–21, 142
'faith in humanity', 31
false beliefs, 156, 157
fascism, 84, 93
federalism, 7, 73, 83
feminism, 100, 131, 134, 136, 139
Ferguson, Adam, 62
feudalism, 154, 156, 157
financial crisis, 172–4
forms, 108–9
fortune, 16
France, 71–2, 77, 78, 134–5
    see also French Revolution
freedom, 7–8, 90–103
    American ideals, 82
    capitalism, 152
    Hobbes, 35, 56, 92
    inequality of, 168
    Kant, 163
    Mill, 98–101, 102, 103
    as non-domination, 96–7, 102
    Paine, 169
    Pateman, 65–6
    positive and negative, 7, 91, 92–7,
        102
    reduction in, 71
    Rousseau, 45, 63–4, 65, 76, 163
    socialism, 168
    triadic view of, 95–6
    see also liberty
French Revolution, 41, 134–5, 147, 148,
    149
Fukuyama, Francis, 71
future generations, 167

Galston, William A., 162–3, 164, 174–5
Gates, Bill, 105
gender, 8, 120, 129–30, 140–1, 143–4
    see also women
genealogy, 46
general will, 64, 72, 77, 86
George, Andy, 152
Glorious Revolution, 3, 58, 158
glory, 6, 12, 17, 18–19, 28, 36
God, 34, 38, 47
    Declaration of Independence, 82
    French Revolution, 147
    Locke, 39, 106, 115, 124, 125
    monarchs' power from, 4, 54, 57, 67–8,
        78, 146
    Paine, 169

Godwin, William, 35, 134
good and evil, 33, 45–6, 47, 48, 49–50
goodness, 2, 7, 13, 41–2, 44, 48–9, 74
Gough, Stephen, 90–1
government
    Aristotle, 111–12, 113
    consent, 52–3, 61–3
    freedom, 97
    liberalism, 162, 165
    Locke, 3, 58–60
    Mill, 100
    Paine, 149, 150, 151, 158
    Plato, 108–9
    Rousseau, 64
    see also democracy; state
Greece, ancient
    democracy, 4, 72, 73–5, 80, 86
    justice, 105–6
    women, 131–2
    see also Athens
Greensboro Four, 52
guardians, 107, 108, 110, 131, 132

Habermas, Jürgen, 140
Hamilton, Alexander, 82
happiness, 28, 30
    Declaration of Independence, 82
    liberty, 91
    private realm, 132
    Rousseau, 41
    utilitarianism, 6, 12, 19–23, 100
Harm Principle, 7–8, 22–3, 84, 91, 98–
    101, 102, 103
health issues, 10–11, 100
Held, David, 73
history and tradition, 150, 161, 166, 167,
    175
Hitler, Adolf, 84
Hobbes, Thomas, 2, 9, 20, 28, 48, 68–9
    on Aristotle, 113
    freedom, 91, 92, 93, 102
    humanity, 6–7, 32, 33–9, 47
    Hume's critique, 63
    ideology, 161
    male view, 130, 132
    obedience to the state, 53–8, 66
    Rousseau's critique, 41–2, 44–5, 65
    social contract, 7, 112
    women, 141
human rights, 39, 60, 115, 147, 158, 161,
    174
    see also rights

humanity, 6–7, 31–50
  Hobbes, 33–9, 47, 48
  Locke, 39–40, 47
  Nietzsche, 45–7, 48, 49–50
  Rousseau, 41–5, 47–9
Hume, David, 7, 8, 53, 61–3, 66,
    117–18

ideologies, 9, 160–75
  definition of, 161
  Marx, 94
  polarization, 3, 27
  see also conservatism; liberalism;
    socialism
impartiality reasoning, 140
individualism, 168, 174
Industrial Revolution, 152, 154
inequality
  gender, 129–30, 140–1, 143–4
  Rawls, 120, 127
  Rousseau, 44, 133, 170
  wealth, 105, 168, 169
  see also equality
interests, 22, 77, 110, 123, 163
An Introduction to the Principles of
    Morals and Legislation (Bentham),
    19, 30

James I of England, 33, 67–8
James II of England, 58
Jansma, Noa, 129–30
Jay, John, 82
Jefferson, Thomas, 81, 82, 130
judiciary, 72, 78
justice, 8, 104–28
  Aristotle, 111–14
  gender differences in reasoning,
    140
  Hume, 117–18
  Locke, 114–17, 125–6
  Nozick, 121–3, 127–8
  Paine, 116, 126–7
  Plato, 107–11
  Rawls, 28, 118–21, 127
  Socrates, 11, 13

Kaepernick, Colin, 51
Kant, Immanuel
  liberalism, 161, 162, 163–4, 175
  politics and morality, 6, 12, 20, 23–6,
    27, 29–30
Kymlicka, Will, 24

Labour Party, 3, 172
land, 115, 116, 124, 126–7, 169
language of politics, 141, 142
law, 52, 64, 65, 74, 139
law and order, 32, 36
laws of nature
  Hobbes, 37–8, 56, 68
  Locke, 32, 39–40, 47, 59–60
  Rousseau, 40
legal systems, 104
legislature, 72, 78
Levellers, 61
Leviathan (Hobbes), 33, 36, 48, 68–9
liberal democracy, 4, 65, 71, 140–1
  see also democracy
liberalism, 35, 161, 162–6, 174–5
  definition of, 164
  democracy, 73
  financial crisis, 174
  Locke, 39, 60, 160–1
  Rawls, 119
liberty
  Burke, 146
  Declaration of Independence, 81
  French Revolution, 147, 148
  Hobbes, 91
  Locke, 39, 59–60, 114
  Madison, 82–3
  Mill, 85, 98–101
  Montesquieu, 77–8
  positive and negative, 7, 91, 92–7, 102
  private realm, 132
  Rawls, 119
  role of politics, 11
  see also freedom
Lincoln, Abraham, 82
Linz, J., 71
Locke, John, 3, 9
  government interference, 149, 158
  humanity, 32, 39–40, 47
  Hume's critique, 62
  liberalism, 160–1, 162, 164–5, 175
  male view, 132
  property, 8, 106, 114–17, 124, 125–6,
    151–2, 154–5
  Rousseau's critique, 65
  social contract, 7, 53, 58–60, 66, 112
  women, 141
logical positivism, 119
Louis XIV of France, 57, 77, 78, 134
luck, 16
lying, 24

MacCallum, Gerald, 7, 95–6, 102
Machiavelli, Niccolò, 6, 11–12, 14–19, 26, 28
Madison, James, 7, 73, 82–3, 86
markets, 152, 174
Marsilius of Padua, 113
Marx, Karl, 2, 8, 146–7, 153–8, 159
  democracy, 84
  freedom, 91, 94
  socialism, 170–1, 175
Marxism, 145, 146, 161
McCain, Franklin, 52
McNeil, Joseph, 52
mental harm, 100
Mill, James, 21
Mill, John Stuart
  biography, 98
  freedom, 93
  Harm Principle, 7–8, 22–3, 84, 91, 98–101, 102, 103
  liberalism, 164
  politics, 28
  tyranny of the majority, 7, 73, 84–5
  utilitarianism, 12, 20–1, 22–3
  voting, 85, 86, 87–9
  women, 8, 85, 130, 131, 137–9, 141–2, 143–4
Milton, John, 97
minorities, 83, 84, 85, 86
mode of production, 153, 154
monarchs
  Aristotle, 113
  English Civil War, 33
  power from God, 4, 54, 57, 67–8, 78, 146
  Rousseau, 41
  separation of powers, 72, 78
Montesquieu, Charles-Louis de Secondat, Baron de, 72, 77–8, 79, 83, 86
moral dilemmas, 5, 22
morality
  Aristotle, 113
  gender differences, 131, 140
  Kant, 6, 12, 23–6, 27, 29–30, 163
  liberal autonomy, 162
  Machiavelli, 11, 18–19
  Nietzsche, 48, 50
  Plato, 107, 109
  Rousseau, 1–2, 42–3
  Socrates, 13
  utilitarianism, 6, 19–23

'naked rambler', 90–1
nanny state, 11
nationalism, 156
natural law, 39–40, 47, 55
natural man, 32–3, 42, 44, 45, 47–8
natural rights, 8, 21, 114–15, 132, 150–1
  see also rights
negative liberty, 7, 91, 92–7, 102
neoliberalism, 164
New York, 10–11, 100–1
Nietzsche, Friedrich, 7, 9, 33, 45–7, 48, 49–50
non-domination, 96–7, 102
Nozick, Robert, 9, 152
  justice, 8, 106–7, 117, 121–3, 124, 127–8
  liberalism, 164

Oakeshott, Michael, 166
Obama, Michelle, 15
Occupy Wall Street movement, 104–5
On Liberty (Mill), 98–9, 102, 103
Oppenheimer, P., 15
de Orco, Remirro, 17–18, 26
original position, 119, 121, 140

pain, 19–20, 30
Paine, Thomas, 9, 82, 126–7, 131, 134–5
  democracy, 73
  inequality of wealth, 169
  liberalism, 164
  Locke's influence on, 60, 149
  private property, 8, 106, 116
  revolution, 146, 149–51, 158
  rights, 20, 21, 28
  socialism, 170, 171
  taxation, 115, 124
passion, 12, 26–8, 117
Pateman, Carole, 7, 53, 65–6
Pericles, 74, 80
persecution, 165
Pettit, Philip, 96, 102
philosopher kings, 80, 106, 109, 110, 123, 131
philosophy, 12, 46, 47, 109, 113
Plamenatz, J., 65
Plato, 2, 9, 12, 80, 113
  Allegory of the Cave, 109–10
  Aristotle's critique, 111
  biography, 106
  democracy, 84
  justice, 8, 105–6, 107–11, 117, 123–4

reason, 94
  Socratic method, 13
  women, 130, 131–2, 141
pleasure, 19–20, 30
polarization, 3, 27
political discourse, 3
politicians, 25, 27–8, 79–80
politics, 6, 10–30
  Aristotle, 28–9
  history of political thought, 3–4
  Kant, 23–4, 29–30
  Machiavelli, 14–19
  Socrates, 12–14
  utilitarianism and happiness, 19–23,
    30
  Walzer, 25
  Weber, 26–7
The Politics (Aristotle), 28–9, 56
Politics as a Vocation (Weber), 26
Popper, Karl, 110
populism, 27
pornography, 100
positive liberty, 7, 91, 92–7, 102
poverty, 94
power
  dominant class, 153, 154
  Hobbes, 34
  ideology, 161
  Machiavelli, 17
  Nietzsche, 33, 47
  separation of powers, 72, 77–8, 79
  sovereign, 53–4, 55–6, 58
prejudice, 147–8, 150
The Prince (Machiavelli), 14–15, 16, 17
producers, 108
proletariat, 153, 154–7, 159
property rights/private property, 8, 11,
    107
  capitalism, 151–2
  communism, 157
  Hume, 117–18
  Locke, 39, 59–60, 106, 114–17, 124,
    125–6, 154–5
  Nozick, 122
  Paine, 106, 116, 126–7, 169
  Rousseau, 169–70
  socialism, 170
proportion, 26–7
protest, 51–2, 104–5
*The Protestant Ethic and the Spirit of
    Capitalism* (Weber), 26
public services, 105, 173

public/private realms, 132–3
punishment, 21, 40, 59, 74, 114, 150–1

racial segregation, 52
Rainsborough, Thomas, 61
rationality, 37, 47
  see also reason
Rawls, John, 9, 24
  impartiality reasoning, 140
  justice, 8, 28, 106–7, 118–21, 123, 124,
    127
  liberalism, 164, 165
  Nozick's critique, 121, 122
  policy issues, 174
  rights, 21
  socialism, 170, 171
  talents, 120–1, 169
Reagan, Ronald, 168
reason
  Enlightenment thinking, 147, 167
  gender differences in reasoning, 8, 140
  Hobbes, 35, 37–8, 39
  Hume, 117
  impartiality reasoning, 140
  liberal autonomy, 162
  men, 135
  Paine, 150
  Plato, 94, 108, 110, 123
  Rousseau, 49, 130, 133
redistribution of wealth, 105, 107, 117,
    122, 170
Reflection on the Revolution in France
    (Burke), 147, 149
religion
  Locke, 114
  Rawls, 120
  right to choose, 150
  sovereign power, 55–6, 58
  toleration, 163, 165
  Western philosophy, 47
  see also God
representative democracy, 7, 64, 72,
    78–81
The Republic (Plato), 13, 14, 106, 109, 131
Republicans, 3, 166, 168
responsibility, 26–7, 28, 54–5, 174
revolution, 8, 135, 145–59
  Burke, 147–9
  Declaration of Independence, 82
  Locke, 58
  Marx, 91, 153–8, 159
  Paine, 149–51

Richmond, David, 52
rights
  Burke, 146, 149, 150, 158–9
  capitalism, 152
  Declaration of Independence, 82
  Enlightenment principles, 167
  Hobbes, 38, 56, 68–9
  justice, 104
  Kant, 30
  legal, 21
  liberalism, 161, 164, 165
  Locke, 59, 60, 114–17
  Mill, 85
  minorities, 86
  Paine, 20, 28, 146, 149–51, 158
  Rawls, 119–20, 127
  role of politics, 11
  Rousseau, 133
  US federalism, 73, 83
  utilitarianism, 21–2
  women, 85, 130, 131, 134–5, 139, 142
  see also natural rights
The Rights of Man (Paine), 131, 134–5,
  149–51
Rousseau, Jean-Jacques, 1–2, 9, 48–9
  democracy, 4, 72, 76–7, 86
  freedom, 91, 93, 94, 102
  humanity, 6–7, 32–3, 40, 41–5, 47–8
  Hume's friendship with, 62
  liberalism, 161, 162, 163, 164, 175
  private property, 169–70
  social contract, 63–5, 66
  on the state, 53, 57
  women, 8, 130, 133–4, 138, 141
Russia, 145

science, 34
Scruton, R., 167
Second World War, 22, 25
self-interest
  conservative view of humanity, 32
  Hobbes, 34, 38, 53
  Hume, 66, 117–18
  Rawls, 119
  Rousseau, 42–3, 64
separation of powers, 72, 77–8, 79
sexism, 130
sexual harassment, 129
Shelley, Mary, 134
Sidgwick, Henry, 21
The Simpsons, 70
Singer, Peter, 21

Skinner, Quentin, 7, 96, 102
slavery, 51–2, 73, 81, 82, 130, 137, 144
Smith, Adam, 62, 152, 154–5
smoking, 99, 100
social contract, 7, 52–3, 66
  Enlightenment principles, 167
  Hobbes, 38–9, 54–5, 161
  Hume's critique, 61–3
  Locke, 39, 53, 58–60
  Pateman, 65–6
  Rawls, 119
  Rousseau, 40, 63–5, 170
The Social Contract (Rousseau), 41, 76,
  170
social man, 32–3, 42, 44, 47–8
socialism, 160, 162, 168–72, 175
  definition of, 170
  financial crisis, 173, 174
  Marx's opposition to, 146, 156, 171
sociality, 112
society, corruption by, 41, 44–5, 48, 76,
  133, 163
Socrates, 9, 49, 74–5
  Allegory of the Cave, 109
  influence on Plato, 106, 107
  politics, 6, 11, 12–14, 27
  Socratic method, 13
solidarity, 75, 168
sovereign power, 53–4, 55–6
species being, 171
spirit, 94, 108
Stalin, Joseph, 84
state
  Aristotle, 29
  conservatism, 168
  Hobbes, 34, 36
  Locke, 114–15, 124
  Marxist view, 146, 153, 157, 158
  nanny state, 11
  Nozick, 122
  obedience to the, 7, 51–69
  Paine, 169
  Plato, 108
  Rawls, 121
  Weber, 26
  see also government
state of nature
  Hobbes, 32, 34–8, 44, 48, 54, 92, 130
  Locke, 32, 39, 40, 59
  Rousseau, 40, 41–2, 43–4, 45, 49
Stepan, A., 71
stewardship, 167

stoicism, 16
The Subjection of Women (Mill), 137–8,
    143–4
sugary drinks, 10–11, 100–1
surplus value, 171

tacit consent, 53, 59, 62–3, 64, 66
talent, 120–1, 169
taxes, 10–11, 105, 164
    American Revolution, 148
    Nozick, 117
    Paine, 106, 115, 116, 124, 169
    Rawls, 121
    socialism, 170
Taylor, Harriet, 137
Thatcher, Margaret, 168
A Theory of Justice (Rawls), 119–20, 127,
    140
Thoreau, Henry, 51–2
de Tocqueville, Alexis, 7, 73, 84
toleration, 161, 162–3, 164–5, 174–5
trade unions, 156, 171
tradition, 150, 161, 166, 167, 175
Trolley Problem, 22
Truman, Harry S., 22
Trump, Donald, 57, 105
Tunisian Revolution, 145
Turing, Alan, 22
Twilight of the Idols (Nietzsche), 46
Two Treatises of Government (Locke), 39,
    58, 125–6
tyranny of the majority, 7, 73, 84–5, 86,
    98

'unexamined life', 13, 75
United Kingdom, 3, 71–2, 78, 168, 172
United States of America
    American Revolution, 134–5, 147,
        148–9, 158
    citizen participation, 75
    civil disobedience, 51–2
    conservatism, 166, 168
    Constitution, 77, 83, 86
    Declaration of Independence, 73,
        81–2, 130
    democracy, 7, 71–2, 73, 81–3, 84, 86
    Enlightenment thinking, 135
    liberalism, 164
    Occupy Wall Street movement, 104–5
    Republicans and Democrats, 3
    the state, 57, 58

universal morality, 20, 23–6, 27, 163
universal suffrage, 4
utilitarianism, 6, 12, 19–23, 85
    democracy, 70
    liberty, 91
    Mill's Harm Principle, 100, 102,
        103
utility, principle of, 19, 30

veil of ignorance, 119, 121, 140
A Vindication of the Rights of Woman
    (Wollstonecraft), 134–6, 142–3
violence, 25, 27, 35–6, 38, 47
virtue, 12, 28–9, 107
virtuosity, 15
Voltaire, 37
voting
    citizenship, 112
    Mill, 7, 85, 86, 87–9
    Rousseau, 77
    women, 85, 137
    see also democracy; elections

Walzer, Michael, 12, 25, 28
war, 34, 36–7, 38, 70
    see also violence
wealth, 121–2, 124, 152
    inequality, 105, 168, 169
    redistribution of, 105, 107, 117, 122,
        170
Wealth of Nations (Smith), 152
Weber, Max, 6, 12, 26–8
The Wilt Chamberlain Principle
    (Nozick), 122, 127–8
wisdom, 110
Wollstonecraft, Mary, 8, 9, 130, 131,
    134–6, 139, 141–3
women, 4, 8, 100, 129–44
    Athens, 73, 131–2
    Mill, 137–9, 143–4
    Plato, 131–2
    public/private realms, 132–3
    Rousseau, 133–4
    voting rights, 85
    Wollstonecraft, 134–6, 142–3
    Young, 140–1
Wootton, D., 67–8
working class, 153, 154–7, 159, 171

Young, Iris Marion, 8, 131, 139, 140–1,
    142